RAINER MARIA RILKE

The Ring of Forms

Er liebte, was ihm ausging, wieder ein
und war nicht mehr im offnen Wind enthalten
und schloss entzückt den Umkreis der Gestalten
und hob sich auf und konnte nicht mehr sein.

(*Narziss* II)

All that went from him he loved back again,
no longer in the open wind contained,
he closed in ecstasy the ring of forms,
cancelled himself and could no longer be.

RAINER MARIA RILKE

The Ring of Forms

BY FRANK WOOD

1970

OCTAGON BOOKS

New York

Reprinted 1970

by special arrangement with the University of Minnesota Press

OCTAGON BOOKS

A DIVISION OF FARRAR, STRAUS & GIROUX, INC.

19 Union Square West

New York, N. Y. 10003

LIBRARY OF CONGRESS CATALOG CARD NUMBER: 78-120681

○⃝ Acknowledgments

I WISH to acknowledge gratefully the many helpful suggestions and ready encouragement extended by two of my colleagues who gave so generously of their time to the reading of the manuscript before publication: Professor Norbert Fürst of the University of Indiana and Professor Victor Lange of Princeton University. I am also indebted to the many Rilke scholars and specialists who, over the years, have provided me with many stimulating and fruitful suggestions.

My further thanks I owe to the director and staff of the University of Minnesota Press for their friendly cooperation throughout.

∞ *Contents*

RAINER MARIA RILKE

The Ring of Forms

o͡o *Introduction*

T H E amplitude of Rilke criticism today, representing so many different points of view and so many conflicting purposes, is perhaps sufficient justification for introducing another study with some comment on the "many Rilkes." Since his death in 1926, the winds of fashion, taste, or personal bias have shifted several times. The first Rilke audience was chiefly concerned with the early poetry, *The Book of Hours* and *The Lay of the Love and Death of Cornet Christopher Rilke*. Later, during the twenties and early thirties, the poet of the *New Poems* became the fashion. Only from the mid-thirties on did the final *Sonnets to Orpheus* and *Duino Elegies* receive the attention they are accorded today.

These various reactions may be accounted for in several ways. The symbolical complexity of the later work, for one thing, made greater demands on the reader who had found himself swept along by the overwhelming music and misconceived religiosity of the earlier poetry. Indeed, the present danger seems to be a tendency to underestimate some of the early things in favor of whatever was written after 1912. Today, with so many more published materials available, both posthumous verse and correspondence, there seems no reason not to accept the whole output, from beginning to end, as thoroughly interrelated and interdependent, the organic expression of an extremely homogenous mind. The "many Rilkes" are actually one, and only with the greatest hazards can the earliest products of his adolescence be divorced from the work of his ripest maturity. In fact, some

3

critics hold that the very latest poems actually revert to, and throw into greater illumination, the work accomplished at the beginning of the century.[1] This unified approach, however, does not preclude the existence of transitions in Rilke's work-development, of sharp though not abrupt "curves" and "returns," such as from the early work to the middle period, and from this to the late work.[2] There is, after 1910, for example, quite clearly a transition in reverse against the *Sachlichkeit* of the Paris period.

A corollary to the above attitude is the insidious habit that has developed of distinguishing an "early Rilke" and a "late Rilke" (with their variants of a "Prague," "Paris," "Muzot" poet, and so on). Perhaps his lifelong association with the arts has had something to do with this kind of classification (as one distinguishes the phases in Picasso's work). Such a procedure ends inevitably in neat and fine cleavages where they do not exist, and with Rilke least of all. Gottfried Benn's by no means facetious comment on this matter is very much to the point: "The tendency is generally as follows: Phase 1: the phase of experiment, effort, beginnings, then Phase 2: 'fulfillment' and the 'true form'. It is only in Phase 2 that Rilke really became 'what in the beginning he believed he was but in fact was not.'"[3] The whole method smacks, to Benn, of "too much eschatology, too much ideology, too much old-fashioned evolutionary theory," all apparently rooted in a persistent German idealism. Benn is right, of course, for such a schema completely destroys the organicity of the art-work. No poet ever wrote more about "roots" and "stems" than Rilke, when introducing the symbolical "tree" of his poetry. Such distinctions are only justifiable as ready signs and aids to facilitate the critical exposition and to save time, and I have used them frequently, perhaps, but always with this proviso. My main approach has been precisely to reveal the interrelatedness of both "early" and "late" in the unraveling of specific themes and motifs. A similar qualification holds true of what Benn calls the "phase of experiment and effort." I have several times used the word "workshop," since in my opinion Rilke's entire creative life was one long apprenticeship, an unending workshop whose doors were opened for only very special exhibits. The term never im-

INTRODUCTION

plies, in my practice, Benn's chronological meaning or anything of the "verticalism" bequeathed by an age of progressive positivism and science.

Such considerations inevitably cause one to reflect on another aspect of considerable interest: the great critical productivity centering around the poet. His bibliography to date fills a huge volume, and the end is not yet in sight. The situation seems to confirm what a recent writer, a poet himself, has said regarding Rilke's being "somewhat of an embarrassment to critics." [4] This is an unhappy though true predicament and, in revenge, it seems as though each critic were bound to single out his own interpretation, his own bias, and play them for all they are worth. To hardly any other modern poet have there appeared so many so-called approaches (metaphysical, hagiographical, Marxist, Freudian, existentialist, and perhaps one day we shall be favored with a Vegetarian one). Here, again, I have eschewed all ideologies, only referring to them where clarification of a passage, or a book under discussion, or a balancing of opposing interpretations might help in understanding the work itself. My limited aim has been, by analyzing persistent themes and motifs in their original context, to give a broader idea of how a great poet can be, at one and the same time, one of the most "paradoxical" and yet most "consistent" personalities of our time. Life itself is a continuous process of paradoxical equations, organically awaiting solution. Since for this subtle creative chemistry the scientific rubrics are lacking, the poet, closer to the matrix of being, may be pardoned if he is unable to supply the logical distinctions for what so far exceeds them. "The living make the mistake of drawing too fine distinctions," reads one of the great *Elegies*.

Here is perhaps the occasion to comment on another topic which has surely intrigued many who have followed closely Rilke's reputation over the years: the question of his popularity. The continual snowballing growth of Rilke criticism does not render the task easier, even if one were bent on this kind of speculation. In drawing a distinction between the Major and Good Poet types, while attacking what he calls the Mythical and Historical types, Karl Shapiro goes on to say: "Rilke, who is probably the best modern poet, is neither ma-

5

jor nor minor nor great . . . He is both emotional and 'intellectual,' both obscure and simple, both metaphysical and symbolist, both formalist and anti-traditional: in short, he is himself, like any poet who abdicates from theory and literary politics." [5] Auden refers to him as "the Santa Claus of Loneliness" and has also been influenced by him, as have other moderns, to a considerable extent.[6] Holthusen agrees that Rilke appeals primarily to the "loneliness" and isolation of modern man and offers some spiritual panaceas for it.[7] There is little doubt that, in an age of spiritual insecurity, world-wide conflict, and "politics" at all levels of life, many readers have derived from the poet confirmation and solace (his correspondence of a lifetime is alone ample evidence of the fact) where the so-called Mythical and Historical mouthpieces have failed. Here he becomes a need, a cult, a religion, and here too, I think, the argument has not been pushed far enough. The emotional accessibility of Rilke to so many readers (who may not at all understand the significance of his symbols nor what the poetry is really about) can be explained in some measure by the fact that his "inverted" Christianity found ready to hand a willing compliance. Strip from his work the disguises and masks, penetrate beneath the nuances and evasions, and a skeletal Christianity stares one in the face. Despite his repudiations of Christ in favor of the artist-god, Orpheus comes in through the back door to take His place. Nor does Rilke's Duino angel emotionally belie the original model, despite repeated protests; more importantly, his very paradoxes and ambiguities sound like glosses on the Pauline epistles. Under this category would fall his relentless pursuit of, his almost martyr-like devotion to, poetry. Even critics who will justifiably hesitate to "define" what he intended with his angel and Orpheus figures will have been at least prepared by a long heritage of Western civilization.

A final reason for his appeal on such a large scale (and all the reasons adduced do not, of course, necessarily imply a better understanding of his work and may, in fact, deflect from it) is the Freudian basis of his art. An exhaustive study has recently been made of the subject, and the data gathered on Rilke that explain him as a clear type of infantile regression is altogether conclusive.[8] Both the repeated emphasis on childhood and the erotic ambivalence in his treatment of certain themes point to a subconscious basis for his art. It is customary to speak today of the lack of communication, owing to the dissociation processes at work in modern society, between the poet and his audience: neither understands the other's language. But on one plane, at least, they may still communicate universally, disturbing as this fact may be: in the realm of the subconscious all men are free and equal. Rilke may seem to resemble, at times, a little boy, surrounded by his toys in a sequestered garden-spot while his playmates have resorted to more manly pursuits. There they are: the angels, trees, unicorns, heliotropes, and roses of his poetry, toys that the others had long since consigned to the attic or the dustbin. Rilke merely asks to be allowed to go on playing his games undisturbed, alone with himself, in his solitude. But precisely because they are also *our* toys, *our* images, *our* symbols, and still supply the basis of undivided consciousness, they are particularly cogent. For "on the plane of poetry," writes one reviewer of Rilke, "the games he played absolved him" from the subconscious self manifested on the human plane in the guise of infantilism.[9]

The picture would be incomplete without some reference to the critical counter-currents that have served to offset so much unthinking adulation and bring the scales more properly in balance. Some critics regard Rilke as an aesthete committed exclusively to poetry and divorced from other human concerns, a danger rather than a model to be followed—indeed, a greater peril to traditional values of truth than even Nietzsche, whose heir he seems in many ways to be. From the orthodox religious point of view, again, he has been attacked as representing a "world without transcendence," to use Holthusen's phrase, a counter-blow to Christian teaching, an example of the kind of monistic thinking we find in so many modern poets.[10] A more cautious and conservative brand of criticism has been sorely needed as an antidote to the extremes present in a considerable portion of the Rilke literature to date.

In the matter of reputation it is often difficult to distinguish between cause and effect, between the popularity of the poetry reacting on the criticism and the criticism reacting back on the poetry. The anomalous feature is that, contrary to the usual course of literary reputations, Rilke's popularity has never been allowed to subside since his death more than thirty years ago. Most writers usually suffer an eclipse temporarily, in the generation after their decease. What Rilke requires is some similar period of fallowness in order that those factors blocking the way to an impartial critical judgment may be eliminated. The signs are not as yet encouraging, though there is evidence that future critical trends will no longer be so concerned with works of a general nature (biographies, philosophical interpretations, and psychological investigations), but with special studies of poems or groups of poems, either for their own sake or in a comparative-literature context.[11] Here much remains to be done. Rilke research still suffers from the handicap that posthumous materials are constantly being published at regular intervals, though the impression they leave is that they will not appreciably alter estimates nor add new dimensions to the great work accomplished with the *Duino Elegies* and *Sonnets to Orpheus*.

To return to the charge that Rilke presents something of an "embarrassment" to the critic, the main difficulty seems to be that the latter is rarely able, to employ a trite figure, to steer clear between the Scylla of pure aestheticism and the Charybdis of ideological commitment. The poet himself, for example, is constantly making statements and value judgments: are these to be taken at their face value, as Guardini and others hold, or closely restricted to the aesthetic reference, as Holthusen, Mason, and Günther maintain? The case is somewhat similar to recent discussions of Keats's *Ode on a Grecian Urn*, except that, wrenched from their context, Rilke's didactic "statements" (*Aussagen*) are much more numerous and often bespeak the poet not entirely dissuaded from accepting the perquisites of the prophet and the seer. Thus it is false to say, in any commonly accepted sense, that "death is the better side of life" and "the crown of living," or that love on earth can never be realized except through "departure" and "absence" from the loved one. Yet, left in their contexts, such statements do not require to be taken literally—they rather refer to the poet's inexorable demand of art, to what Yeats called "the fascination of what's most difficult" in the practice of poetry. On the other hand, such devotion to poetry and its craft

8

seems far removed from what we usually understand by art for art's sake. If Rilke's undeviating devotion to a single purpose has been able to reflect back so generously on our life and experience today, there must be reasons for it which cannot be entirely laid at the door of aestheticism.

A preoccupation with such controversial issues, fortunately, does not fall within the province of these investigations, and I have left it to the poetry itself to do the talking. We can hardly go far wrong in retracing its growth and examining its structure for those ingredients the poet wrought so consistently and patiently throughout a lifetime into the Ring of Forms.

I
○○ *The Early Workshop*

I<small>F</small> Hugo von Hofmannsthal, the Austrian poet, had
died at the age of twenty, as Hermann Bahr once exaggeratedly remarked, he would have been the most beautiful figure in the world's
literature. If Stefan George, his great contemporary, had written no
more than the early *Hymns*, the stamp of his highly individual art
would have left some vestiges on posterity. If Rainer Maria Rilke's
reputation, however, were to be measured solely by his early poetry,
it would hardly have survived a temporary sensation on the part of
a few friends and acquaintances, chiefly restricted to Prague. Rilke
always admitted that he had written too much too early, and later, as
a full-fledged craftsman, he concurred with George's early warning
(at their first meeting in the Boboli Gardens in Florence) against premature publication. Toward the end of his life he repudiated most of
the work with which it began. Such disapproval is expressed in a late
letter to one of his first critics, in the form of hostility to any attempt
to "dig out" and "interpret" his beginnings: "Insofar as you begin
from this point, I must deny the correctness of your presentation.
These specimens unfortunately on hand have actually no validity,
are in absolutely no sense the beginning of my work, rather the extremely private conclusion of a juvenile and adolescent indecision
. . ."[1] What the poet once had to say of *The Notebooks of Malte
Laurids Brigge* can be applied to most of these earlier efforts: "The
accents are all over the wrong vowels," for all these "minor impotent
products were only ideas, little emergency lies for the purpose of self-

10

assertion and self-preservation." [2] These statements are not only indicative of a highly critical mind, but particularly of the distance that mind had to travel in order to produce the *Duino Elegies* and *Sonnets to Orpheus*.

Despite the fact that the bulk of this early output is discouragingly second-rate, the poetry sentimentally immature, the prose morbid and fantastic, the stage experiments either derivative or melodramatic, it is nevertheless of considerable importance for the full picture of Rilke's poetic development in relation to the Ring of Forms. The youthful poetry of most major writers is usually demarcated from their mature work by abrupt transitions; the art of Rilke from beginning to end evolves almost foetus-like, with almost biological consistency, from original cell to mature organism. Here, in embryo, are the themes, metaphors, symbols, paradoxes, the very vocabulary of the great work to come. We are confronted with the half-shaped torsos and unfinished designs of an early workshop, whose inchoate and fragmentary masses yet give us some idea of the refinements eventually to emerge.

POETRY

To say that much of Rilke's early verse is impressionistic, interspersed with sentimental balladry, naturalistic sketches and pictures, is to point to the poverty of the literary traditions of his youth in Prague (somewhat analogous to the exhausted literary tradition faced by the young William Butler Yeats). If he did not wish to fall back on the epigonal romanticism of the preceding decades, the German poet at the end of the nineties was forced to identify himself with the already moribund naturalistic movement or with the new and vaguely understood symbolist doctrines imported from France. If the heavy hand of naturalism proved to be dispiriting and paralyzing in its effects, symbolism in its turn was open to the charge of a vague mysticism, ambiguity, and antisocial perversity. The striking significance of Nietzsche's work had not yet penetrated the consciousness of youth, and Stefan George's symbolism still belonged to the future. It was indeed for the young poet of Rilke's generation no unalloyed pleasure, and frequently a source of confusion and peril, to pendu-

11

late anxiously between the extremes of vulgarity and materialism on the one hand, refinement and mysticism on the other.[3]

More important still, in Rilke's case, were two other factors which had a lot to do with the genetics of his early verse; the one a biographical factor connected with his home life, particularly his mother; the other significant for the shaping of his poetic idiom, not only in the early stages but for years to come. Rilke's lifelong and unremitting dedication to poetry is readily explained as an outgrowth of a fixation implanted in him by his romantic and unpredictable mother, Phia Rilke. Hence the goal he set for himself in his earliest poems was "fame," not "art," a fulfillment of childhood dreams and wishes. In the privately printed *Life and Songs* (1894) we are expressly informed that the genius is not necessarily dedicated to failure, that if an age does not succeed in creating its great men, the individual will create a great age. The frustrated romanticism of his mother, in addition to the disappointments of his own military career as well as those of his father, led psychologically to the interweaving of both hero and poet themes we meet at almost every stage of his career.

The local impoverishment of the German language, furthermore, as a result of the conflicting national interests in the Prague of Rilke's childhood, is in great measure responsible for the deficiencies of the poet's language, vocabulary, and ideas.[4] The great miracle of Rilke's life is that he achieved so much with so little to start with: an inadequate idiom, a fugitive inspiration, and the lack of a consistent background in tradition, poetic or otherwise. Only through unremitting toil and patience were these defects gradually overcome, long before he met with the example set by Rodin's slow striving. But these early efforts are not without their redeeming graces. For despite the paucity of vocabulary and ideas, Rilkean concepts never "thin out" or "disperse," as is frequently the case with other poets in their evolution.[5] The narrowness of linguistic range makes for a concentration that leads to an increasing deepening of, a greater technical precision in dealing with, specialized fields of experience.

It is not surprising, therefore, that Rilke's earliest efforts in verse should resemble a pastiche of various elements: imitations of songs and ballads of an earlier age, with the old stereotypes and clichés retained; attempts in the neo-romantic fashion of the nineties with its unassimilated moods and metaphors ("Day's choral song ebbs out/in breathless rapture. . ."), and others again with an obvious naturalistic flavor. Usually the subjects selected are drawn from the Prague environment: the Hradschin, St. Vitus' cathedral, St. Wencelas' chapel, historical figures like Wallenstein and Rudolf of Hapsburg, rustic festivals and All Souls' vignettes. Rilke's interest in these materials was neither patriotic-nationalistic nor narrowly regional, rather it was intuitive and personal. In poems on the Hradschin and Rudolf, as in his later comments on Tolstoi and the Russian Easter, he already seems to be visualizing preliminary versions of the "Things," the *Dingobjekte* of *New Poems*. Of all Rilke's earlier verse *Household Gods* is the least tiring and monotonous for the reason that to the poet's tender nostalgia is added an unusual boyish, masculine note absent from the following collections. Here he tried seriously to identify himself with his environment, though it was only a transient phase, and the poems are accordingly closely structured around the details and surfaces of the objects described.

In the early verse Rilke's metrics and verse forms are often derived from old models—Eichendorff, Lenau, Storm, and later Liliencron —while Heine's influence is evident in poems like "The Saints" and "On Attending the University," with its brusque humor in the terminal *pointe*. Not infrequently the early verse structure bears little relation to the content, though a notable exception is the "Folk Lay," with its lilting rhythm expressive of the sad impersonality of a people's sorrow:

> Mich rührt so sehr
> böhmischen Volkes Weise,
> schleicht sie ins Herz sich leise,
> macht sie es schwer . . .

> > Song of the Czech folk
> > so deeply stirs me,
> > softly into the heart it steals,
> > making it heavy . . .

When the feeling is not thus clarified, we have the appalling sentimentality of "The Angel" or the sheer melodrama of "The Young

Sculptor." Words still bog down in undisciplined emotions and the saccharine smoothness of the lines is unrelieved by any inner development. Not Lenau's chronic melancholy nor the brooding pessimism of Leopardi informs this verse, but rather the morbid attachments of adolescence. By contrast, "Village Sunday" and "Little Dratenik" are sunlit genre-pictures, though still imperfectly realized and very un-Rilkean in tone. Gradually through *Household Gods, Dream-Crowned* (1897), and particularly *Advent* (1898), the impersonal images become more individualized as the poet becomes more conscious of self in relation to the non-self, of the world of nature with himself as center and the world of actuality so unbearably real and paradoxical.

What the reader chiefly carries away from this early poetry is its unmistakable melodic pattern, which immediately distinguishes a verse of Rilke from those of his contemporaries. This pattern is determined not only by externals of rhythm and meter, but by interior structural devices such as alliteration and assonance, frequently overworked:

> Hart am Kirchenaltargitter,
> wo die Ampel flammt, die matte,
> schläft ein alter, alter Ritter
> unter grauer Wappenplatte . . .

> Close by the altar's grill,
> where the lamp burns dim,
> sleeps an old, old knight
> under gray, armorial stone . . .

Rilke's virtuosity in rhyming is perhaps his most conspicuous early stylistic feature. There is a noticeable effort to avoid the mechanical stereotypes of most beginners and to forge out on paths of his own. Because of this excessive rhyming, however, the reader often forgets what the poet is trying to say in the poem itself. End rhymes and interior rhymes may be used to good effect in poems of humorous intent, as in "Saints":

> Grosse Heilige und kleine
> feiert jegliche Gemeine;
> hölzern und von Steine feine,
> grosse Heilige und kleine . . .

Great saints and small
all people intone;
wooden ones and those of stone,
great saints and small . . .

But a too great virtuosity, especially when combined with foreign word elements (later employed with great tact and sensitiveness), easily degenerates into mannerism (cf. "At St. Vitus'" where a rhyme-medley of three languages is employed: *Idiom, Dom; Erotik, Gotik; Casus rei, roi soleil*).

Much of the vocabulary consists of affected neo-romantic hand-me-downs (*Lichtgeglänz, glastend, Goldglast*), although his striving for originality is evident in the bold innovations at compounding (*grünspanngrüne, Waldseereines, Kerkereinsamkeiten, Blätterleichenschau*). Over and above these elements, however, for the reader of the mature Rilke certain words strike out with symbolic import. Stereotypes like "diamonds," "amethysts," and "rock crystals" were already part and parcel of the neo-romantic canon, but when we encounter "chrysanthemums" and "a little white rose with a red halo," or read of an "angel of coarse clay," of numerous Madonna figures, particularly of a "stone Apollo" and a silent Triton in a poem called "Fountain," we are inclined to regard them as signposts and arrows pointing through the long Rilkean "forest of contradictions" toward some of his favorite symbols and themes.

Such examples suffice to make clear how rigorously the youthful Rilke, despite all handicaps, submitted himself to the discipline of creating a poetic language, his *own* language. Yet, generally speaking, at this stage his verse shows a too pronounced facility, ending in monotony, often becoming a musical description rather than an imaginative shaping of theme. One might hazard the opinion, in view of his persistent stress on the plastic aspects of poetry, that already his musicality was seeking its opposite, the firm dike against the flood of words, in his choice of subject matter from the arts. Personal affiliations with some of the local Czech artists and art movements indubitably account for such an "arty" exhibition as

Am Häuschen lehnte die Melone
dort wie auf einem Bilde Dows . . .

THE RING OF FORMS

> The melon leaned against the cottages
> as if in a painting by Dow . . .

from "Abendgang." A similar emphasis informs the series "Charcoal Sketches in Callot's Manner." Yet this same youthful interest in the fine arts as a reservoir of materials for poetry was to lead, by various detours, through the portrait poems of *The Book of Images* and *New Poems* to the Fifth Duino Elegy with its variations on Picasso's painting, "Saltimbanques."

The second collection, *Dream-Crowned*, (*Traumgekrönt*), has justly been called a transitional work. Undisciplined longing is here the matrix from which issue poems of no high order of merit. "My heart is like a forgotten chapel" is a poorer version of what Hofmannsthal accomplished so well in "Early Spring" with similar motifs, while "I wished that instead of a cradle/they had made me a little coffin" speaks for itself. The traduced-maiden theme, a great favorite with naturalist writers, is effectively treated in the nineteenth poem, which, despite the sentimentality, is remarkable for its economy as well as for the peculiarly Rilkean phrasing of the love-idea ("Love or whatever you call it"). The prevalent idea of "longing," *Sehnsucht*, is unquestionably fluid and vague, yet the verse structure itself is more disciplined than in the previous collection. The urge to overdo rhyme and rhythm is avoided, though the tendency toward multisyllabic word-compounding is even more evident than before. The most important poem for Rilke's evolution is the opening "King's Song" (*Königslied*):

> Darfst das Leben mit Würde ertragen,
> nur die Kleinlichen macht es klein;
> Bettler können dir Bruder sagen,
> und du kannst doch ein König sein . . .

> You may endure life with dignity,
> the petty alone make it small,
> beggars can say to you Brother,
> and a king you still can be . . .

This is not the flabby, colorless idealization of the poet we might have been led to expect, but that of one seriously dedicated to his task, one whose "divine silence" is sufficient "purple and ermine."

16

THE EARLY WORKSHOP

The poems in the third youthful collection, *Advent*, and onward through the final volume of youthful poetry, *Early Poems* (originally called *In Honor of Myself*), grow one into the other by easy transitions. *Advent* is still a very immature work, though the longing which provides the emotive drive is desperately searching for an objective correlative. That the poet has not yet found it is evident from the frequent use of the stereotype "methinks" (*mir ist*) at the beginning of many of the poems. The mood is a personal one, stated rather than organically identified with the subject of its concern. Uncertainty of tone and viewpoint is implicit in the colloquial grammar and the occasional omission of sentence subject, devices extremely effective in the folk song. Personifications and even faint allegories are more conspicuous than metaphorical or symbolical units. Rilke is the simile-poet par excellence,[6] and his skillful use of this figure, for many poets a dangerous snare, is peculiar to his best style. But in the early work the simile is still wooden and insistent, especially in the harness of a tiresomely repeated imagery (a dark gothic chapel, for example, likened to the soul's interior).

Faint echoes of Faust's passionate commitment to life may be heard in the opening poem of *Advent* until we recognize that the Rilkean movement and purpose are headed in a different direction (Faust was distinctly committed to life *in* time and his longing was of a quite different order):

> Das ist mein Streit:
> Sehnsucht geweiht
> durch alle Tage schweifen.
> Dann stark und breit,
> mit tausend Wurzelstreifen
> tief in das Leben greifen—
> und durch das Leid
> weit aus dem Leben reifen,
> weit aus der Zeit.

> > That is my strife:
> > to longing dedicate,
> > to roam through all the days.
> > Then, strong and broad,
> > to reach deep into life

17

with a thousand branching roots—
through sorrow
ripening far out of life,
far out of time.

Already the imagery anticipates certain lines from *The Book of Hours* and the entire poem is actually a pre-form of the even more complex and typical title poem of *Early Poems*. Already Rilke is passing from the optimistic standpoint of the "life philosophy" of his age to one of doubt and resignation. No longer is he the "worldwide wanderer" of *Dream-Crowned*; his emotions are more dependably at home in the twilight realm "between day and dream," for "the day is small and stingy, and the night is wide with silver borders, almost like a legend." His growing preference for the romantic night-concept is unambiguously expressed in a single verse, a pathetic comment on his broken childhood: "I felt so strange and abandoned." From the treatment of the night motif in the early poetry there is a gradual shift from the descriptive mood-aspect, half playful and coy, to one whose reference is darkly and suggestively allied with the deeper poetic intent. Not yet does night receive its apotheosis, as in *The Book of Hours* or the "night cycle" of his last years; for the poet the evening is either "mild and mine" or "heavy," sometimes close to the sinister: "The night is like a sable city." The night-concept serves the poetry in a fashion quite different from its use in Novalis' hymns, for example, and his term "solitude" is only distantly related to romantic usage. The healthy freshness of Tieck's "forest solitude" has little in common with Rilke's "holy solitude," a state of peaceful suspense before the desires of life invade the untouched garden.

In *Advent*, furthermore, we may distinguish several dim proto-forms of later poems (cf. "Love Song" and "The Lute" in *New Poems*). The collection as a whole suggests a patient waiting and groping, nicely conveyed by such lines as "The evening listens into the house/and those within listen out." The few travel poems, residues of the first Italian journey of 1898, are of no great significance. The first poem of the first section called "Mothers" merely substantiates the statement that Rilke's mother and her world "remained the core of his life, a core around which formed myriad accretions, but

18

which nevertheless secretly influenced his every moment."[7] From here to the Third Elegy is but a step seemingly, and yet what a large one:

> Mutter, *du* machtest ihn klein, du warsts, die ihn anfing;
> dir war er neu, du beugtest über die neuen
> Augen die freundliche Welt und wehrtest der fremden . . .

> Mother, you made him small, it was you that began him;
> he was new to you, you arched over those new eyes
> the friendly world, averting the one that was strange . . .

The original title poem of *Early Poems*, "In Honor of Myself," whose pre-form we have met in the opening poem of *Advent*, discloses the very core of Rilke's feeling out of which his greatest poetry evolved. The core is, in the language of physics, the force that starts the poetic object rolling in a *perpetuum mobile* without end or goal, ever directed toward the open and infinite:

> Das ist die Sehnsucht: wohnen im Gewoge
> und keine Heimat haben in der Zeit.
> Und das sind Wünsche: leise Dialoge
> täglicher Stunden mit der Ewigkeit.

> Und das ist Leben: Bis aus einem Gestern
> die einsamste von allen Stunden steigt,
> die anders lächelnd als die andern Schwestern,
> dem Ewigen entgegenschweigt.

> This is longing: to live in fluctuation
> and have no home in time.
> And these are wishes: soft dialogues
> of daily hours with eternity.

> And this is life. Until, from a yesterday,
> the most solitary of all hours rises,
> which, with a smile unlike its sisters',
> in silence meets eternity.

If Rilke's art, like his life, was dedicated to the fluid contour, the "nuances" of experience, the implications are all at hand: longing and homelessness as requisites for quiet dialogues with eternity until the most solitary of yesterday's moments mounts to meet it. Just as later both God and Love become directions and not goals in his

19

thinking, so here all desires are "in process," continually weaving back and forth. The verses quoted also lend substance to the criticism that what Rilke wants to say absorbs so completely the verse structure into itself that the reader is often overwhelmed by the idea without thinking of the language in which it is clothed. On closer analysis, the quoted verses reveal structural defects which the later Rilke would hardly condone (the repeated copulas and the profusion of definite articles). The reference to "soft dialogues" involves a typical Rilkean paradox, occurring again and again in his work, as in the Paris "Roman Fountain" poem ("Silencing towards the gently speaking one").

Compared with *Advent*, a darker tone emerges in *Early Poems*, a tone that "borders, unaware, upon the tragic." [8] The poetry is still entirely intuitive in character, but the poet is less addicted to facile images, rather questioning the ultimate goals toward which the current of his longing is bearing him. The deliberate assertion of will in the opening lines of the first three poems is a forecast of a struggle with still unseen problems. The intuitive calm, where ego and world are identified, proceeds from a kind of idealistic monism that Rilke retained, with variations, throughout his career. On the technical side, foreign words tend to disappear from the poetic structure and excessive rhythmical or figurative language is generally avoided. A new verse pattern emerges to replace the old four-line stanza: a five-line stanza in alternate rhyme, the penultimate verse rhyming with the first and serving as a barrier to the accumulated emotion before the final release. [9]

The repeated emphasis on the nuance, the volatile and vanishing, in this early poetry permits us to observe the evolution of certain favorite and fundamental attitudes which begin as *aperçus* and gradually solidify to form the core of Rilke's aesthetic. He was not slow, for example, to arrive at the conclusion that "You mustn't try to understand life/then it will become a festival" ("Du musst das Leben nicht verstehen,/dann wird es werden wie ein Fest"). The "festive" idea of life as understood by children and primitives (an idea that goes back to Hölderlin) means aesthetically a return to innocency, a stripping bare of all inessentials, a rebirth into new modes of feeling and creating. The twenty-first of the *Sonnets to Orpheus* (Part I), some twenty years later, reveals how consistently the poet shaped this early theme. Moreover, the rejection of the everyday world of adult feelings is closely associated with Rilke's early concern with the language of poetry. The *word*, for the symbolists, was the symbol of deeper and larger causalities and relationships, reaching back ultimately to the Magian ground of all being.[10] Rilke's early soft-pedaling of the meaning involved in everyday word usage is an attempt to bridge the gap between the "thing" to be expressed and the idiom specifically appropriate to that experience. He dreads the words people ordinarily use because they are too crudely articulate (*deutlich*): "And this is called dog and that is called house/and here it begins and there it ends." Here, *in ovo*, is the "interpreted world" (*gedeutete Welt*) of the First Elegy, in which humankind is not entirely at home. The following companion piece to the just quoted lines, expressing his preference for the homely, inconspicuous words of speech to stereotypes and clichés, is a clear statement of Rilke's concern with the materials of poetry:

> Die armen Worte, die im Alltag darben,
> die unscheinbaren Worte, lieb ich so.
> Aus meinen Festen schenk ich ihnen Farben,
> da lächeln sie und werden langsam froh . . .

> The humble words that famish in dull day,
> the inconspicuous words are what I love.
> I give them hues out of my festivals,
> and then they smile and slowly become gay . . .

Rilke characteristically personalizes the "words" of this poem, lending them something of his own shy readiness for renewal after banality. One might contrast the intention behind his "humble words" with Wordsworth's idea of poetic diction. Where Wordsworth proposes for poetic idiom the "simple and unelaborated expressions" chosen from "the very language of men," [11] Rilke is interested in a "language of things," a language unknown to rustics and simple folk but bearing the stamp of already highly specialized modes of thinking. Rilke's "inconspicuous" words ("roots," "tree," even "time" and "space") are heavily charged with particular meanings, symbolic connotations, and indirect references. They mark off quite clearly the evolution in poetic idiom during the century between the two poets.

We do not expect to find the old-fashioned love lyric in symbolist verse, and Rilke's complex love-idea as it developed later is hardly more than adumbrated in the early poetry. Number eighteen of *Dream-Crowned*, for instance, concluding with a melancholy quatrain, deals with a passing adolescent stage of the unreal, nostalgic variety. Yet in one direction the love theme already admits a certain complexity, transcending mere longing to seek its objective by a curious inversion. In the section "Girl Figures" and "Girl Songs" he transfers his own emotions to young maidens who patiently wait for the beloved. They are never satisfied because, like the poet himself, they are caught between dream and resignation. This vicarious reaction of love is the first stage in the crystallization of Rilke's ultimate conception of love from the woman's standpoint and in terms of her emotional reference. The girls' feelings are divided between anxiety and desire to be released from their state of longing. Like boats chained to the shore they wait for wind or storm to release them from their moorings. Sometimes an unknown singer passing with his lute has estranged their hearts from living, often they share the feeling that life has completely passed them by. Their susceptibility to music relates the emotion of love to art and, like Rilke's own art, love is only a direction and not a goal. The tensions of love so conceived require that it remain unsatisfied. The poems called "The Girls' Prayers to Mary" go even further in relating love to what we should with some caution call the religious factor in Rilke's poetry. For always the figures of Christian mythology and dogma are utilized as ultimate symbols of the aesthetic standpoint, growing out of the human concern, as in the following poem "Pietà":

Wie kam, wie kam aus deinem Schoss,
Maria, so viel Lichte los
und so viel Gram?
Wer war dein Bräutigam?

How came, how came from out thy womb,
Mary, so much light
and so much gloom?
Who was thy bridegroom?

These prayers to the Virgin, who replaces indifferent parents as confidant, have little to do with religion and a lot with the eroticism of adolescence. The Virgin is regarded as one who has likewise passed through a similar stage of adolescent indecision and yearning, passively accepting ineffable love with its attendant sufferings. Thus the Virgin of dogma has become, in one sense, an early forerunner of Louise Labé and the Portuguese Nun, and in another, of various subsequent poems dealing with Christ.

Just as the girls are the central figures of *Mädchengestalten*, so the Virgin receives more attention than either God or Christ. Yet setting aside frequent sentimental references to nuns and field Madonnas, saints and churchyard graves, we find at least two *Early Poems* in which the controversial Christ-figure makes its first appearance, both as the Man of Sorrows on his wayside cross and as the King of Children ("Thou King of Children that Thou art"). God is mentioned sparingly, chiefly as reference in a flight of daring figures where the voice of an invisible nun, "like a half-erased face," rises above the other voices to lay itself against God's ear "like the hollow of a seashell." Such tropes point to skillful use of simile in cases where other poets might easily overdo it. The concluding number of *Early Poems* defines the poet's conception of God, at this early stage, as one of pantheistic immanence, a God actuated only by the progressive experience of the heart. The poem is important in that the author is concerned to eliminate formal Christian attributes and predicate God's power not on revelation but on individual human experience:

> Du darfst nicht warten, bis Gott zu dir geht
> und sagt: Ich bin.
> Ein Gott, der seine Stärke eingesteht, hat
> keinen Sinn.
> Da musst du wissen, dass dich Gott durchweht
> seit Anbeginn,
> und wenn dein Herz dir glüht und nichts ver-
> rät, dann schafft er drin.

> You must not wait for God's first step to say:
> I Am.
> A God who will his power confess is
> meaningless.

> For know that through your life is
> breathed God's air from start of
> time.
> And when your heart ablaze does nought
> betray, he labors there.

The poetry is singularly didactic, yet it offers in attentuated form the gist of the poet's ideas of poetry and life, which expanded in different directions as his poetic experience deepened. His heterodox view of God is posited at the very outset in his refusal to regard the creator as an absolute in a state of stasis. Nowhere in Rilke's poetry is there endorsement of the divine personality as the great I AM. Verses three and four simply take up the old romantic concept, adapted by Hölderlin and Shelley, of the indispensability of the human factor in God's awareness of self:

> Denn weil
> die Seligsten nichts fühlen von selbst,
> muss wohl, wenn solches zu sagen
> erlaubt ist, in der Götter Namen
> teilnehmend fühlen ein andrer.
>
> (Hölderlin, "Der Rhein")

Rilke's terms *durchweht* and *Anbeginn* are key-words for his conception of poetry. Like the poetic idea, God is without contours, a quality of experience, the unhistorical *anima* beyond definition and without termination. The verb *wehen* is characteristic and related to an increasingly prominent series (*fallen, werden, wachsen, atmen*), which leads with ever greater complexity of meaning to the *Duino Elegies* and the *Sonnets to Orpheus*.

In the section "Angel Songs" the treatment of the angel-figure is an early illustration of the poet's practice of using religious terminology to reduce the distance between man and God, not so much for the purpose of closer communion as for offering a challenge to the muse. In allowing his guardian angel to escape to the freedom of the skies, the poet is aware of the angel's unhappiness in being cut off from human concerns. In the final poem "Prayer" the apostrophized figure carved in ebony is a forerunner of his inaccessible Duino counterpart, without the latter's symbolic implications:

THE EARLY WORKSHOP

Ernster Engel aus Ebenholz:
du riesige Ruh.
Dein Schweigen schmolz
noch nie in den Bränden
von Büsserhänden.
Flammenumflehter!
Deine Beter
sind stolz
wie du.

Solemn angel of ebony:
stupendous repose.
Never thy silence
melted in ardent flames
from penitent hands.
Thy worshipers
are proud
like thee.

One is already struck by the fact that in the early poetry no really human type appears, a corollary to the often-repeated complaint that Rilke worded significantly in 1914: "My feelings overleaped humans and I would only be satisfied with salvation at the hands of the angel." Poetic concern with words and art-expression enhances the role of nature at the expense of man. But of what kind of nature?

Rilke's conception of nature was always highly personal, without Wordsworth's simple literalness or Goethe's organic simplicity. He writes, in fact, about certain select objects in nature rather than about nature itself. Particularly in the workshop the pathetic fallacy is strained to the limit; the face of nature is only what the poet has put there. One has only to consider the late *Elegies* to measure the change in Rilke's nature concept. If he began with an identification of the poet with nature, in the end he arrived at the complete suspension and transformation of nature into invisible relationships (*Bezüge*). An example of the purely descriptive nature poem, the following has sacrificed nothing of the old magic of alliteration and assonance, and the tone of fading and hopeless waiting is unequivocally built round the major vowel *a*:

Im flachen Land war ein Erwarten
nach einem Gast, der niemals kam;

25

> noch einmal fragt der bange Garten,
> dann wird sein Lächeln langsam lang.
>
> Und in den müssigen Morästen
> verarmt im Abend die Allee,
> die Äpfel ängsten in den Ästen,
> und jeder Wind tut ihnen weh.

> In the flat land an expectation
> for some one guest who never came:
> once more inquires the timid garden
> and then its smile grows slowly lame.
>
> And in the evening idle marshes
> impoverished lies the avenue;
> the apples on the branches quake,
> hurt by each passing gust of wind.

In a much better poem than the last, the poet desires to merge with the garden and its dreaming fountains, to surrender to the winds and shiver with the pale, spring beeches. However subjective and sentimental, it nevertheless gives voice to the dilemma of a whole young generation: the loss of a common ground of experience and the search for something to take its place:

> Kann mir einer sagen, wohin
> ich mit meinem Leben reiche?
> Ob ich nicht auch noch im Sturme streiche
> und als Welle wohne im Teiche,
> und ob ich nicht selbst noch die blasse, bleiche
> frühlingfrierende Birke bin?

> Can anyone tell me whither
> I reach with my life?
> Whether in the storm I still do not shiver
> and dwell in the pond as wave,
> and whether myself am not the pale, bleached
> spring-freezing birch tree?

The poem is predominantly built around two sounds: the short vowel *i* and the dipthong *ei*, the latter in emphatic rhyme position and repeated four times, bedded between the softer, lower tones of the first and last verse-rhymes with their naïve, questioning uncertainty. The pauses and breathing are especially important for the effect. The poem further illustrates Rilke's management of the run-on line and the use of inconspicuous words in emphatic positions. No less striking are the consonantal effects with their recurrent labials and liquids. Two other major Rilkean themes in the early poetry have been left to the last, not because they are less important, but because at this stage they are not as well articulated as in later periods. The almost total absence of the death theme (I do not mean the graveyard atmosphere of *Advent*) would seem surprising since Rilke had already begun to read Jacobsen as early as 1897. He was still too much concerned with immediate orientations, too eager to resolve his pressing emotional conflicts in publishable poetry to evolve the great vision of death of *The Book of Hours*. Wherever death as theme does occur in this youthful work, it is rather in the prose tales or diary entries. As for the childhood theme, on the other hand, the poet had not yet achieved the necessary distance from his own childhood which made possible the *Notebooks of Malte Laurids Brigge* in the next decade. A recent critic has stated that the childhood theme may be developed in three directions.[12] Childhood is, first, the paradise of unconscious, integral existence open to all experience. It has, again, its status in conflict with the adult environment, where it generally suffers and is misunderstood. And, finally, childhood may be regarded as an awakening from the early paradise into reality, the mystery of human growth as a progress, in Hofmannsthal's sense, from the pre-existential phase to the mundane plane. Rilke's early poems partake of all three conceptions in small and varying degree, but for the most part the second version of the theme seems to prevail. The awareness of the Other, the uncomprehending world outside, takes either the form of self-warning or of metaphorical withdrawal into the solitude of a youthful mind. Only after Russia and Worpswede, however, which provided phases of experience essential to his development, could Rilke fully realize that his lost childhood was to be the very wellspring of his poetry.

DRAMA AND PROSE IN THE POETIC PERSPECTIVE

Valuable sidelights are thrown on the early workshop by a consideration of Rilke's youthful efforts in drama as well as prose. That

27

from 1895 to 1902 he wrote at least eight short dramas and a substantial number of prose tales is strong indication that he believed it possible to realize himself artistically in genres other than poetry, though the aftermath was to cure him slowly, almost reluctantly, of this illusion. Not that he was never fully conscious of the main direction of his talent. "Short stories are fragments, poems are continuations," he wrote his publisher in 1897, ". . . with a book of short stories in my hand I am a suppliant bowing before the inane,—with poems in my heart I am king of the sentient."[13] He was never able to write a completely successful drama or novel (if we except the *Notebooks*), yet his persistent interest in dramatic and epic forms until the end of his life is reflected in his poetry. The theater especially furnishes one of the outstanding symbols of his poetry, and his early experiments in drama allow us indirectly to follow this interest in, and adaptation of, typical poetic themes.

Rilke's early bathetic and sentimental plays, now entirely forgotten, derive from a curious concoction of Hauptmann and Maeterlinck, naturalism and symbolism. The central dramatic conflict usually arises from the resistance of the heroine to the sale of her virtue for purely economic reasons. These Helenes and Maries, confronted at last with brutal realities instead of with shining knights in armor or wandering minstrels, are still the expectant dreamy girls of "Maiden Songs." Their loss of chastity turns out to be a vain, irreparable step, leading to a spiritual desperation whose consequences are easily linked with Rilke's vaguely crystallizing love theme. The chastity theme not only points up his untiring criticism of the discrepancies existing between the role of sex in life and his own conception of love; it also provides a bridge to the unrequited-love theme, which receives its first significant statement in the *Notebooks*. The loss of chastity is the negative aspect of a conception of love that transcends physical possession and enters the paradoxical situation where love is construed as a flight from the object beloved. The emphasis in these plays rests on the female characters, while the male protagonists function chiefly as sensuous, vulgar puppets. At heart, and in his own odd way, Rilke was always something of a social revolutionary, but the psychological subtleties of his vague social theorizing were hardly calculated to capture the attention of an audience. In fact, the failure of the first performance of his social drama *Equal and Free* (in Prague, 1901) may have cured him forever of his "revolutionary disease" and furthered his decision to leave the country.

Rilke's last play, *Daily Living*, was likewise a scandalous failure on the Berlin stage in 1901, yet more could hardly have been expected of a conglomeration of naturalistic techniques imposed on the thought-patterns of Maeterlinck. One or two new themes, however, fresh from the heart of his personal experience, bring new life into the pattern. The scene is laid in the studio of the artist Georg, and the central problem is one of communication—communication between the artist and his model, between the artist and his sister, between the artist and his sweetheart Helene.[14] The human isolation in Rilke's play is revealed in the inadequacy of words to convey real feelings, a metaphysical reality, which—for all the characters except Mascha, the model—signifies a state of mind beyond convention, a hypostatization of Rilke's evolving attitudes toward his own solitude as an artist. The *real*, as contrasted with the *actual*, lies in the expectation of some filled dimension of experience. Helene is speaking for the author in saying that possibly the task of modern art is to find for each experience its proper time-beat. Helene's case is likewise a variation on the chastity theme. Her rejection of Georg's offer of marriage is motivated by the fact that, in a previous two-hour conversation with him, she had spiritually experienced all that marriage could possibly offer, anticipating and advancing beyond mutual love, companionship, even physical possession. One can hardly resist finding in this situation a forerunner of Eurydice in the 1904 poem "Orpheus. Eurydice. Hermes" (*New Poems*):

> nicht mehr des breiten Bettes Duft und Eiland
> und jenes Mannes Eigentum nicht mehr.
> Sie war schon aufgelöst wie langes Haar
> und hingegeben wie gefallner Regen
> und ausgestellt wie hundertfacher Vorrat . . .

> No longer the broad couch's scented island
> nor yonder man's possession any more.
> She was already loosened like long hair

29

and given far and wide like fallen rain
and dealt out like a stock of various goods.

Both Helene and Georg's sister, Sophie, are prototypes of the unrequited lovers who have transcended conventional love to enter upon a life of greater spiritual achievement. In the end, Georg is brought to understand Mascha's love as something plain and casual as the "things" of everyday.

Yet, like the "things" of Rilke's poetry, Mascha is singularly complex. When Georg confesses his desire to create a different type of art to express the world's longing—"the unexpected"—Mascha's naïve remark that "an unexpected death is the best" becomes a serious Rilkean *aperçu*. A typical paradox again looms out of Georg's conception of the artist as one who suddenly "says something only conceivable as silence." Nor are we taken entirely off our guard by his professed intention to paint a Christ conceived not as a human being but as a landscape, a landscape waiting in serene expectation of the future.[15]

Perhaps a brief summary of some of the ideas on drama, taken from the early workshop, will help toward a fuller understanding of Rilke's early aesthetic. As early as 1897 he was writing with devastating irony of the naturalistic school of Sudermann and Otto Brahm, which ignored the timeless inner reactions of the artist for casual externals.[16] Rilke insisted that the "new" drama was to devote itself to a new style or form. In the artistic presentation the modern dramatist's task was to develop the spiritual possibilities of the most insignificant subject and lay bare its maximum contours (an insignificant object or event, for example, might paradoxically assume proportions of the first magnitude). Form or style was not determined by arbitrary incidents introduced from the outside (the machinery and *décor* of naturalism), but by an interior stress of suggestive silences and articulations. Modern poets, went the thesis, had lost faith in word values. Though the public might believe that dramatic development depended on the literalness of a passage, the poet was aware that "the action is in the silence, the words its postponement."[17] Works had their own resonance and antecedents in poetry while ordinary stage language was merely the worn coin of communication. The real poet distrusted "the word," which often operated as a wall rather than a channel for vital expression on the stage. Ideal drama would consist solely of inner events.

That much of this theorizing, under the shadow of Maeterlinckean theatricalism, would nullify the possibility of spoken drama altogether, is further clear from two essays on the value of the dramatic monologue.[18] The monologue spoken without an audience in mind, Rilke held, was truer to inner experience than dialogue. He even went further in the direction of total suspension of oral drama by deploring the over-emphasis on the spoken word. What he seriously proposed in place of ordinary dramatic speech was "a space above and between words in the broadest sense," a very obvious application of his poetic practice to the stage, as the following passage reveals:

For my purpose, in order to be 'realistic', the stage has not merely one wall too few (the fourth), rather three walls too many. I want space for everything that participates in our rounds, everything by which we are affected and determined from childhood on. This has just as much claim on us as the words themselves. As though we were to read in the list of *dramatis personae*: a wardrobe, a glass, a sound, and the many purer and softer gradations between them. In life everything has the same value, and a *thing* is no worse than a word, a fragrance or a dream. Gradually this justice must become mandatory on the stage . . .[19]

Such speculation parallels an ever-growing tendency in his poetry to isolate the object from its human reference by placing it off in space. Here, in embryo, are the elements of the objective poem (*Dinggedicht*), the symbolical wall (*Wand, Vorwand*) of Malte's amphitheater at Orange with its multiple meanings for that invisible drama; and, finally, the unpretentious objects of our world that the Ninth Elegy seeks to transform and thus preserve in the precincts of the human heart:

Erde, ist es nicht dies, was du willst: unsichtbar
in uns erstehn?—Ist es dein Traum nicht,
einmal unsichtbar zu sein?—Erde! unsichtbar!
Was, wenn Verwandlung nicht, ist dein drängender Auftrag?

Earth, is it not this what you wish: an *invisible*
rebirth in us?—Is it not your dream

to be once invisible?—Earth! invisible!
What is your urgent command if not transformation?

Yet Rilke was logical enough to perceive that such wordless drama as he advocated must end in Maeterlinck's *Drames pour Marionettes* because, as he expressed it in a variant of Kleist's famous essay, "the soul of nature was easier to discover than the soul of man." [20] And by 1902 he had, outwardly at least, bid farewell to this "theater of the soul" or "dialogue of the second degree." So far is he from thinking in terms of any practical theory of drama or theater that he anticipated years in advance that peculiarly Rilkean symbol which was to appear later in the essay "Some Thoughts on Dolls" (1914) and, again, in the Fourth Elegy of the year following: the puppet with its single face and permanent expression, its economy of movement and concentration of emotion, a variant of the death-mask theme and as revealing for Rilke's poetry as the Byzantium symbol for the poetry of the later Yeats.

A quick glance at the prose workshop (the items were published in 1928 as *Early Tales*) again clarifies from another angle the ideas, images, themes, and other structural characteristics that went into the making of Rilke's poetry. Of the three collections, the one called *Around Life* (1898—a better translation would be *By-Passing Life*) was finished while he was still in Prague. At the most one may perhaps agree that these little narratives show "considerable freedom of movement, an easy and humorous way of looking at people from every angle," and that Rilke is here "the grand seigneur, who later was concealed behind the religious seeker." [21] Yet the tone is surely derived from an already outdated romanticism, and the sting of tragedy is perhaps blunted by the author's playful distance from his subject.

Religious dualism (and religious subject matter enjoyed a unique vogue in literature as the old century waned and the new got under way) emerges from two such different stories as "The Christ Child" from this collection and "The Apostle" (from *Little Novellas*). A weaker version of Hauptmann's *Hannele's Journey to Heaven*, "The Christ Child" is the sentimental account of a mistreated stepchild who, on the afternoon before Christmas, wanders off into the snow-laden woods to light her own Yule tree and is discovered asleep by two orphan children. So far it is unadulterated Dickens and Andersen at their worst. One feature, however, is significant and thematically important. The remembered beauty of the Christ Child seen in the woods by the children contrasts sharply with the brutal, factual recording of the girl's death in the hospital as the story opens: " 'Dead' stood in indifferent, brutal, damply shining letters in the thick green hospital case-book. And in the same line: II Floor, Room 12, No. 78. Horvant, Elizabeth, father forester, Aged 9." This indictment of what *The Book of Hours* will shortly term "the small death" (*der kleine Tod*) precedes by only a few years its more ironic statement in the Malte reference to the "dying in 559 beds, factory style, naturally."

"The Apostle" presents the other side of Rilke's religious conflict (he later regarded it as "my half profoundly serious, half satirical profession of faith").[22] One evening a pale, serious stranger enters the dining room of a boardinghouse, sits down at the table (an ironic distortion of the Last Supper), and launches into a vitriolic attack on Christ and the practices of Christian charity. I have come, he says in effect, to kill love in the world. Mankind was still immature when the Nazarene wasted his gift of love on a race of cripples, weaklings, and misfits. Only the strong have the right to live, only the strong reach the promised land by disengaging themselves of these human impediments. Such a conception is a blend of Nietzsche and Dostoevsky. It may seem illogical that, in one breath, Rilke could reconcile Nietzschean aristocratism with a kind of Christian socialism, but the situation is psychologically validated in much of the literature of his day, specifically in his own Paris poetry where sympathy for the poor and oppressed goes hand in hand with the cult of isolated and impoverished genius. The story offers another instance of the ambiguity of the Christ-figure in so much of his poetry.

One other story in *Around Life* should be mentioned for the light it throws on the genesis of a well-known Rilkean metaphor. In "All in One" an invalid woodcarver, disappointed in love, grimly continues to carve the features of his sweetheart in his Madonna figures who are significantly referred to as "dolls" (*Puppen*), one of the stage

33

properties of another story of the period, "Mrs Blaha's Maid." The tale's crude gothic symbolism is involved with the identity of the artist's love and work, and points in the direction of the poet's concern with the puppet as aesthetic symbol.

The two *Prague Tales* (1899), finished when the author already had Prague behind him, parallel, in point of development, the poetry of *Household Gods*. Both tales are attempts to identify immediately with the Prague environment. While less typical than the earlier prose volume, the *Prague Tales* nevertheless offer unsuspected glimpses of Rilke's mind. Here, for the first time, the death motif, intertwined with that of love, comes to the fore as it had failed appreciably to do in the early poetry. King Bohusch, the hunchback in the story by that name, and his sweetheart Frantischka arrange a rendezvous in a cemetery as a last refuge of silence and a promise of a wider life. Such love is not merely a pallid reflection of morbid concerns, for the real object of King Bohusch's affections is not the dimly conceived Frantischka but the Princess Aglaja, a forerunner of Abelone and the unrequited lovers. Aglaja's disruption of the hunchback's childhood dream by taking the Barnabite vow induces Bohusch to rail against church and state, which leads directly to his doom.

In the second tale, "Brother and Sister," Ernst Land, the young druggist who rooms with the Wankas, can only complete the circuitous route of love by seeking the forlorn childhood he had missed (evidently a strong autobiographical motif). The lost-childhood theme and Luise's fever fantasies link scenes from the Danish novelist Jacobsen with Malte's fever extravaganzas in Paris. The emotional *pointe* of the tale is the fruition of Luise's love as a result of the preceding deaths in the family.

When a Czech character in one of the tales remarks that "we have only old men and children," concluding on the very Rilkean note that "we experience our beginning and our end at the same time," not only are we reminded of Kassner's reference to a "father-world" (*Welt des Vaters*), a realm in which the poet seemed to be at home, but of the lines of the Fourth Elegy, "O trees of life, when will your winter come?" [23] Of equal interest is the fact that in the *Prague Tales* the darker atmosphere of *The Book of Hours*, along with the idea of

34

a God "underground" to replace the one in the skies, is already beginning to emerge.

Three other short stories (from the later collection *The Last of Their Line*, 1902) deserve brief mention for the additional light thrown on the love-death theme. In "The Lover," Helene is caught between the extroverted love of her fiancé, Hermann Holzer, and a spiritual affinity for his friend, Ernst Bang (the names are intentionally symbolic). Hopelessly Helene yields in the end to Holzer, healthy exponent of the modern and decrier of the past, while the sensitive, poetic Bang leaves the scene in horror. That this triangular episode will eventuate in the misery of all concerned is clearly implied; for to love in the accepted sense, according to Rilke, is to "possess," and in becoming her husband's toy Helene will sever her heart's loyalty to past and childhood, depriving her death of its ultimate florescence out of living.

In the longer title story of the collection *The Last of Their Line*, Harold Malcorn renounces his love for the healthy peasant Marie. Both Harold and his mother are victims of the claims of an artistocratic past with its fascinating legend. The son sacrifices his present affections and responsibilities to a remote past in his own memory and thus anticipates Malte's more successful explorations in the realm of childhood (even the spectral presences of Ulsgaard Castle are suggested by the melodramatic entry upon the scene of the ghostly Walpurga). Harold's desire to recapture his childhood is significantly associated with an ambition to create, but the crux of his aesthetic is sheer "Beauty." Rilke was long to experiment with the aesthetics of Beauty before locating it on the fringes of Terror. But the main emphasis is still on childhood, as though he were first probing the terrain in prose before working the theme into the structure of his poetry.

LOVE AND DEATH
Two other products of Rilke's pen, a story and a verse drama in one scene, extend a little beyond our present period. But since they are usually included with the earlier work and serve, moreover, as transition pieces to what was to come, they may be considered here.

35

THE RING OF FORMS

The White Princess (first draft 1899; revised 1904) is a lyrical drama of the type we have come to associate with the younger Hofmannsthal: there are even curious parallels with the later Hofmannsthal play *Electra*. The sixteenth-century Italian setting and the melancholy tone, however, are more reminiscent of Maeterlinck than Hofmannsthal, nor does the work display the latter's broad grasp of reality and greater poetic condensation. What is of chief interest is its themal relatedness to the already discussed "Girl Songs" and "Girl Figures," to a story like "King Bohusch" and, finally, to a whole galaxy of heroines in Rilke's later prose and verse who reject love's consummation for the destiny they may not escape. The White Princess fails to signal to her lover as the plague invades her domains. "Who lives is helpless and alone," says her young sister, Mona Lara. Reviewing her unhappy married life, the Princess is aware that "death is in life," each interweaving "as the threads run through a carpet," like the "silken thread, you have entered into the weaving" in the twenty-first Orpheus Sonnet of Part II. She is speaking also within the framework of the later *Elegies* in stating that her past miseries "were not to be missed from the melody of her great joy." Also involved is the distinction between the everyday death (in her case, possibly the loss of chastity) and the Rilkean conception of it expanded in *The Book of Hours*. The passage finally concludes with a concern for the "inconspicuous" words already alluded to, the language of poetry. One could point to many other stylistic features of *The White Princess* as bearing directly on the basic ingredients of poetry.

Of similar psychological kinship is the short story, "The Gravedigger," in *Little Novellas* (first version 1899; printed in 1903). The theme is death in a plague-ridden Italian town and is evidently indebted to Jacobsen's "Plague in Bergamo." One is at first overwhelmed by the morbid treatment, the fascination of the horrible until typical Rilkean substrata are identified.[24] The work is based on actual experiences recorded in Rilke's Smargendorf diary.[25] The new gravedigger who has turned the whole churchyard into a flower garden cannot, in the end, compete with the violence of the plague nor with the superstitious rage of the town's inhabitants. Unable to

36

cope with the corpses thrown at him, he throws aside his spade and "slowly leaves his garden and walks into the night: conquered as one who came too early, far too early." The details are macabre enough in all conscience and the story is open to various interpretations. Perhaps the flower beds symbolize art, "an attempt to encompass everything—even the unpleasant—by loveliness." [26] In any case, a grim polarity exists between life and death, not yet reconciled as in the later poetry, for the gravedigger, symbol of life, must yield in the end to the greater adversary. Several things stand out among others: the solitude of the creative life as suggested by the disruption of real spiritual communication among the characters; the gravedigger's departure as "one who came too early" reflects on the Prodigal Son theme of the *Notebooks*; and, finally, the morbid episode of the roses, reworked from a draft recorded in the *Worpswede Diary*, expands, as the years go by, into the death-mask theme, through which Rilke repeatedly sought to convey his conception of the creative life. [27] The rose symbol itself occurs at every stage in his career, with ever increasing complexity, until it comes to rest in the epitaph in the churchyard at Raron as "the rose of pure contradiction/Desire/To be nobody's slumber/Under so many eyelids."

It must seem evident, after what has been said, that the artistic values emanating from the early workshop are practically nil. It is, indeed, more like an old curiosity shop whose evidences the poet was wise to repudiate later. The work as a whole makes rather painful reading; never are we allowed to forget Rilke's greatest hazards at this stage: an exaggerated sensibility and an overflowing intuitiveness. Yet as a study of some of the major themes and motifs immaturely groping toward ultimate expression the workshop can hardly be neglected. The center of gravity of this analysis rests precisely on the extreme homogeneity of Rilke's evolution as a poet. If nothing else, the workshop period glaringly reveals the immense progress still to be made in the years that lay ahead.

II

o⚬ *The Dark God*

THE year 1899, to judge quantitatively, was one of the utmost productivity. Rilke's writing expanded in several directions, all of which, though not in equal degree, were to furnish permanent strands in the pattern of his work: the already discussed *Early Poems*, a sequel to the aesthetic experiences of the Italian journey of 1898; the first part of *The Book of Hours* following the first Russian visit; then *The Lay of the Love and Death of Cornet Christopher Rilke* and *Stories about God*, besides many poems taken up in *The Book of Images*. The abrupt and often incredibly rapid productivity is explained by the patient hoarding and waiting concentration that preceded.

It has been customary to exaggerate, often sentimentally rather than critically, the part played by Russia in Rilke's life in the sense of a neat, clearly defined dividing line between the work done before and after his Russian experience. It is generally forgotten that not only Italy but Smargendorf and Worpswede also played their parts, quite aside from the fact that his inner development had, of its own accord, attained to a fairly rich and complex level. His self-education (it was mostly that) had made immense strides from the time he left Prague in 1897 to study in Munich and Berlin, to travel in Italy, and to make two brief visits to Russia in 1899 and 1900. The *Tuscan Diary* is adequate proof of this process, and *The Book of Hours* its first large-scale expression.

38

THE DARK GOD

In connection with the work of this time as compared with that preceding, it has been remarked that "consciousness had awakened and Rilke's problems were beginning to emerge in his work." [1] The essential conflict contributing to this emergence may be recognized by contrasting two passages, one from the *Tuscan Diary*:

Know, then, that Art is this: the means whereby the lonely, the solitary, fulfil themselves. What Napoleon was outwardly is what every artist is inwardly . . . Know, then, that the artist creates for himself, for himself alone. [2]

The other is from a Russian letter of the year following:

Russia became reality for me, but at the same time the profound and daily realisation that reality is something distant which comes infinitely slowly to those who have the power to wait. Russia, the land where people are lonely, each with a world in himself, each full of darkness like a mountain, each deep in his humility, without fear of lowering himself, and consequently pious. People full of distance, uncertainty and hope: growing ones. And over all an unfixed, eternally changing, growing God. [3]

The change has been regarded as one from a "newly discovered romantic pride" to "an attitude of unbounded humility more in accordance with his nature." [4] That the poet himself felt these attitudes to be complementary rather than discordant is clear from another Russian letter: "I experience my stay here . . . as a rare completion of that Florentine spring, the influence and effect of which I have described to you," adding, as if to show toward which side of the equation he inclined, "A friendly disposition has led me to the next things, further into the depths, into the greater simplification, the lovelier simplicity." [5] Heerikhuizen remarks quite justly: "As the Renaissance had first appealed to his sense of beauty and individualistic pride, Russia now appealed to the dark, mystical unity of things, to his wish to relinquish himself to something greater than himself in a fanatical humility, and to his feeling of brotherly kinship with all men." [6] When he writes from St. Petersburg, May 27, 1899: "For all things are in existence in order to become to us images in some sense," [7] we have a fairly good clue as to what disposition Rilke made of Russia—and

39

indeed of every other experience—in the scheme of poetry. Russia, Worpswede, Paris, and Muzot alike were simply cadres into which he tirelessly fitted an ever changing kaleidoscope of images out of his total experience.

The Book of Hours is organically uneven, the product of different levels of feeling. The last section, written in Paris in 1903, is superior in inner organization to the first part of 1899, while the intervening section of 1901 is roughly transitional. In order to get at the quality of Rilke's "felt thought," the ideas in the first part will be discussed at greater length, always at the risk attendant on paraphrase, than it aesthetically deserves in proportion to the other two. Its early popularity can now be understood since it contains a good share of the aestheticism of Rilke's age, the retreat to a "hushed cult of beauty, a religious sensuality, a retreat out of the profane into an exquisite cloistral art," [8] rendered familiar by many *fin de siècle* writers. The title derives from the *horae canonicae* of the medieval church, the French *livres d'heures* of the fifteenth and sixteenth centuries, decorated with costly miniatures and imitating the older Latin breviary. Since their content consisted of the prayers of the monks, in a purely liturgical style and not signifying personal recourse to God, a title implying such formal relationship might seem ill-suited to a book of poetry so obviously personal in content. It was not so much the content of the old liturgies that supplied Rilke with the title as the poetic connotations associated with the word "hours."

Structurally the work resembles an opera libretto with recitative, chorus, instrumentation and melodic effects, implied or explicit, all supplied by the same person. This is clear from an examination of the earliest draft of Part I ("The Book of Monkish Life"), whose poetry is interspersed with prose comments referring to "the monk" in the third person. The aesthetic conception of this *soi-disant* monk is reflected in the following rubric: "The monk was almost an artist. Although he allowed himself to be formed by his verses instead of forming them." [9] The dramatic nature of the original conception is apparent in the inclusion of a virtual dramatis personae of brother monks as well as God himself.

In the *Tuscan Diary* the poet had remarked that, in their moments

THE DARK GOD

of supreme adoration, the old monks were impelled solely by the
longing to find themselves (*die Sehnsucht nach sich selbst*). In this
sense *The Book of Hours* is the most subjective of Rilke's works, a
daring effort to relate the artist to his world in terms ultimately reducible to solipsism. Reciting a cadenced litany, the artist-monk ex-
plores his relationship to the artist-god, his symbol. He is speaking
primarily to and for himself, immersed in a brown twilight, invoking
an invisible interlocutor. The argument assumes the form of separate
prayers and meditations in varying metrical patterns, always interrupted by the protagonist's fearful obsession with the problem of in-
venting new attributes to convey his conception of the "dark god,"
in keeping with the imperfective nature of the Russian experience.[10]
Neither deity nor monk exist independently; the one is dialectically
necessary to the other, held in balance by a common tension:

> Doch wie ich mich auch in mich selber neige:
> mein Gott ist dunkel und wie ein Gewebe
> von hundert Wurzeln, welche schweigsam trinken . . .

> No matter how I hearken to within:
> my god is darkness and a complex network
> of countless roots forever silent drinking . . .

No one today regards Rilke, as was formerly the case, as a mystic
in the traditional sense of the term. His concern is not with the divin-
ities of either Eastern or Western churches, but with his own inspiration. Instead of the humble passage from human to divine modes of
experience, as with Eckhart or St. John of the Cross, *The Book of
Hours* presents a merging of divine and human merely as a function
of creative power. The once-sought analogies between the Rilke of
this stage and Angelus Silesius, for example, or even with the attempts of ancient Talmudists to name the ineffable are only superficial, and this applies also to generalizations about the *coincidentia
oppositorum* and the Hegelian dialectic. Rather, a view of poetry is
projected under a religious guise; religiosity is here the product of
artistic consciousness; the divinity a catalyst in a solution of many
lofty, if somewhat specialized images, modified by impressions of
Tolstoi, Jacobsen, the Old Testament, and hours spent before Renaissance paintings and Russian icons.

THE RING OF FORMS

THE NEW GENESIS

The Book of Hours begins with cosmogony and ends with an adaptation of the legend of St. Francis to the poet's vision. In his cell the monk addresses himself to a power known only through the attributes of metaphor. The Rilkean god is the "neighbor god," the "mysterious one," the "sooty old man sleeping on a stove," the "peasant with a beard," the "darkling foundation of the world," the "thing of things," but his real presence is enclosed in the tension of antinomies and paradox:

> Du bist der Tiefste, welcher ragte,
> der Taucher und der Türme Neid.
> Du bist der Sanfte, der sich sagte,
> und doch, wenn dich ein Feiger fragte,
> so schwelgtest du in Schweigsamkeit.

>> You are the *deepest* one to *soar*,
>> the *divers'* envy and the *tower's*,
>> the *gentle* one who *spoke* his name,
>> yet if a coward *asked* the same,
>> then *silence* was your revelling.

Here the emphasized words (my italics) stand to each other in the condition of paradox and contradiction. In George's *Star of the Covenant*, on the other hand, the figurative language serves a quite different purpose:

> Ich bin der Eine und bin Beide
> ich bin der Zeuger bin der schoos
> ich bin der degen und die scheide
> ich bin das opfer bin der stoss . . .

>> I am the One, I am the Two,
>> I am the womb, I am the sire,
>> I am the shadow and the true,
>> I am the faggot and the fire.

George's metaphors merge the contradictions of experience (the pronoun is therefore *I* and not *You*, for the Ego and the Other coalesce into One in George's social humanism). Unity is stressed through repetitions of subject and predicate, suggestive of litany or ritual chant. George's certainty stems from psychological and aesthetic premises quite different from Rilke's search for the artist-god.

42

THE DARK GOD

In a sense one may speak of baroque metaphors in Rilke's poetry, here as well as later. The use of paradox, oxymoron, catachresis, of Christian, pluralist, and mystical figures reminds us that in baroque poetry, as well as in baroque religion, the truth about God may be expressed through anagogical images as well as by couplings of contradictions and contraries.

One can readily conceive of the god of *The Book of Hours* as "the guest always in transit." His beginnings lie partly in the poet's anxiety, partly in the conviction that, whether we will it or not, God is constantly growing in us. In the Rodin period this deity will become synonymous with "things" (*die Dinge*), in the poet's maturer poetry with the "pure relationships" (*reine Bezüge*). The first book's opening lines invite particular consideration:

> Da neigt sich die Stunde und rührt mich an
> mit klarem, metallenem Schlag:
> mir zittern die Sinne. Ich fühle: ich kann—
> und ich fasse den plastischen Tag.

> Now the hour bows down, it touches me, throbs
> metallic and lucid and bold:
> my senses are trembling. I feel my own power—
> on the plastic day I lay hold.

The language explicitly draws on plastic, visual imagery to convey a distinctly acoustic effect. Indeed, the protagonist is primarily a painter, evidence of the poet's absorption of his Russian experience to a good extent through the fine arts. The entire work is better understood from this art-aspect than from any attempt to read mysticism into it. This *seen* universe with its metallic bell-tolling and its "plastic" daylight tries to come to terms with an almost exclusive susceptibility tò music. From the start Rilke's poetry is a persistent contest between music and plastic form (in another context, between time and space).

The second quatrain provides a key to the poet's novel cosmology in the attempt to create a poetic myth:

> Nichts war noch vollendet, eh ich es erschaut,
> ein jedes Werden stand still.
> Meine Blicke sind reif, und wie eine Braut
> kommt jedem das Ding, das er will.

> Until I perceived it, no thing was complete,
> but waited, hushed, unfulfilled.
> My vision is ripe, to each glance like a bride
> comes softly the thing that was willed.

This private universe with its own version of Genesis is a poetic declaration of independence from all previous practices, norms, and beliefs. "Art is childhood," he had written in the *Tuscan Diary*, in rejection of the cultural past and the stock evaluations of this heritage, "Art means not knowing that the world already *is* and making one. Not destroying what one finds left but simply finding nothing finished. Nothing but possibilities. Nothing but desires."[11] In the act of creation

> Gott spricht zu jedem, eh er ihn macht,
> dann geht er schweigend mit ihm aus der Nacht.
> Aber die Worte, eh jeder beginnt,
> diese wolkigen Worte sind:
> von deinen Sinnen hinausgesandt,
> geh bis an deiner Sehnsucht Rand;
> gib mir Gewand. . . .

> God speaks to each only before he's made,
> then silently goes with him from the night.
> But the words before each one begins,
> these nebulous words are said:
> emissaries of your senses go
> to the margin of your longing's reach,
> give me figure and dress. . . .

Again there is speech amid silence, and the idiom conforms to an already familiar pattern: "silently," "cloudy," "longing," "garments," etc. The equating of God with the world is made possible through *things*, and the texture of experience as a whole, heralding the opening lines of the First Elegy, is seen to consist of both Beauty *and* Terror. The terms "night" and "darkness" are more than costume or mask, symbols rather of more primitive layers of experience as contrasted with over-civilized, over-illuminated modern "culture." When Novalis hymns night, on the other hand, it is a metaphysical realm in the other world; Rilke's night is an aesthetic element limited to this world.

The historical orientation of this cosmology sets off the High Ren-

aissance against Russian Byzantinism, light and color against tone-
less dark, clear contours against shifting nuances, West against East,
contemporary art-forms against the greater potentialities yet to come.
Michelangelo by name, and Botticelli by implication, are the only
artists mentioned in the *Tuscan Diary* who are exempt from Rilke's
condemnation of the Renaissance. For him the fifteenth century
marked the great watershed in the history of Western civilization,
long before Hulme and other modern thinkers took up with the idea.
If God is still lost in "the forest of contradictions" and the Logos
Son still an impediment to progress, the Virgin at least comes off
with one of Rilke's finer lyric passages, typical of his early style at its
best and anticipating the later *Virgin Songs.* Ironically, his "Nativ-
ity" with its flowing music, bloom and color, its swaying Virgin so
intimate with fruition, is actually much indebted to Renaissance
painting seen through Pre-Raphaelite eyes:

> Da liessen sie sie gehn und schweben
> und treiben mit dem jungen Jahr;
> ihr dienendes Marienleben
> ward königlich und wunderbar.
> Wie feiertägliches Geläute
> ging es durch alle Häuser gross;
> und die einst mädchenhaft Zerstreute
> war so versenkt in ihren Schoss
> und so erfüllt von jenem Einen
> und so für tausende genug,
> dass alles schien, sie zu bescheinen,
> die wie ein Weinberg war und trug.

> And then they let her grow and sway
> and burgeon with the youthful year;
> her humble helping Virgin day
> was royalty and magic here.
> Then through all homes the spirit wrought,
> like feast-day bells demanding room,
> till she whose girlhood was distraught
> was so intent upon her womb
> and so replete with One alone
> and ample now for thousands more
> that for her shining all things shone
> who like a vineyard waxed and bore.

45

THE RING OF FORMS

The Michelangelo motif of the first section receives considerable importance when taken in conjunction with the St. Francis adaptation in the final "Book of Poverty and Death." By way of Michelangelo and St. Francis the curve is already prefigured from Russia to Muzot, from the Byzantine monk in his closed cell to the Orpheus of the *Sonnets*.

To find symbolic equivalents for the many contradictions of living the protagonist-monk resorts to the allied fields of sculpture and painting. Despite occasional fumbles he usually succeeds in describing his object in some plastic, spatial form. The certainty of his vision is predicated on his knowledge of a new dimension—*Raum*, "space" —perhaps the most universal and complex of all Rilke symbols, for a broader, more timeless life. Symbols and images ordinarily expressing the god-artist relationship are conceived of as objects (walls, towers, etc.). The "dark" source of the monk's inspiration embraces "forms and flames, animals and myself," an early intimation of many themes of the Paris *New Poems*.

The justification of the Rilkean God's existence rests on empirical foundations, on the use to which he is put, as one uses a tool or utensil, a carry-over from *Early Poems*. The Rilkean artist achieves through action, the work of loving hands, and not through cerebration. Behind such ideas lurk Bergson, the life-philosophers, and other metaphysical theorists of the day.

Except for the "tree" and "space" metaphors, probably no figure is so conspicuous as that of the "cathedral." Trembling creative hands labor at the cathedral of God whose final ornamental touches the monk conceives himself as lending:

> Werkleute sind wir: Knappen, Jünger, Meister,
> und bauen dich, du hohes Mittelschiff.
> Und manchmal kommt ein ernster Hergereister,
> geht wie ein Glanz durch unsre hundert Geister
> und zeigt uns zitternd einen neuen Griff.
>
> Wir steigen in die wiegenden Gerüste,
> in unsren Händen hängt der Hammer schwer,
> bis eine Stunde uns die Stirnen küsste,
> die strahlend und als ob sie alles wüsste,
> von dir kommt wie der Wind vom Meer.

THE DARK GOD

Dann ist ein Hallen von den vielen Hämmern,
und durch die Berge geht es Stoss um Stoss.
Erst wenn es dunkelt, lassen wir dich los:
und deine kommenden Konturen dämmern.

Gott, du bist gross. . . .

    We are all workmen: prentice, journeyman,
    or master, building you—you towering nave.
    And sometimes there will come to us a grave
    wayfarer, who like a radiance thrills
    the souls of all our hundred artisans,
    as tremblingly he shows us a new skill.

    We climb up on the rocking scaffolding,
    the hammers in our hands swing heavily,
    until our foreheads feel the caressing wing
    of a radiant hour that knows everything,
    and hails from you as wind hails from the sea.

    Then hammerstrokes sound, multitudinous,
    and through the mountains echoes blast on blast.
    Only at dusk we yield you up at last:
    and slow your shaping contours dawn on us:

    God, you are vast. . . .

The short dimeter at the end not only provides metrical variety but serves also to introduce the theme of God's stature in the lines that follow. Characteristic, again, is the rhythmic pattern, lines flowing into each other, the one pulling the other after it, so to speak. The lines further illustrate Rilke's choice of the participial form of the epithet, even of the substantive—a practice to become increasingly more complex and diversified as his work developed. The figure of the "cathedral," as elsewhere that of the "tree," merely emphasizes two aspects of the creative process. The artist's achievement is in the terms of organic form but the drive comes from the matrix of all creation, whether we call it "divine afflatus," as did the Augustans, or, with the Freudians, the subconscious, or Rilke's tree growing darkly, root-borne downward, yet brushing the heavens with its crown.

    Much in the first section still betrays the early workshop, many thoughts are still unrealized poetic constructions. The death factor is only vaguely worked out "because death's note would claim a higher key," though at least one of its aspects, the petty bourgeois death so excoriated in the *Notebooks*, receives significant statement:

> Ich kann nicht glauben, dass der kleine Tod,
> dem wir doch täglich überm Scheitel schauen,
> uns eine Sorge bleibt und eine Not.

> I do not hold the belief that petty death
> into whose face we daily gaze askance
> should bide a trouble to us and distress.

More important are Rilke's variations on the time factor. The monk contrasts the time-bound knowledge of man with the dark, unknown god, time with eternity, diffusion with concentration, and his commission from his deity is to depict time as his deepest sorrow: "You bent me slowly out of time/in which I climbed unsure." In demanding "space" rather than "time," he is Rilke playing off plastic expression against musicality (not fully realized until the *Sonnets to Orpheus*). Rilke actually lends spatiality to his time concept, for time is transient and "many-figured," but we are "the veins in the hard splendor of God's basalt." With the time factor, in turn, is associated the element of dread (*Angst*) which came to play so large a part in Malte's Paris experience. Even the monk's "neighbor-god," the poet's artist-surrogate, is filled with anxiety for the very postulates of his existence: "What will you do, God, when I die?" In the hour of "incomprehensible anxiety," when God demands back from all things his completed image, Rilke's Last-Judgment theme is already prefigured.

THE PETTY DEATH

In "The Book of Pilgrimage" the number of fragmentary themes of the preceding section is greatly reduced; we come closer to the poet's own person and thought operating on a more immediate present. The scene is more localized, East and West intermingling: the flight of autumn leaves in the high wind suggesting Russia and Westerwede, contrasted with unhealthy urban conditions of modern life (Paris).

In reintroducing himself, the monk—a relatively more colorful speaker than in the first part—again emphasizes his peculiar relationship to the god-symbol: "I am the same one still who kneeled," an indication that Rilke intended the three books to be interrelated. In disclosing the diffusion and disintegration of the modern soul, the monk unbares the poet's own agonies and fears, personality conflicts and anxiety neuroses. He is a being "scattered, myself divided piecemeal by my enemies, the laughter of all laughers, the drink of all drinkers, collected from courtyards out of rubbish and old glass shards." Like a "house gutted by fire" or a "plague-ridden city," he gropes for his god-symbol as a warrant of coherence and unity in living where all seems to be chaos. The symbol again is primarily aesthetic, with merely ethical overtones; the monk seeks neither solace nor sanctification, but simply someone "who will regard him as a simple object," i.e., the *Kunstding* itself.

Of further modifications of the symbol the most striking is the paradoxical father-son relationship in which the usual orthodox roles are reversed. The artist, committed to his own Genesis, will not permit the father to be more than the son. Artistic self-justification had already elicited the statement (*Tuscan Diary*) that the father represents the past while the creative future belongs to the son. The polemics against Christianity throughout the book are to be understood as a maneuver not primarily to destroy it but to make room for a certain conception of poetry. This is all that is meant by such lines as "All who seek you, tempt you." Yet the sensitive Rilke apparently felt some slight twinge of conscience, for his monk explicitly abjures any charge of blasphemy—quite unnecessarily since purely artistic orientation and not the orthodox sonship of Christ is in question— God as "the nuance of nuances," as Mason puts it.[12] The poet is giving us a description of a certain kind of poetic awakening: first awareness on the poet's part increases sensitivity to surroundings, and the percipient is disturbed "by neighbor and clock"—psychic conflicts inducing "anxiety" but culminating in the creative process itself. A conglomeration of accidents and tricks, anxieties and petty joys, an attic storeroom of lifeless things (*ungelebte Dinge*), man does not live his own life; and the feebly stated hypothesis that God may live it for him is only another way of bringing the artist back into the picture.

Taken literally, such *aperçus* seem to have more biographical and psychological interest than anything else. Yet beneath the surface may be detected an important statement about poetry. Human activity today is tragically devoid of symbolic representation—"an activity without image," as Rilke was later to call it. Hence the monk is "farther from humans than from things," for men are visualized "as children already disguised in masquerade, as masks articulate, as visages mute." Rilke's important mask theme is already breaking through in the early poetry.

The monk's conviction that all life is somehow miraculously lived raises the question, by whom? The answer is: if not by man, then by the *Dinge*, the concrete "things" of this world with its woods and flowers, waters and animals. *The Book of Hours* as a whole is indeed "a surprising series of poetic variations on the theme: what is *das Ding*?" [13] The formula reads: *God* equals *Ego* equals *Things*. Ancient hylozoism was something else again. Rilke's objects are not merely animated by nature forces but preferred to human behavior patterns —a stinging indictment of the hyperintellectual temper of the times. He frequently refers to the "law of gravity" (*das Gesetz der Schwere*), to which his things stand in docile submission. Falling, they are carried into the heart of the world, guarded by some "winged goodness," the gravitational pull of God's world. Unable or unwilling to surrender to these shrewd energies (the "tree" again is functional model), men crowd themselves into a narrow space devoid of all freedom. The images used are those of unhurried falling or hovering in the air, like the leaves in the well-known "Autumn" poem from *The Book of Images*. Ethically Rilke pleads for a type of piety (*Frömmigkeit*) that will harmonize the individual with his universe, and to this end renunciation and dispossession are essential. Men have no claim to the really important elements of their living; nothing they lay hands on really belongs to them, though they commonly speak of *my* life, *my* wife, *my* dog, even *my* God.[14] Such renunciation is ultimately linked with his difficult conception of love as maintaining a certain distance from its object.

To offset this negative criticism of an age, we are offered a some-

THE DARK GOD

what vague, because essentially message-type, prospect for a rebirth of feeling and spiritual orientation. The world, the monk concludes, is at the mercy of money-violence and of the mob. As a sort of parable of the simple life, he cites the longing of the "noble metals" to return to the ancestral stone (an old romantic motif). The new religion, of course, will have no accommodation for churches that "hang on God as though he were a fugitive." Their place will be taken by homes inviolable as cathedrals, accessible to all. And in this envisaged creative relationship to earthly things the majesty of death will not be desecrated by piteous cravings for the hereafter:

Kein Jenseitswarten und kein Schaun nach drüben,
nur Sehnsucht, auch den Tod nicht zu entweihen,
und dienend sich am Irdischen zu üben,
um seinen Händen nicht mehr neu zu sein.

No waiting the beyond, no peering toward it,
but longing to degrade not even death;
we shall learn earthliness, and serve its ends,
to feel its hands about us like a friend's.

The Rilkean god himself is never really "owned," and is therefore "the guest forever wandering," in poetry a symbol of "nuances" and of "openness," described as follows in the antithetical pairs (my italics) of the verse structure:

Ein Ausgestossener und ein Vereinter,
gesammelt und vergeudet doch zugleich;
ein Lächelnder und doch ein Halbverweinter,
klein wie ein Haus und mächtig wie ein Reich.

An *exile* and yet one *restored*,
at once *collected* and *dispersed*,
all *smiles* and yet with *tears* half-versed,
house-small and yet an *empire strong*.

The concluding vision of the pilgrims, particularly of the antics of an epileptic monk, is shot through with revealing motifs and figures: the "crooked marionette" (*schiefgeschobene Marionette*), the god unheeding as in Michelangelo's stone until the monk presents himself naked to him, all important ingredients to be met with later in prose and poetry.

51

THE RING OF FORMS

THE GREAT DEATH

Two years later, during eight April days of 1903, the final section, "The Book of Poverty and Death," completed the cycle of what Rilke was to call, after the event, somewhat deprecatingly, "prayers" (*Gebete*). Because of fresh insights into poetry gained from the Paris experience the thematic sequence is more clearly enunciated and worked out than in the preceding sections. The death theme, merely hinted at before, at last receives its definitive statement.

Life and death are the reverse sides of an identical coin, mortality one of the conventional symbols invented to designate the phenomenal side of what we do not clearly understand. Death is not the final extinction of personality but the goal and fruition of experience, the crown and seal of living, functional as life itself. Out of our being we create our death, create it as we go along. If death is made to appear dour and repulsive (despite the enticements of morticians), it is because, like fruit picked out of season, we have not fully ripened, are still green or withered away. Though metaphysical speculation has long been familiar with this attitude, it is Rilke's special contribution to have degeneralized it, applying it to individual experience. Rilke does not flay life to propitiate a lugubrious other-worldliness, like the preacher who cried "In the midst of life we are in death." Nor like Pascal, for whom death was in life from the drawing of the first breath, did he make of it a continuous preparation for the body's holocaust, alone acceptable to God. His death-metaphysic is another aspect of his aesthetic, as is the St. Francis motif at the end of the book. It is perhaps possible to link the idea with Nietzsche's Eternal Recurrence, as Heller has done, who goes on to say: "We shall come to see Rilke as the St. Francis of the Will to Power." [15]

It is logically consistent for the monk to advocate the destruction of a civilization that does not encourage such insights. In excoriating the modern city he corroborates not merely the poet's private agonies of maladjustment and frustration but those of our whole modern culture. The melody part of the final section suggests the possibilities of a more vital future as the bass hammers away at mass civilization, accused and condemned. The cities, the monk perceives, are dissolved in chaos, the gestures of their inhabitants heavy with the sordidness of their lives. But Rilke's children standing in dark doorways, knowing nothing of flowers and fresh air, of the possibilities of health and happiness, derive not from social humanitarianism but from Baudelaire. All this concern with social disintegration is rooted in aesthetic soil. Only in a very limited sense may Rilke be regarded as a forerunner of Expressionism; in any case he singles out the spiritual effect of the social circumstances rather than their material consequences.[16]

> Und ihre Menschen dienen in Kulturen
> und fallen tief aus Gleichgewicht und Mass,
> und nennen Fortschritt ihre Schneckenspuren
> und fahren rascher wo sie langsam fuhren,
> und fühlen sich und funkeln wie die Huren
> und lärmen lauter mit Metal und Glas.

> Their denizens slave as some culture's basis
> and break all balance and all measures mass,
> and vaunt the progress of their creeping paces
> and because that which once was calm now races
> glitter like whores with pride upon their faces
> and still redouble roar of steel and glass.

The "traveled faster where they once traveled slower" will become twenty years later, in the airplane age, a warning to youth against "attempts at flight into mere swiftness" (*Sonnets to Orpheus*, Part I, 22), while the "roar of steel and glass" will be reflected in the technical confusions of the machine age (*Sonnets* I, 18, 23, 24). The vowels run in parallel alternations of *u, ei, a*, as in the final two verses, leaping from the dark closed vowel to the brighter open one. The juxtaposition of opposites (*Fortschritt-Schneckenspuren, rascher-langsam*, etc.), together with repetitions of word stems with alliterative overtones (*fahren-fuhren*) serve to link the four middle verses together. The contrast of "falling" and "balancing" again repeats the symbolic pattern familiar to us. The use of such devices, however, may often become mannered (the *Huren-Kulturen* rhyme was certainly providential) and tonal values are sometimes exaggerated in the breathless run-on lines—here the copulative is repeated six times! A letter from Rome (1903) specifically attributes the "style and poverty" of this early verse to "this fluid forming and disintegrating."[17]

Its effect may account in some measure for the reaction of many Germans of the first World War generation to Rilke's poetry generally. "There were times," writes one of them, a competent Rilke critic, "when one forgot *The Book of Hours*, wanted to forget it, when the melodic beauty of young Rilke's verse in its swaying pliancy was intolerable to us." [18]

The poet's prescription for the New Adam tallies fairly well with the popularizations of the vitalists and life-philosophers from Nietzsche through D. H. Lawrence. The healthy mind must first have a healthy body; false hypocrisies and shame reactions regarding sex are bitterly attacked, as in the exacerbative prose of the *Worker's Letter* twenty years later. Rilke is not usually at ease in the phrasing of sex ideas, here particularly crass as issuing from one who has just been supposedly conversing with God:

> Mach Einen herrlich, Herr, mach Einen gross,
> bau seinem Leben einen schönen Schooss,
> und seine Scham errichte wie ein Tor
> in einem blonden Wald von jungen Haaren,
> und ziehe durch das Glied des Unsagbaren
> den Reisigen, den weissen Heeresscharen,
> den tausend Samen, die sich sammeln, vor. . . .

> > Make thou One lordly, Lord, and make him great,
> > give him a womb as wondrous as his fate.
> > And let his phallus like a gate of awe
> > by a blond forest of young hair protected . . .
> > the thousand seeds of consecration draw.

The New Man is also to possess the "solitude of a star" during his impressionable years so that the fullness of manhood may later be restored through the gift of recall and unconscious association. Such ideas are at the bottom of Auden's reference to the poet as "The Santa Claus of Loneliness" and Holthusen's to "the patron-saint of the loneliness of modern man; not as an advocate of a spurious retreat into other-worldliness, but as the authentic opposite of the mass-mind and of the civilization of machines and ideologies." [19] The reference to unconscious associations in connection with childhood is, of course, the Archimedean principle of all Rilke's poetry. The most signal achievement of the New Man, however, is to be the gen-

THE DARK GOD

eration within himself of "death the master." Rilke substitutes for
the ancient Messiah-expectation the "father birth of death," the artist-god of the *Tuscan Diary*. Wherever the network of his thought
may lead, we always arrive back where we started from: the premise
of aesthetic experience leading to the Ring of Forms.

The motifs of the modern city and of the New Adam lead consistently to the poverty theme which concludes the book. Though
the days of wealthy tribal chieftains, dynastic rulers and merchant
princes are over, they at least compelled life to "be infinitely broad,
heavy and warm." The modern rich, on the other hand, have no
status at all. Only the poor (a variation of the social theme beloved
of naturalist poets at the end of the century) have any chance of a
new life, "the privilege of being as poor as they really are." The aris-
tocratic-aesthetic bias is not only revealed in the definition of poverty
as "a great radiance from within" (similar phrasing was used later to
characterize Van Gogh) but in the choice of metaphors, for here the
literal couplings of "The Book of Monkish Life" have been suc-
ceeded by the mystical tropes of Christology: "The great Rose of
Poverty," "The Beggar with the Hidden Face," "The Leper with the
Rattle," "the Homeless One." The apotheosis of St. Francis at the
end, in emphatic position, betrays to what extent Rilke was willing
to accept the linkage between ideas of religion and art through the
agency of poverty. Already Christian and orphic features are inter-
mingled in the jubilant description of the saint's death and his pantheistic reversion to nature. The conception is closer to the Greek
version of the sacrificial death of Orpheus than to anything readily
associated with the Italian saint:

> Und als er starb, so leicht wie ohne Namen,
> da war er ausgeteilt: sein Samen rann
> in Bächen, in den Bäumen sang sein Samen
> und sah ihn ruhig aus den Blumen an . . .
> Was fühlen ihn, den Jubelnden und Jungen,
> die Armen, welche harren, nicht von fern?
>
> Was steigt er nicht in ihre Dämmerungen—
> der Armut grosser Abendstern?

> And when he died, as lightly as unknown,
> he was distributed: the brooks

> carried his seed and trees intoned it
> and from the flowers it quietly gazed at him . . .
> Why do the poor, who wait on him, not feel
> far off this jubilant and youthful one?
>
> Why mounts he not into their twilight hours—
> Poverty's great evening-star?

It is easy to point out, as Rilke himself seemed willing to do, more obvious defects in the work as a whole. The poetry has been well likened to those "acted poems" of the Mysteries in the Rue Saint-Denis, described in the *Notebooks*, that "continually added to and extended themselves, growing to tens of thousands of verses . . ." [20] The great rapidity with which the individual sections were written is certainly one of the causes of the formal looseness the poet himself deplored. There is no definitive "sinking into" a theme to develop its resources and close off its contours. Years later his French translator records Rilke's own impressions: "When I wrote *The Book of Hours*, I had the feeling that the act of release had been accomplished so easily that I could no longer stop writing. The book, by the way, is not a collection, from which a page or a single poem may be removed, as one plucks a flower. More than any other of my books it is a song, one indivisible poem, in which no strophe can be moved from its place, as little as the veins of a leaf or the voices of a choir." [21]

Essentially, however, the poet was faced in this case with a psychological difficulty. The monk, for example, is frequently uncertain whether he is the voice of the poet or of the anchorite. The real saint would have been confused by these occasional discrepancies, but *The Book of Hours* was conceived on the plane of aesthetic symbolism where the poet and his diction should be organically unified. In her recently published memoirs Lou Andreas-Salomé has graphically described the psychological conflict taking place in Rilke at this time (i.e., the Russian experience), a conflict caused by the increasing divergence between "experiencing" (*Erleben*) and "forming" (*Gestalten*).[22] It was, indeed, a new beginning in which "a deep and intense feeling of vocation" is revealed, and equally true that the gulf between the poet's intensity of feeling and his "god," the nuance of nuances, is only too frequently bridged by an unceasing number and

THE DARK GOD

variety of images, and by the dynamic quality of the rhythms. For that matter, the poem itself is its own best critic: "For my voice grew in two directions/and has become a fragrance and a crying."

GOD FOR THE BOURGEOIS: FESTIVAL OF DEATH

The *Stories about God*, at one time more popular than *The Book of Hours* and stemming from the same spiritual climate, continues the argument on the "paradoxical identities of life and death." [23] The pseudo-mystical sublimity has merely been replaced by a mixture of fairy tale and parody. The framework itself is a playful irony, for these whimsical tales told to adults who are supposedly to repeat them for the benefit of children are directed, of course, at the adults themselves—a kind of attempt to *épater le bourgeois*. Such is the effect upon the reader, though the poet's later gloss (Jan. 25, 1921) gives a quite accurate account of their genesis: ". . . these youthful phantasies were improvised out of an instinct. If I were to define this more closely, I should like to regard it as being occupied in removing God from the sphere of rumour into the realm of direct and daily experience; and suggesting with every available means a naïve and active 'using' of God as it seemed assigned to me in childhood . . ." [24]

Only two of the stories are of particular interest for an understanding of the poetry. The prose story of Michelangelo, of one stubbornly at work in his workshop to shape the stone to his indomitable will, is an aesthetic version of Jacob's wrestling with the angel. Here an attempt is made to correlate in plastic terms both the god-symbol and the artist. Was Rilke perhaps acquainted with the sculptor's own sonnets where the future hidden stone is prophetically envisioned in the purity of new-hewn marble?

> Non ha l'ottimo artista alcun concetto,
> Ch' un marmo solo in sè non circonscriva
> Col suo soverchio; e solo a quello arriva
> La man che ubbidisce all' intelletto.

and again:

> . . . Ma nel secundo poi di pietra viva
> S'adempion le promesse del martello;

57

E sì rinasce tal concetto e bello,
Che ma' non è chi suo eterno prescriva.[25]

Through the workings of God in himself, the artist achieves creation, the productive act releases the inner prompting. Already God and artist have become the selfsame person as seen from different vantage points.

In the tale "How Old Timofei Died Singing" the glorification of folk minstrelsy and oral transmission of song contains a certain amount of *pro domo* pleading, especially in the semantic emphasis on "the little words that die in daily life." "But the words people use now," comments the author-narrator, "these heavy, unsingable words, were hostile to it" (i.e., the oral art of the past),[26] "and removed from it one mouth after the other." Behind the story as façade the poet presents his own idea of the anonymity of art, its uncommittedness to temporary situations, its dedication to the open horizon and the full nuance.

By comparison, *The Lay of the Love and Death of Cornet Christopher Rilke* is, despite the poet's belittlement in after years, a little masterpiece of episodic richness and ingenious rhythmical construction. The twenty-seven short vignettes are written in rhythmical prose. The poetic form of *The Lay* fits into no ready stereotyped pattern.[27] To call it a ballad conjures up the war-poem fallacy. Its effective form is quite different even from the varieties of rhythmical prose that were cropping up at the century's turning.[28] The variations in form proceed from one vignette to another, from impressionistic prose to definite prose rhythms with internal rhyme as the tension reaches the climax of love and death. The poem's form is organically related to its dramatic tensions—which is perhaps one reason why it has been so long a favorite with many people.

The sweeping dramatic curve of the story of an alleged ancestor who encounters death in a seventeenth-century campaign against the Turks may easily tempt us to forget that the work is imbued with characteristic Rilkean themes, however unrepresentative it may be in other respects. In his search for ancestral connections, for a traditional link with the past, Rilke, like Nietzsche before him, indulges in romantic myth-making. However spurious in fact, this sense of traditional values became an important ingredient in his poetry, as in the beautiful Orpheus Sonnet I, 17:

> Zu unterst der Alte, verworrn,
> all der Erbauten
> Wurzel, verborgener Born,
> den sie nie schauten.
>
> Sturmhelm und Jägerhorn,
> Spruch von Ergrauten,
> Männer im Bruderzorn,
> Frauen wie Lauten . . .

> Undermost he, the earth-bound
> root of uprearing,
> multitudes, source underground,
> never appearing.
>
> Helmet and hunting-horn,
> words of the aging,
> rage between brothers-born,
> women assuaging . . .

Heller's interprctation of the final tercets in the Nietzsche context as indicating an aesthetic based on a Dionyso-Apolline mergence is, I think, basically sound.[29]

More important than this effort to fixate his present in the rich past of Europe is Rilke's treatment here of one of his basic themes. He depicts the transition from childhood to adulthood of a young man (of the later Malte, perhaps, or of the "hero" of the *Elegies*), suddenly wrenched from the mother and girls singing in the harvest fields at home to encounter mature love and death as overwhelming destinies. The description of the love-hour in the tower before the fatal engagement is a variation of the "new creation" idea. "And yet they fear nothing,/for nothing confronts them, no/yesterday, no morrow, for time has/collapsed and they blossom out of its/ruins." The fruition of death, after such love, is a "festival," the crown of living. Death culminating amid the sixteen Turkish blades reintroduces the opening imagery of childhood:

> Aber, als es jetzt hinter ihm zusammenschlägt,
> sind es doch wieder Gärten, und die sechzehn
> runden Säbel, die auf ihn zuspringen, Strahl um

> Strahl, sind ein Fest.
> Eine lachende Wasserkunst.

>> But as they strike together behind him
>> he knows there *are* gardens and
>> those sixteen sabres that strike down
>> upon him, stroke after stroke, are a
>> feast.
>> A laughing fountain that plays.

How beautifully the "laughing fountain" paves the way to the art-object of the Paris poems and to the "Fountain-Mouth" of the *Sonnets* "that can respond/so inexhaustibly to all who ask/with one, pure, single saying . . .") Little question that *The Lay* is informed with "intuitive ingenuousness" and a "somnambulistic sureness" placed in the service of dramatic vision.[30] There is little question also that the commercial success of this minor work helped to ensure the poet's financial rating with his publisher for many years to come.

III

o͜o *Experiment in Objectivity*

R ILKE referred to *New Poems*, written between 1903 and 1907, as new "in more than one sense," without enlarging upon his meaning. We also know, from a remark made to his French translator, that many of them "wrote themselves, in final form, often several in one day." [1] However that may be (and the letters of these years hardly corroborate the statement), the "new" poems are not only products of a more deliberate craftsmanship but equally signs of a technical awareness and sensitivity unknown to *The Book of Hours*, where objects are almost one-dimensionally treated and hardly emerge from the brown half-lights the poet throws about them. They are conditioned by an eclectic selection of materials and new forms of perception, practiced with examples in mind of very immediate models. Compression of statement and elimination of subjective states of mind is carried perhaps as far as it can go. To agree with some critics who regard *New Poems* as a diversion, an aberration from the main course of the poet's development as intuitional poet toward a forced intellectualism, is to draw the line too fine, to forget that without this discipline we should hardly have had the *Duino Elegies* nor the *Sonnets to Orpheus* as they are now. [2] On the other hand, no one today regards them as "mountain peaks, real and solid against the sky," as contrasted with the mystical "uncertain stratosphere" of the later poetry. [3] They are simply part of the homogeneous development of a poet who remained ever the same even as he changed.

61

The correspondence records in detail the background of these years when Rilke was absorbing through every pore the spiritual climate of a city so fruitful and persuasive for the artist, on so many levels. *The Book of Images* in part, as well as *New Poems*, commemorates the lovely, worthwhile moments of an already jeopardized civilization, many of them now beyond recapture. Yet if in our memory, beyond time and chance, the panther of the Jardin des Plantes still watches the bars of his cage file past his weary eyes, while the merry-go-round in the Luxembourg Gardens still flashes its reds and greens and grays, with "now and then a snow-white elephant," it is because of the careful poetic organization of the poems in which their destinies appear.

The emphasis in *The Book of Hours* on "earth-borne" objects patiently reposing in their own heaviness now proliferates in several directions. The indefinable "neighbor-god" and artist-monk make way for the anonymous observer of flowers, animals, statues, Gothic cathedrals, and Biblical figures. In this experiment Rodin served primarily as catalyst. What further helped to direct attention away from extreme subjectivism were associations and changes in Rilke's life during the transition years from 1899 to 1902. Travels played a large role here, while his stay in the art colony at Worpswede (1901–2) brought him face to face with the creative problems evident around him in the daily struggles of brother artists. In order to gauge his progress in at least delimitating his objectives one need but read the Worpswede monograph series (or the often fragmentary, often sentimental Worpswede letters and diaries, which nevertheless reveal great flashes of insight and comprehension where poetry is concerned) against the earlier *Tuscan Diary*. One of the most instructive aphorisms in the diaries, in view of the role played by paradox in Rilke's work, defines almost canonically a certain quality of mind as the matrix of the full Ring of Forms: "I fear in myself only those contradictions with an inclination to reconciliation. It must be a very narrow spot in my life if the idea should occur to them to shake hands, from one side to the other. My contradictions shall hear of each other rarely and only in rumors." [4]

EXPERIMENT IN OBJECTIVITY

Hofmannsthal's remark about Victor Hugo that there was nothing in the mature man not already present in his youth is eminently true of Rilke's poetry and its theory.[5] His ideas on poetic perception, only vaguely foreshadowed before, gradually assume more and more definite outlines. In 1899 he was already stating a view of poetry which, despite later qualifications and additions, was to suffer little basic change:

Everything was at first arranged to conceal from me the beauty of things. Gradually I learned to experience them as exceptions. And precisely during these days I recognize more clearly than ever their infinite regularity [*Gesetzmässigkeit*]. It seems to me to be a cruel lack of charity on the part of the eye to make any selection between things that are beautiful and those which are not. Each thing is merely a space [*Raum*], a possibility, and it is my task to fulfill them either perfectly or defectively. For since humans and human conditions are both self-assertive and perpetually self-confusing, by what standard shall one be measured, unless it be that of willing objects [*Dinge*]?[6]

If we add to this statement of 1899 a single, strangely worded passage from the correspondence of 1907—anticipating the Cézanne experience by several months—we have some measure of the refining process going on in his thoughts about poetry:

Perception [*Anschauen*] is such a remarkable thing, about which we know so little; our perceptiveness is directed entirely outwards, and when it seems so most of all, things apparently happen inside us which had been waiting for just this minute of escape from observation; and as they develop within us, autonomous, inviolable and strangely anonymous, their significance slowly evolves in the object outside us: we discover the only possible and powerfully convincing word for the event acknowledged with such inward joy and reverence, without any intervention of our own, and understanding comes gently and from far off, under the sign of an object still strange to us and liable to be snatched away again the very next moment.[7]

Such a theory of art-perception seems related to associational theories of aesthetics based on analogies, spiced with paradox and intimations of later Expressionist techniques. The important terms are "anonymous" and "autonomous," signifying the independence of poetry from anything like a "public" occasion.

THE RING OF FORMS

The Book of Images (1902; second enlarged edition 1906) serves as a transition to *New Poems*. Though partly overlapping in time, the two collections show wide disparities in unity, concentration, and attitude. The tone of the transitional work is still frequently that of *The Book of Hours*, the technique often uneven or unfinished (cf. *Bangnis*—"Anxiety"); and while the run-on lyric monologues of the earlier work have been broken up into shorter individual poems, the rhythms are still loose, the object often inadequately realized, the meters transitional and experimental. Yet the *Book of Images* contains some of the really superb poems familiar to most Rilke readers; we are at least aware that a poet, and not a stylized monk, is speaking. Poems like "Moonlight," "The Knight" with its companion piece "L'Envoi," "Autumn Day," and "Annunciation" are deservedly cherished and are the best of a certain type of early Rilkean lyric. One would never charge these poems with the obscurity that appears to envelop so much of the later poetry. Rilke's autumns are those we have all felt, and even his personified "Knight" is a plausible, untechnical version of the complex death theme. A frequent resemblance to ballads or ballad form indicates their musical nature. There are, for example, repetitions and refrains in "Annunciation," while "Madness" contains both the refrain and dialogue of balladry. Sometimes the ballad is expanded into loosely contrived legends ("The Last Judgment," "Charles XII Rides into the Ukraine," "The Tsars"). Besides ballads there are poems of an autobiographical tinge, expressing, however, an aesthetic intention, such as "The Scion"—*Der Letzte*. This poem's musical virtuosity is striking in the finale, with its hovering short vowels:

> Denn was ich fortstelle,
> hinein in die Welt,
> fällt,
> ist wie auf eine Welle
> gestellt.

> For what I put out from me
> into the world
> falls,
> as if upon a wave
> placed.

EXPERIMENT IN OBJECTIVITY

"The Scion" and "Serious Hour" do not quite disguise a certain sentimentality common to some poems of this period. The same flaw is
conspicuous in the last five lines of an otherwise fine poem ("Autumn
Day"). Yet even here the flat, placid movement of the *a* and *au*
vowels, together with shifting metrical accents, serves excellently to
retard the whipped-up movement of the preceding strophes. The
movement itself is dependent on the use of internal rhyme, with identical rhythmical phrasing (*Auf den Sonnenuhren* . . . *Auf den Flu-
ren*) in close sequence, while the pervading syncopation suggests perfect harmony of structure with meaning. The antinomies "heavy-
light" throw a bridge back to the good, heavy *Dinge* we are urged to
emulate, and to the Dark God versus the Lucifer of Light of *The
Book of Hours.*

In the practically flawless "Autumn," however, Rilke avoids the
pitfalls of "Autumn Day":

> Die Blätter fallen, fallen wie von weit,
> als welkten in den Himmeln ferne Gärten;
> sie fallen mit verneinender Gebärde.

> Und in den Nächten fällt die schwere Erde
> aus allen Sternen in die Einsamkeit.

> Wir alle fallen. Diese Hand da fällt.
> Und sieh dir andre an: es ist in allen.

> Und doch ist Einer, welcher dieses Fallen
> unendlich sanft in seinen Händen hält.

> The leaves are falling, falling as from far,
> as though above were withering farthest gardens;
> they fall with a denying attitude.

> And night by night, down into solitude
> the heavy earth falls far from every star.

> We are all falling. This hand's falling too—
> all have this falling sickness none withstands.

> And yet there's always One whose gentle hands
> this universal falling can't fall through.

The effect is again achieved through repetitions (the word "falling"
repeated seven times), alliterations, assonances, internal rhymes, a

practically disyllabic vocabulary, and broken lines which interpose
pauses to provide answers to implied questions before rolling on to
the serene plane of the final strophe. The initial metaphor comes to
rest through the interlinked chain: *leaves* equals *the human hand*
equals *the hand of God*. Even this "coming to rest" is a typical Rilkean resolution of conflict, for the poem's after-vibrations are still
produced by the tensions of paradox in "falling" and "holding."

The manipulation of imagery now ranges beyond its vague usage
in the earlier poetry. Fountains are described as "incomprehensible
trees of glass" ("Of Fountains") or, bolder still, "wounded windows
beat their timid wings" in the outburst of sunshine after rain ("An
April"). Such imagery does not altogether belie its impressionist heritage, particularly the curious simile in the poem "Progress," accurate
though baffling, which magnificently describes a certain "slippery"
quality of Rilke's own poetry, the nuance at its best: "and into the
broken-off day of ponds/my feelings sink as though mounted on
fish." The use of foreign words in rhyme position continues, though
sometimes appearing mannered, as in "About Girls" where *Brokat*
rhymes with *bat*, indicating an empty spot and a stylistic defect.

A good transition poem is "The Last Judgment," a curious unfolding of the theme announced in *The Book of Hours* and a preliminary
version of its namesake in *New Poems*. The slightly mannered attitudes and vocalic tricks of language are, for a moment, caught up
with sharp Baudelairean precision in the ghastly description of the
dead, which can only be rendered literally in English:

> So ringen sie, die lange ausgeruhten,
> und packen sich mit ihren nackten Zähnen
> und werden bange, weil sie nicht mehr bluten,
> und suchen, wo die Augenbecher gähnen,
> mit kalten Fingern nach den toten Tränen.
> Und werden müde. . . .

> And so they wrestle, the long rested-out,
> and snatch each other with their naked teeth
> and become startled when they bleed no more
> and in their yawning eye-sockets search
> with frigid fingers for dead tears.
> And become tired. . . .

EXPERIMENT IN OBJECTIVITY

Another poem, "Picture of My Father as a Young Man," has been compared to the work of sixteenth-century painters like Parmeggiano and Bronzino, exhibiting a similar dread of transiency and mortality, along with a feigned attitude of composure and security.[8] A sequence of nine monologue poems in the concluding section ("The Voices"), besides giving Rilke's own version of some Baudelaire models, gives us an idea of his approach to human subjects. The best among them are "The Drunkard's Song" and "The Idiot's Song." Other poems, like "The Reader" and "The Spectator," crystallize clearly into a theory of poetry and of the poet in relation to life. In the latter, for instance, the artist's struggle with his materials is likened to the ambiguous wrestling of Jacob with the Angel:

> Wie ist das klein, womit wir ringen,
> Was mit uns ringt, wie ist das gross . . .

> How small the strife that occupied us,
> how great is all that strives with us . . .

In defeat lies victory, the vanquished challenger emerges from the fray, reborn and erect:

> Sein Wachstum ist: der Tiefbesiegte
> von immer Grösserem zu sein.

> He triumphs now in being defeated
> by the unconquerably great.

In time the Kalckreuth *Requiem* will conclude with the memorable lines "Who speaks of victory/surviving is all," and twenty years later one of Rilke's last poems ("In a Dovecote") brings the same theme home to rest in all its final complexity.

RODIN

Evaluations of poetry based on the practices of other arts and artists is a highly questionable approach to criticism, but with *New Poems* such procedure has much to say for itself. It is not, of course, a question of so-called literary influences, but one of effort, directions, sympathies, and mutual interests that draw artists of a period together.[9] It is no disparagement of Rilke's stature to say that he was constantly sensitive to what other artists were pursuing and achieving. If his tireless groping for the ultimate formulation of his vision almost necessitated at times a temporary watchfulness for maturer guides, the core of the experience is nevertheless the poet's own. What is unique is the highly individual residue of this experience once it has filtered through the poetic organization. Externals have been absorbed into the poem's inner organization, human agents and cultural associations become peripheral factors. For a study of the intention behind *New Poems*, a consideration of Rodin, Baudelaire, Van Gogh, and Cézanne is exceedingly helpful.

Shortly after arriving in Paris, Rilke enumerated what he considered, for his own purposes, the two outstanding achievements of Rodin: the discovery of a new technical foundation for art and the freedom with which to express himself fully in the chosen medium. In the first instance, Rodin's conception of *modelé* was the study of objects, not for their colors or contours but for the variable expression of their surfaces. Here lay the key to their essence, a theory related to Verlaine's

> Car nous voulons la Nuance encore,
> pas la couleur, rien que la nuance,

and indirectly to Mallarmé's concern with the physical properties of things: "the terror of the forest or the mute thunder at large among the foliage, not the intrinsic thick wood of the trees themselves." [10] Rodin could hardly have met a more receptive disciple, whose own practice was already committed to *modelé*.

As for the second factor, Rodin merely confirmed Rilke's conviction that, as creator, he must find the center of life in work and radiate from there outward into experience as far as possible. How Rilke must have enjoyed Rodin's saying that whenever he read the *Imitatio* of Thomas à Kempis he always substituted the word "sculpture" for "God"! [11] The much talked-about "*travailler, toujours travailler*" had already become a part of Rilke's working equipment, even in Worpswede if not before. He was soon to perceive that what he had to learn from Rodin was not so much a treatment of materials as an interior adjustment to the poetic process itself. The aesthetics of poetry are not those of sculpture—Rodin's example made him signally aware of the problems of poetry as a craft. Never again, he remarked, would he be able to write a sequence of poetry in a spate of days and nights (like *The Book of Hours* or *Stories about God*), for writing poetry was writing beyond time, against time.[12] To Rodin's advice to frequent the Jardin des Plantes we owe the "Panther" poem and numerous others of this Paris period. And since, for Rodin, it was but a step from the nature-fact to the art forms of antiquity, Rilke now became aware of the great classic tradition of art which lay behind the Renaissance.[13] How much this classic strain, completely transformed and almost preclassic, has filtered down into *New Poems, Sonnets,* and *Elegies* is evident on every hand.

Poems like "The Panther," "The Gazelle," and "The Unicorn" were not the first "objective" poems to come from Rilke (cf. *Advent*: "A white castle in white solitude"). Yet the emergence of the Rilkean *Dinggedicht* does mark a turning point in the development of the German lyric after a century and a half of glorious achievement.[14] From the time of Lessing and Goethe poets had shied away from the treatment of the concrete object *qua* object. Investing the poem with their own feelings and reflections about the object, they cultivated an impressionistic, speculative type of poetry which dominated the greater part of the nineteenth century. Here the object became the prey of free fantasy, the evoker of moods and meditation. Only occasionally, in Mörike's "To a Lamp" or C. F. Meyer's "The Roman Fountain," did the object proper provide the central focus. In France similar tendencies in the direction of the plastic poem may be traced from Hugo's *Légende des Siècles* to Leconte de Lisle's *Poèmes Barbares*. A closer study of techniques would disclose some interesting analogies between Rilke's *Dinggedicht* and Hopkins' idea of "inscape." For if Hopkins' "inscape" is, as a recent critic states, "any kind of formed or focused view, any pattern discerned in the natural world," or better, any range of meaning "from sense-perceived pattern to inner form," some essential properties of the Rilkean *Kunstding* are disclosed.[15] Both poets desire to record "inscapes" and to employ words as objects.

Rilke's perception of objects at this stage (*reines Anschauen*) reveals a dominant plastic interest. Good examples are "Tanagra," "L'Ange du Méridien," and "The Rose Window." The three "Buddha" poems betray a penchant for exotic art, more striking, perhaps,

69

in "The Mountain," a reminder of Japanese drawings of Fuji by Hokusai. In fact, Rilke's attitude toward most of his models is similar to that of the painter in this poem, whose success in capturing the evasive subject—"indifferent and far and without intention"—is ensured only after repeated strivings. The titles themselves of many *New Poems* suggest the labeled products of museums and art galleries that emphasize the species rather than the individual ("Blue Hydrangea," "Black Cat," "Persian Heliotrope"), often provided with subtitles as to place of origin ("The Flamingos. Jardin des Plantes" or "Roman Fountain. Borghese"), sometimes with the scientific rubric attached ("The Gazelle: Antilope Dorcas").

The pure "objective" poem, is of course, an impossibility, for if the subjective elements are altogether eliminated, nothing is left but *décor*. A modern critic's remarks on the pure "physical" in poetry are pertinent, even to the phrasing, to Rilke's position. While condemning the attempt of Imagists "to present things in their thinginess or *Dinge* in their *Dinglichkeit*," John Crowe Ransom comes very close to describing Rilke's poetry: "The way to obtain the true *Dinglichkeit* of a formal dinner or a landscape or of a beloved person is to approach the object as such and in humility; then it unfolds a nature which we are unprepared for if we have put our trust in the simple idea which attempted to represent it." [16] There is subjective intrusion, for example, in the sestet of "Blue Hydrangea" and conspicuously in the entire framework of "Archaic Torso of Apollo," from "We did not know his legendary head" to "You must change your life." Yet wherever the injection of the self does occur in poems of this period, the intrusion, with some glaring exceptions, is never a didactic overlay, but the natural outgrowth of the poem's accumulated energy. The "Archaic Torso of Apollo" gives us much more than purely visual perceptions in the Parnassian sense; the illumination spreading downward from the "unheard-of" head through the flexure of the chest to terminate in a smile in the area of sex: such experience can only terminate in the abrupt, half-line command "You must change your life." One might further contrast the statue's "inward bent glance" (*zurückgeschraubt*) with the eyes "turned around" of the bodies in the poem "Morgue," a kind of inverted perspective as

70

EXPERIMENT IN OBJECTIVITY

in "L'Ange du Méridien," "The Death of the Poet," and certain other poems.

The theme of animal consciousness, a permanent thread in the design of Rilke's poetry, early and late, can be studied in the familiar and much-discussed "Panther" poem:

Sein Blick ist vom Vorübergehn der Stäbe
so müd geworden, dass er nichts mehr hält.
Ihm ist, als ob es tausend Stäbe gäbe
und hinter tausend Stäben keine Welt.

Der weiche Gang geschmeidig starker Schritte,
der sich im allerkleinsten Kreise dreht,
ist wie ein Tanz von Kraft um eine Mitte,
in der betäubt ein grosser Wille steht.

Nur manchmal schiebt der Vorhang der Pupille
sich lautlos auf—. Dann geht ein Bild hinein,
geht durch der Glieder angespannte Stille—
und hört im Herzen auf zu sein.

His glance, so tired from traversing his cage's
repeated railings, can hold nothing more.
He feels as though there were a thousand cages,
and no more world behind them than before.

The padding of the strong and supple paces,
within the tiniest circle circumscribed,
is like a dance of force about a basis
on which a mighty will stands stupefied.

And only now and then a noiseless lifting
of the eye's curtain, till an image dart,
go through the limbs' intensive silence drifting—
and cease forever in the heart.

The panther's universe is bounded by the bars of his cage, beyond which lies the nothingness of our world. The perspective is the reverse of the usual one: across the tired, static vision the bars themselves are seen to file in endless procession. The vocalic repetition (*Stäbe-gäbe*) increases the wearisome monotony. Paralyzed and passive, the animal cosmos still possesses its own immovable center, an enormous will, able to hold in suspense its own mysterious operations. Like the potter's wheel, the centripetal pull of this will holds

71

the movement down to the smallest radius, "a dance of power about a center." The idea is carried out in the regal prolongation of the adjectives: "Der weiche Gang geschmeidig starker Schritte," followed by the monosyllabic dominance of a blind, central agency. Suddenly the blank stare is interrupted, the curtain of the pupil lifts to receive an arrow-like image, the powerful limbs suspend their motion as if inclining an ear to its inward flight, and the dwindling image reaches the heart, where it is suddenly halted, in the shortest verse of the poem. By implication the procession of bars continues across the vision, and the caged pacing resumes.

The panther's actual movements have nothing to do with the poem's meaning, which is left open and may be interpreted in various ways. A thoroughly literal mind might find his humane feelings enlisted against cruelty to animals, or the animal's plight may be read as a symbol of the isolation of royalty, of the "marked" individual, as in "The Staircase of the Orangerie": "Like worn-out kings who finally slowly stride/without a purpose, only now and then/to show the bowing suite on either side/the loneliness within the mantle's hem." Or one may link the panther's situation with the stubborn determination of the poetic volition: life centered in the work and radiating thence outward. Another reading may establish a connection between the object and man's isolation in a world of cages.

"The Panther" has its own embryology in keeping with the crystallizing tendencies of the poet's mind. In a little-known prose sketch, "The Lion Cage" (1902–3), a lioness is seen to pace her "hopeless, ridiculous guardsman stretch" about her mate (the roles are reversed), a stride "which repeatedly sinks back into the same footsteps." She "paces and paces, and often her distracted mask, round and full, appears as if crossed out by the cage bars." [17] The situation is further exploited in the poem "The Aschanti." What happens in the "Panther" poem when the arrowy image has flickered out, the treatment in "The Aschanti" at least allows us to visualize:

> Und sie brennen wie ein stilles Feuer
> leise aus, und sinken in sich ein,
> teilnahmslos dem neuen Abenteuer
> und mit ihrem grossen Blut allein.

EXPERIMENT IN OBJECTIVITY

In their great golden eyes a steady fire
Now glancing out, now sinking like a stone;
No urge to new adventure, no desire,
They bide with their great beating blood alone.

About the only thing shared in common by Rilke's poem and Blake's "Tyger," which it inevitably recalls, is the "fearful symmetry," a symmetry as differently motivated and developed as the age of Blake was different from that of Rilke. The tiger "burning bright in the forests of the night" has become the weary panther whose only forest is the maddening procession of bars, beyond which lies nothing. The "immortal hand or eye" becomes in downward transcendence "a great will," the high and open has become enclosed and secretive, the divine replaced by the indigenous energies of the subject. The glorious object of wonder and admiration has been converted to a symbol of the exile and enslavement of the modern. Images and metaphors once drawing their substance from a divine smithy now connote mechanical motion, almost robotism. Blake's symbols are such that the mind leaps to immediately, while the symbolic implications in Rilke's poem are not fixed and often leave us asking if we have taken the right turning.[18]

In another animal poem, "The Unicorn," a perfect balance is maintained between dancing, buoyant grace, and the vertical rigidity of the horn, a "tower against the moon":

> . . . Der Beine elfenbeinernes Gestell
> bewegte sich in leichten Gleichgewichten,
> ein weisser Glanz glitt selig durch das Fell,
> und auf der Tierstirn, auf der stillen, lichten,
> stand, wie ein Turm im Mond, das Horn so hell,
> und jeder Schritt geschah, es aufzurichten . . .

> The ivory framework of the limbs so light
> Swayed like a balance delicately deflected,
> There glided through the coat a gleam of white,
> And on the forehead where the beams collected
> Like a tower in moonlight stood the horn so bright,
> With every footstep proudly re-erected . . .

A good contrast to Rilke's poem is the sonnet-sestet of Hérédia's "Fuite des Centaures":

73

THE RING OF FORMS

Parfois, l'un des fuyards de la farouche harde
Se cabre brusquement, se retourne, regarde,
Et rejoint d'un seul bond le fraternal bétail:
Car il a vu la lune éblouissante et pleine
Allonger dérrière eux, suprême épouvantail,
La gigantesque horreur de l'oeuvre Herculéènne.[19]

The Parnassian poem is a painting or vignette, only the concluding line producing a mysterious magic with reference to the mythological foe. Rilke's unicorn is not contained within mythological, Christian, or other allusion; we are simply given to feel, through the poem's movement, that out of the reconciliation of opposites (dancing buoyancy and changeless rigidity), the inner sense has uncovered a new and important range of feeling. The paradoxical relationship is continued in an altogether different set of terms in the fourth Orpheus Sonnet (II), on the same subject, twenty years later.

After the animals come the flowers, a most unlikely material, one should think, for strictly objective treatment. Rilke is, in fact, less successful in poems like "Persian Heliotrope," "Blue Hydrangea," "Rose Bowl," and "Opium Poppy" than perhaps a painter might be in the same genre.[20] "Blue Hydrangea" is a color poem, a study in pastel nuances pushed to the utmost, again emphasizing the emergence of new life from dessication and death. But the situation is too artfully contrived, too close to the studio and the deliberate arrangement; the poet insists too much on our seeing the object (hence the awkward repetitions in close proximity: *Spiegeln-bespiegeln*). There is more than a formal difference between this poem and the later Orpheus Sonnet II, 21:

Singe die Gärten, mein Herz, die du nicht kennst; wie
in Glas
eingegossene Gärten, klar, unerreichbar.
Wasser und Rosen von Ispahan oder Schiras,
singe sie selig, preise sie, keinem vergleichbar . . .

Sing those gardens, my heart, poured as into a
glass,
gardens you have not known, transparent, untrampled.
Waters and roses of Ispahan or Shiras,

74

EXPERIMENT IN OBJECTIVITY

blissfully sing them, praise them, the unexampled . . .

In "Rose Bowl" an image of outer world-furor serves to introduce experience at the flower-center. Fullness and sweetness are conveyed through graded nuances in color words and tactile images. One figure impinges upon another, and the polarity of stasis and mobility is canceled in a plethora of sensuous data. Even here the object does not fully yield itself, for the continuity is broken by a fictitious interlocutor or reader: "For now you know how that may be forgotten . . ." The poem's conclusion is likewise a less successful version of the later transformation theme, and one reason for its failure is, perhaps, its distance from Rilke and closeness to Hofmannsthal. The title is significant, because the poet is speaking not of the "rosebush" or the "rosebud," but of the "bowl" which "contains nothing but itself," a spatiality "lying without care in the open roses." The importance of the rose motif for Rilke has already been mentioned, and a nice critical exercise in the flower genre would be to compare his flower poems with Blake's "O Rose, thou art sick," for example, or with modern specimens from the poetry of D. H. Lawrence, Marianne Moore, and Edith Sitwell.

The use of nonhuman objects to convey states of human consciousness is nothing new in poetry. Rilke resorts to it constantly, from a vision of the Birth of Venus to an azure cup of Chinese porcelain filled with butterflies. His analogies are impressive because his similes are actually metaphors. The Buddha in the poem by that name remains "remote and slothful as an animal"; a woman's destiny is likened to that of the royal drinking goblet, once tasted and now a mere showpiece in the cupboard; the movements of a Spanish dancer flash like the initial sputterings of a sulphur match. Conversely, inanimate objects are animated by human metaphors, for the reality of the "thing" has nothing to do with scientific naturalism or verism. A piece of lace, delicate toil of hands and eyes gone gradually blind, symbolizes a human destiny snatched from transiency: "no easier than life and yet completed and beautiful"; a cathedral snobbishly draws itself up in the folds of its buttress-cloak over the lowly village housetops; the pattern of the staircase at Versailles is one of lonely majesty in a white ascent toward a predestined goal; the lute is the lover whose purpose is consummated by sexual union with its mistress.

In addition to cathedrals and statues, animals and flowers (and humans treated more like animals and flowers), many of the *New Poems* deal with Biblical, particularly Old Testament themes. French critics tend to interpret this interest as a step in the direction of the French plastic tradition in poetry, as a tendency to synthesize the epochs of Western civilization in the manner of Hugo's *Légende des Siècles*.[21] German symbolist poetry also, in the work of the early Stefan George, attempts to come to terms with the Western tradition, but Rilke, more than George, ignores historical considerations as such. His practice is to seize on a certain historical or legendary episode, remove it from its own setting to a realm beyond historical time, and surround it with the poet's own aesthetic atmosphere. The burial of "Egyptian Mary" is a good illustration, since the point of view is not determined by the actual circumstances, but evidently by the suggestiveness of medieval bestiaries or books of heraldry:

Und ein Löwe kreiste; und ein Alter
rief ihn winkend an, dass er ihm helfe:
(und so gruben sie zu zwein.)

Und der Alte neigte sie hinein.
Und der Löwe, wie ein Wappenhalter,
sass dabei und hielt den Stein.

And a lion circled, and there sought her
one grown old who called for his assistance:
(and they dug in unison.)

And the ancient laid her there alone.
And the lion, like a shield-supporter,
sat near by and held the stone.

The Old Testament poems reveal his alleged preference for pre-Christian Judaism and the old Hebraic God to whom one "belonged," as he put it later, on tribal grounds, as a child to its father (an echo of the father-son relationship in *The Book of Hours*).[22] Against a primitive tribal background the relationship between God and man is caught at a moment of highest tension; the poet "human-

EXPERIMENT IN OBJECTIVITY

izes" the relationship, and his figures hold a "reckoning" with the Divine. The prophet in "Jeremiah" entreats the Lord to let his fearsome voice return, over the ruins of the world, to the voice of childhood, which was "a howling from the very beginning." Saul's misuse of his spiritual mission ("Saul") has deprived his life of all authenticity. In the final verses, "Saul among the Prophets," the "dripping prophetic mouth" of the third stanza is figuratively related to the theme's broader meaning in the fifth. Poems like "Abisag," "Absalom's Downfall," "Lament for Jonathan," and "David Sings before Saul" display, for all their excellence, a similar crass eroticism as in *The Book of Hours*. The burden of David's song is envy of the older man's sexual prowess ("Your nights, o king, your nights . . .").

The New Testament poems are mainly concerned with a few orthodox figures like Christ, the saints and angels. Apart from a technical mastery of sound effects, a little overdone, the "Last Judgment" serves as an intermediary link between the earlier, similarly named poem in *The Book of Images* to the later "Harrowing of Hell." The abrupt and constantly repeated vowel sequence (*o, a, o*), bedded among sharp plosives, conveys the sense of horror and disgust we associate with a Hieronymous Bosch painting and is impossible to reproduce adequately in English:

> So erschrocken, wie sie nie erschraken,
> ohne Ordnung, oft durchlocht und locker,
> hockten sie in dem geborstnen Ocker
> ihres Ackers, nicht von ihren Laken
>
> abzubringen, die sie lieb gewannen . . .

The "humanized" Christ in these poems is assigned an equivocal role. Since the Old Testament God and His creatures lived in patriarchal harmony, asked Rilke with his terribly Christian conscience, why a paraclete? Poems like "Pietà" and "The Garden of Olives" are almost parodies of the gospel versions. Christ is merely the human sufferer whose vain struggle terminates in waste and betrayal (cf. "The Apostle"). The Magdalene in the "Pietà" cries:

> O Jesus, Jesus, wann war unsre Stunde?
> Wie gehn wir beide wunderlich zu Grunde.

77

O Jesus, Jesus, what hour was our own?
How strangely both of us are being destroyed.

Rilke's use of religious themes is always directed to aesthetic ends. "Wherever the poet chooses Christian themes for his work," writes Holthusen, "he strips them of their sacred meaning, substituting for it psychological speculations, sometimes with a devastating effect." [23] The meaning of "The Resurrection" is directly opposed to that of D. H. Lawrence's story *The Man Who Died*. Together with "Don Juan's Election" (*Don Juans Auswahl*), the poem belongs to the themal complex of the unrequited lovers, here deliberately formulated in the thought of Christ himself in relation to Mary Magdalene:

Sie begriff es erst in ihrer Höhle,
wie er ihr, gestärkt durch seinen Tod,
endlich das Erleichternde der Öle
und des Rührens Vorgefühl verbot,

um aus ihr die Liebende zu formen,
die sich nicht mehr zum Geliebten neigt,
weil sie, hingerissen von enormen
Stürmen, seine Stimme übersteigt.

Later, in her cave, she recollected,
and perceived how, strengthened by his death,
oil's relief he had at last rejected
and presentiment of touch and breath,

that from her he might create the lover
whom a loved one can no longer bind,
since, upswept by forces far above her,
she has left his voice so far behind.

BAUDELAIRE

During the early Paris years Rilke discovered in Baudelaire a new source of affirmation. In their several ways, two major modern poets, Rilke and Eliot, have been drawn to the French writer. Baudelaire comes to occupy an important place in the thinking of both, understandable enough in view of his significance for the tradition of modern poetry. In dealing with symptoms of decay (*Verfalls-Symptomen*) in modern life, both Eliot in London and Rilke in Paris testify eloquently to Baudelaire's heritage.[24] In Rilke's case the experience of

78

the horrible and repulsive assumed a form of vicarious suffering terminating in an all-inclusive aesthetic doctrine; with Eliot a kind of "obsession with putrefaction," partly transcended in poetry, partly a cynical commentary.[25] Eliot's various essays, read against Rilke's Baudelaire poem and references in private correspondence as well as in the Rodin book, point up the difference quite clearly. What Eliot derives from Baudelaire is an idea "of salvation from the ennui of modern life" through damnation, the capacity for damnation.[26] The satanic and diabolic *fin de siècle* spiritual climate is interpreted in orthodox fashion as a struggle for salvation, in a more or less restricted religious sense. Rilke's emphasis is on the aesthetic and creative side of Baudelaire, whom he addresses in a poem itself aesthetically displeasing in its bad consonantal effects:

> Das Schöne hat er unerhört bescheinigt,
> doch da er selbst noch feiert, was ihn peinigt,
> hat er unendlich den Ruin gereinigt:
> und auch noch das Vernichtende wird Welt.

> Beauty he certified beyond belief,
> but since himself still hymns what gives him pain,
> he purified destruction endlessly:
> and what may still destroy becomes a world.

Both Rilke and Baudelaire succumbed to the fascination of the horrible, the daily aspects of misery and squalor in Paris streets. Did not Malte Laurids Brigge, in his hour of deepest distress, later evoke the spirit of Baudelaire from *Le Spleen de Paris*?[27] In his Rodin book Rilke had pointed out the kinship between Rodin and Dante through the medium of Baudelaire.[28] To Rilke the satanic poet seemed an important phase in the sculptor's own schooling, a precursor in the application of plastic principles to art. Baudelaire had unfortunately left off where Rodin's art essentially began.[29] Isolated, self-contained in the marble of words, his poetry represented a static, closed universe compared with the open contours and unlimited nuances of Rodin's *modelé* surfaces. Yet as Rodin's influence wanes, Baudelaire is shifted (from 1902–7) more and more into Rilke's focus. The sculptor's significance had been, after all, more of a formal nature; Baudelaire, the poet, laid bare the very abysses and dilemmas of art.

79

THE RING OF FORMS

Rilke's comment to his wife on Baudelaire's prayer from *Le Spleen de Paris* unveils his aesthetic orientation (the reference to Russia in this connection is significant):

... And the conclusion is enormous, rising and issuing forth like a prayer. A Baudelairean prayer, a real, simple prayer, handmade, awkward, beautiful as the prayer of a common Russian. It was a long journey for Baudelaire, and he did it all crawling on his knees . . .[30]

The focal point of Rilke's interest is the controversial poem "Une Charogne." In the *Notebooks* centering in this period, Malte Laurids Brigge writes:

Do you remember Baudelaire's incredible poem, "Une Charogne"? Perhaps I understand it now. Except for the last verse he was in the right. What should he have done after that happened to him? It was his task to see in this terrible thing, seeming to be only repulsive, that existence which is valid among all that exists. Choice or refusal there is none. . . .[31]

In a letter to Clara Rilke, during the Cézanne phase of 1907, Rilke further enlarged upon the subject:

I had to reflect that without this poem the entire evolution towards factual expression [*sachliches Sagen*] which we think we now detect in Cézanne could never have been started. This poem had to precede in all its inexorableness. First it was necessary for artistic perception to so control itself as to see in the horrible, only apparently repulsive experience the valid connection with all living essence. The artist is as little permitted to ignore any aspect of existence as he is to make an arbitrary selection. The rejection of any part of it at any time removes him from the state of grace, making a sinner of him through and through.[32]

"We are not free to select or reject our materials!" The final stanza of Baudelaire's poem sinned, however, in this regard by permitting human limitations to impose important restrictions:

> Alors, o ma beauté! Dites à la vermine
> Qui vous mangera de baisers,
> Que j'ai gardé la forme et l'essence divine
> De mes amours décomposés![33]

Baudelaire's religiosity is sometimes a matter of considerable con-

EXPERIMENT IN OBJECTIVITY

troversy even today. His sense of charity seems often vitiated by bitterness and cynicism, virulent passions and private prejudices.[34] It is debatable in some cases whether or not he does not vicariously enjoy the vices of his characters while acknowledging their virtues. Rilke's aesthetic, on the other hand, demands "openness," "humility," "piety," in relation to human experience. Like St. Julian the Hospitaler, one must take the leper into bed with one's self. His frequent use of the word "piety" (*Frömmigkeit*) is misleading; it has no orthodox religious meaning, as he made clear to a clerical acquaintance in later years.[35] In his vocabulary it suggests a number of things, chiefly—as we have seen above—complete surrender to the object under consideration, in a state of total empathy and "without taking sides." One might even extend it to cover an exacting working method which might be circumscribed with such terms as "aesthetic distance" or even Rodin's "long patience."

Perhaps the poem "The Stylite" (*Der Stylit*), too long to be quoted in full, bears the closest analogy to "Une Charogne." The theme has less to do with the legendary stylite than with a symbolic rendering of a conception of art. Like Empedocles in Hölderlin's drama, the stylite has betrayed himself by dwelling too long among people. As he gradually loses consciousness of the world below his lofty perch, the strife between his essential vulnerability and his worldly reputation for saintliness lashes forth with demonic fury. The remote, flapping figure, "conversing with the whole of heaven," is the very antithesis of the staring, minuscule mob below. The last four lines match Baudelaire in repulsive analogies, but they clarify what was meant by "self-surrender" as "the gradual beginning of saintliness":

> Aber wenn er oben, fast verdammt,
> und von ihrem Widerstand zerschunden,
> einsam mit verzweifeltem Geschreie
> schüttelte die täglichen Dämonen:
> fielen langsam auf die erste Reihe,
> schwer und ungeschickt aus seinen Wunden,
> grosse Würmer in die offnen Kronen
> und vermehrten sich im Samt.

> But when up there, damned almost,
> and flayed to bits by their contrariness,

81

> he shook and shook the daily devils,
> alone with outcries of despair:
> slowly there fell upon the nearest row,
> heavy and awkward from his sores,
> large worms into the open coronets
> to propagate themselves in velvet.

The effect of repulsiveness is helped by the choice of epithets but particularly by the reversal of meaning, the paradox in the last two lines: the dropping worms fall into "open coronets" of the shining princes at the column's base and are "multiplied in velvet." Here Rilke takes the step beyond Baudelaire.

Several *New Poems* unavoidably recall Baudelaire's titles ("The Cat," "The Swan," "The Balcony"). Rilke's "Black Cat" has the Rodinesque firmness and visual plasticity of "The Panther" but somehow lacks the rich suggestiveness of "Le Chat." Or compare *Der Blinde* ("The Blind Man") with Baudelaire's "Les Aveugles," or even the childbirth passage from *The Book of Hours* with "Crépuscule du Matin." However successful Rilke may have been in dealing with inanimate subjects, defects occur where the interest centers on human beings (the poor, the blind, the outcast, the insane, etc.). The poem, "One of the Old Ones," which begins "Abends manchmal (weisst du, wie das tut?)," describes the antic gestures of begging old women enticing the passer-by along the building fronts:

> Mit dem Rätsel ihrer Räude,
> mit dem Hut, dem Umhang und dem Gang.

> Mit der Hand, die hinten unterm Kragen
> heimlich wartet und verlangt nach dir:
> wie um deine Hände einzuschlagen
> in ein aufgehobenes Papier.

> > Often evenings (you know how that feels?)
> > she suddenly stands still, beckoning and watching,
> > and a smile, completely patches,
> > is shot at you from under the little hat.

> > Behind her are the buildings in a block
> > interminable, down which she coaxes
> > with the enigma of the scabby itch,
> > with the hat, the cape, and the slow walk.

EXPERIMENT IN OBJECTIVITY

> With the hand behind the collar's nape,
> waiting secretly and craving you:
> as if to wrap your hand
> in a picked-up piece of paper.

Such a poem is packed with skillfully handled incident and detail, and the trailing rhythm beautifully supports the theme. Yet critics have argued, as though it were a particular merit, that in these old women Rilke saw his own destiny, tormentors imposed upon him, symbols of the Other (*Gegenüber*), the Adversary threatening his own vision of experience.[36] Precisely because he is thinking of his *own* destiny, his *own* problems and anxieties, the poem sacrifices much of its organic unity and integrity while the quasi-religious humantarianism easily degenerates into self-conscious dramatization, or even a gratuitous pose.

> Often evenings (you know how that feels?) . . .

What is the function of the rhetorical parenthesis except to focus attention upon the poet through the reader, rather than upon the victim of the experience? The same stricture applies to the poem "The Blind Man" (compare Baudelaire's "Les Aveugles"), where the reader is given the neural processes of the poet himself describing the antics of the blind. The worst offender in this regard is "The Beggar." The glaring contrast of poet and mendicant (and this in the words of the latter!) is almost fatuous:

> Dann weiss ich nicht sicher, wer da schreit,
> ich oder irgendwer.
> Ich schreie um eine Kleinigkeit.
> Die Dichter schrein um mehr . . .

Many of the admittedly vivid descriptions of the poor and delinquent in the *Notebooks*, one might add, suffer from a similar delimitation. As long as the objective poem dealt with inanimate objects or even with historical or Biblical subjects it was usually successful. At such a historical distance, where spatial and temporal immunity were provided, the poetic particulars assumed a new and probable significance, bathed in their own light and adjusted to their own proper dimensions. Rilke was not so successful in handling the world of people, for despite his repeated protests against a partial adaptation

83

of poetic materials, he sometimes got beyond the range of such materials altogether:

... my relation to my models is certainly still false, especially as I really can't use any human models at all yet (the proof: I am not making any yet) and shall be occupied with flowers, animals and landscapes for years to come. (The opening scene of *Alcestis* is perhaps my first reach into the world of 'figures').[37]

The statement is ambiguous because a good half of the *New Poems*, already on the press at the time, deal with human models (the earlier "Orpheus. Eurydice. Hermes" is a much better poem, incidentally, than "Alcestis"). But what Rilke apparently meant by the terms "use" and "make" was that he had been unable to give his human models the objective firmness he had achieved with the other "things." [38] For this a shorter but perhaps more intense apprenticeship was needed.

VAN GOGH AND CÉZANNE

At the height of his Cézanne experience, in October of 1907, the poet summarized the subjective impressionism of his pre-Paris work:

... but in those days Nature was still a general incitement for me, an evocation, an instrument on whose strings my fingers found themselves again; I did not yet sit before her; I let myself be carried away by the soul that issued forth from her . . . I went along with her and saw, saw not Nature, but the faces she inspired in me. How little I could have learned then before Cézanne, before Van Gogh. From the amount Cézanne gives me to do now, I notice how very different I have grown. I am on the road to becoming a worker, on a long road perhaps, and probably just at the first milestone; but nevertheless I can already comprehend the old man who has gone on somewhere far ahead, alone. . . . [39]

He had just completed the first part of *New Poems*, many items of Part II were likewise already written, the *Notebooks* were in progress: what was the meaning of this sudden experience with painting?

The Van Gogh interest is of lesser interest for the poetry, though it is sometimes tempting to press analogies between the bright, hard brilliance of the painter's work and poems like "Poppy," "The Last Judgment," or even certain passages in the *Notebooks* (the flowers that "stood up and said Red with a frightened voice"). Van Gogh merely reinforced what was already a part of Rilke's poetic perspective, painting an old horse, a series of parks, a hospital interior, without partiality or prejudice: [40] "He doesn't take sides, certainly not that of the parks, and all his love is directed towards the nameless and thus concealed, not *shown* but *had*." [41] Though Rilke accepted Van Gogh with reservations (his art was too conscious, too violently subjective), the relation does link the Franciscan poverty theme of *The Book of Hours* with the "factual expression" learned from Rodin and Baudelaire.

The Cézanne letter-series of October 1907 is an important document by itself. Though initially drawn to the psychological aspects of the painter as person, as H. Meyer's investigations show, [42] Rilke's interpretations were of an aesthetic rather than existential nature. In contrast to all the other exhibitions in the current *Salon d'Automne* he found "all reality" on the side of Cézanne. [43] He referred to the "good conscience" of the painter's reds and blues, to the still lifes of "inedible fruits, so wonderfully preoccupied with themselves." [44] And then he records Cézanne's frenzied reaction to the mention of Balzac's Frenhofer in *Le Chef d'Oeuvre Inconnu* who struggled in vain "over an impossible task, through the discovery that there are actually no contours but rather many vibrating transitions." [45] Cézanne "compels" his motifs "to be beautiful, to mean the whole world and all happiness and glory, and doesn't know whether he has brought them to doing that for him." [46] The factual expression Baudelaire initiated with "Une Charogne" appears to have been carried a step further in Cézanne's unemotional treatment of colors, completely "taken up" in the painting, without tag-ends left outside. For "the painter (any artist whatever)," continued Rilke, "should not become conscious of his insights: without taking the way round through his mental processes, his advances, enigmatic even to himself, must enter so swiftly into the work that he is unable to recognize them at the moment of transition . . ." [47]

Rilke anticipated independently the discoveries found in the work of Cézanne, who merely clinched what Rodin, with his often idealistic, often historical orientations, had failed to accomplish: the impersonal presentation of "monstrous reality" (*ungeheure Wirklich-*

keit) in its singular oneness. Rilke is not at all interested in the painter's technical problems, and what Cézanne called *réalisation* Rilke characteristically translated in his own sense as a "Thing-Becoming" (*Dingwerdung*).[48] But the painter aided him in breaking definitively with romantic impressionism ("One painted: I love this") and moving toward a new impersonality ("Here it is").

It would be as useless in Cézanne's as in Van Gogh's case to single out any *New Poems* as companion pieces to the former's paintings, because an alleged identity of subject matter with title means very little.[49] Rilke's "The Seduction," for example, has nothing to do with a mythological seduction portrayed by Cézanne. His "thing" poems are "symbolic" poems as well (*Sinngedichte*), symbolic of the creative process itself.[50] The real question is how, in what manner— since the resources of language are different from the painter's line and color—he manages objectivity (*Deutungslosigkeit*) in the direction he considered Cézanne to have followed.

There are interesting interrelationships between the painter and a group of poems ("The Mountain," "The Dog," "The Child," "The Ball"), written only a week before the first mention of Cézanne in the letters. The "Mountain" poem, already referred to, illustrates the difference of intent in Hokusai's hundred and thirty-six drawings of Mount Fuji and in Rilke's verses on that subject. The Japanese painter's mountain is the unvarying focus in the midst of changing and extended foregrounds; Rilke's becomes a symbol of the artist's tireless pursuit of "factual expression." In the poem "The Dog" there are further interesting corollaries. The letters dwell specifically on Cézanne's "doglike" existence, the way children threw stones at him "as at a bad dog"; on the "factuality of his perception" in one of his self-portraits, "like that of a dog seeing himself in a mirror and thinking: there is another dog." [51] Rilke was much concerned with the dog-symbol in after years ("neither animal nor man, a lamentable and pathetic hybrid"), and erected a monument to it in Orpheus Sonnet I, 16. In the present context the dog is a symbol of the artist absorbed in his work, unrelated to the human world, without other credentials than an indecisive success at the cost of human status. To be completely comprehended within the human equation would

EXPERIMENT IN OBJECTIVITY

be, for both artist and dog, not to exist at all (*denn er wäre nicht*):
Dog equals *Cézanne* equals *Rilke* equals *Art.*

THE DEATH MASK

The "mask" is one of Rilke's most cogent and enduring devices for
presenting the authenticity of true *Innenraum* in opposition to the
superficial and the sham. For this reason it is primarily associated
with the death theme, which contains in itself the other two great
themes of "love" and "life." Behind the mask, symbol of the evanes-
cent and unreal, lies death, the genuine and enduring. The mask
seems also at times to be a sort of protective device, a curtain rung
down to conceal the paradoxical drama being enacted behind it: the
drama we have just seen in relation to the dog—*Nicht ausgestossen
und nicht eingereiht*; to the ball—*zu wenig Ding und doch noch
Ding genug*; and to the mountain—*teilnahmslos und weit und ohne
Meinung.* Death, on the other hand, has no literal meaning but is a
convertible term for the aesthetic principles or soil from which the
poetry derives.

The *Worpswede Diary*, the *Notebooks*, the *Elegies*, and the *Late
Poems* all contain some reference to the death-mask. In the *New
Poems* it broadens to include matters of clearly aesthetic concern.
The poet's euplastic skill interweaves both mask and death motifs in
a variety of contexts and situations. In "Experience of Death"
(*Todeserfahrung*), death "does not share with us" and we know nothing of it. Again, as so often, the "theater" perspective in the poetry is
in full evidence. Death requires neither our "admiration, love nor
hate," since a "masked-voice of tragic lament so strangely distorts
it." Ourselves are mere "actors" for applause; unreality is the stage,
the disguise, the heavy gestures, the incomprehensible script, and,
later, the "puppet." If here the negative aspect, the mask, holds the
center of the stage, in a much better lyric, "The Death of the Beloved" (*Der Tod der Geliebten*), the accent falls on what the former
poem only permitted one to glimpse, that "strip of reality," "green
of real greens," "real sunshine," and "real forest." To be sure,

Er wusste nur vom Tod, was alle wissen:
dass er uns nimmt und in das Stumme stösst . . .

87

> He only knew of death what all men may:
> that those it takes it thrusts into dumb night . . .

But immediately the lover realizes that his beloved has not been indifferently "snatched away" (*fortgerissen*):

> und glaubte nicht und nannte jenes Land
> das gutgelegene, das immer süsse—.
> Und tastete es ab für ihre Füsse.

> and paid no heed to them, and called that land
> the fortunately-placed, the ever-sweet.—
> And groped out all its pathways for her feet.

He is able to comprehend what Orpheus of the *New Poems* failed to do when Eurydice returned to the shades ("Orpheus. Eurydice. Hermes"):

> Sie war in sich. Und ihr Gestorbensein
> erfüllte sie wie Fülle.
> Wie eine Frucht von Süssigkeit und Dunkel,
> so war sie voll von ihrem grossen Tode,
> der also neu war, dass sie nichts begriff . . .

> Wrapped in herself she wandered. And her deadness
> was filling her like fullness.
> Full as a fruit with sweetness and with darkness
> was she with her great death, which was so new
> that for the time she could take nothing in . . .

Against the "mask" is arrayed fullness and sweetness. All three poems are born of a similar conception and related, not only through the recurring imagery (*süss, fortgerissen, Frucht, sanft, leis*), but perhaps even more through the "quality" of the action, the "scenic arrangement."

"The Death of the Poet" finally brings together and marries the mask and death motifs, relating the theme to what Rilke considers the poet (and poetry) as such to be:

> Er lag. Sein aufgestelltes Antlitz war
> bleich und verweigernd in den steilen Kissen,
> seitdem die Welt und dieses von ihr Wissen
> von seinen Sinnen abgerissen,
> zurückfiel an das teilnahmslose Jahr.

Die so ihn leben sahen, wussten nicht,
wie sehr er eines war mit allen diesen,
denn dieses: diese Tiefen, diese Wiesen
und diese Wasser waren sein Gesicht.

O sein Gesicht war diese ganze Weite,
die jetzt noch zu ihm will und um ihn wirbt;
und seine Maske, die nun bang verstirbt,
ist zart und offen, wie die Innenseite
von einer Frucht, die an der Luft verdirbt.

> He lies. His pillowed features now appear
> pale and denying above the silent cover,
> since the whole world and all this knowledge of her,
> torn from the senses of her lover,
> fell back again to the unfeeling year.
>
> Those who had seen him living saw no trace
> of his deep unity with all that passes,
> for these: these shadowy hills and waving grasses
> and streams of water running were his face.
>
> O yes, his face was this remotest distance,
> that seeks him still and woos him in despair;
> and his mere mask, timidly dying there,
> tender and open, has no more consistence
> than coreless fruit corrupting in the air.

Here the poet's countenance, once animated with the experienced glow of the "things" to which all senses have fully surrendered, has become a dead mask, like the husk in "Experience of Death." Once the real face (*Gesicht*, not *Antlitz*) has been torn off in death, like the rind of a fruit, leaving the tender pulp exposed, the mask shrivels and dies (the "timidly dying there" picking up the opening figure "pale and denying above the silent cover"). The poem's major figure is carried through on three etymologically and connotatively different levels: *Antlitz, Gesicht,* and *Maske.* Finally, the use of alliteration in this particular poem is thoroughly integrated with its texture, as Belmore has shown, and no longer employed wilfully as in the earlier verse.[52]

But the death-mask figure is not yet put to rest and, after Spain and Duino, expands in several directions, notably in the poem "The

Deathbed Portrait of Keats" of 1914. Its genesis may be traced in the letters (1907–14), from his definition of art as an indiscriminating transformation of the world "into the dimensions of the wonderful" (*ins Herrliche hinein*) to the complaint that the elegiac note had too long predominated over that of jubilation.[53] The very vocabulary reflects the change. Where he had formerly used the verb *singen* (to sing) or, more narrowly, *feiern* (to celebrate), to define the poet's relation to his materials, the preferred word is now *rühmen* (to praise). Not only does the Keats poem again illustrate the poet's habit of translating other artist's experience into his own terms, but it offers a new application of the theme of "The Death of the Poet." The countenance of the dead Keats, the Rilkean *Rühmer*, is neither recusant nor despoiled, but pacified, almost reconciled. Nor is this countenance, symbolically Rilke's conception of the poet's mission, a mere recorder of objective nature, a bare accessory. Death has left behind more than the shriveled pulp of a fruit. The poet has achieved independent status for himself, the tension between the two poles has been absorbed into the inaccessibility of suffering—an echo of "The Harrowing of Hell" poem written a few months earlier. The imagery not only draws on the earlier Paris poems, but points ahead to *Elegies* and *Sonnets*. The stilled voice of Keats already vibrates with the hopeful undertones of the Orpheus threshold figure (Sonnet II, 15):

O Brunnenmund, du gebender, du Mund,
der unerschöpflich Eines, Reines spricht,
du vor des Wassers fliessendem Gesicht,
marmorne Maske . . .

O fountain mouth, you mouth that can respond
so inexhaustibly to all who ask
with one, pure, single saying. Marble mask
before the water's flowing face . . .

"Face" and "mask," faithful until the end, are at last reconciled in the orphic realm of "relationships," the ontological premise of all Rilke's later poetry.

LANGUAGE

Like the painter in "The Mountain," Rilke wrestles with language that it may yield up its secrets and give him the *Kunstding* in all its purity. If there are two styles of poetic language, the "light" and the "heavy," as Belmore maintains in his close study of Rilke's language, Rilke's is "heavy" in the sense that his words interact or "light each other up with reciprocal reflections," as Mallarmé expressed it.[54] The bold experimentations with the texture of poetry are directed toward making the words express not only themselves but themselves in relationship to other words (the "constellations of language," he might later have said). The peculiar atmosphere that results may be seen by comparing, for example, C. F. Meyer's poem "Roman Fountain" with Rilke's similarly named one from *New Poems*. Rilke's basins are not so much receptacles of constant motion as of a nuanced give-and-take, a quiet dialogue between one level and another, conceived in a new dimension that recalls the timeless preoccupation of the smiling angel in "L'Ange du Méridien." What is this heaven so gently reflected, so mutely, almost coyly displayed "as if in the hollow of a hand"? And what the unhurried secret that the contented water, as if wrapped in a dream, delivers finally to the lowest basin "smiling with nuances"? Over and beyond the simpler relationships of Meyer's poem, Rilke's suggests a set of references to an entirely different order of experience.

What devices does the poet employ as antidotes to the confessed fluidity and thinness of the early poetry? A long chapter would be required to cover in detail, as Belmore has done, the complexities of this language.[55] But one of its more conspicuous aspects, the vocabulary, will strike the ordinary reader at once. Its development is almost in inverse direction to that of most poets, who start with a relatively limited number of concepts and expand them as their work evolves. Rilke's range of vocabulary is fairly wide at first, but toward the end, at the time of the *Elegies*, *Sonnets*, and *Late Poems*, it narrows to a more select word-grouping, often repeated and charged with special vibrations of meaning. The emphasis is rather on depth than on range. But in *New Poems* the vocabulary is still "varied and rich," containing both "simple and elaborate words," with particular stress on nouns and verbs in the diction. In the case of verbs, prefixes elicit fresh nuances from combinations like *ent-*

golden, verblühen, überstimmen, erflehen. Particularly the nouns Rilke selects with care, and if a noun is not ready to hand, he resorts to "combining," generally with a verb or with another noun. These rhetorically periphrastic and elliptical devices are signs of an effort to break through the abstractions of the poetic idiom of his day and to keep the language horizons "open," to use a favorite word of Rilke's. Thus the mountain is described as "the thing clothed with outline" (*der mit Umriss Angetane*), the swan's effort is through the medium of the "still unperformed" (*noch ungetanes*), the women appeal to the poet as the "you-sayer" (*du uns Sagender*). The use of the gerund, in place of the usual substantive, especially in combinations with the copulative "to be" or the verb "to stand," introduces an existential force of increasing effectiveness, as in the third stanza of "The Rose Bowl":

> Lautloses Leben, Aufgehn ohne Ende,
> Raum-brauchen, ohne Raum von jenem Raum
> zu nehmen, den die Dinge rings verringern,
> fast nicht Umrissen-sein wie Ausgespartes
> und lauter Inneres, viel seltsam Zartes
> und Sich-Bescheinendes bis an den Rand . . .

> > Living in silence, endless opening out,
> > space being used, but without space being taken
> > from that space which the things around diminish;
> > absence of outline, like untinted groundwork
> > and mere Within; much that is strangely tender
> > and self-illuminating to the brim . . .

Later, the varied combinations will operate from multiple levels of feeling, and the poet will speak, in the *Elegies*, of "the animal's state of being-sad" (*das Traurigsein des Tieres*), a conception different from the animal-in-the-abstract ("the sadness of animals," *die Trauer von Tieren*) or even in the concrete ("sad animal," *trauriges Tier*.)[56]

Especially in *New Poems* a preference for foreign words, used indiscriminately before, becames part of a deliberately considered technique. More than anyone, Rilke helped to free the older rhyme patterns of German verse, chiefly through the use of foreign words, from the monotony and stereotype into which they had sunk during the nineteenth century. The contrasting effects of Germanic and Romanic word stems, either in composition with the same word (*mit dem Apfel in der Apfelpose*) or in juxtaposition (*als ob sie kreisten, willig, primitiv*) opens the idiom to more of the resources at the disposal of English verse.

Very infrequently does the practice verge on mannerism—even in a poem like "The Flamingos" the somewhat precious *ins Imaginäre*, "into imaginary space," is justified by the Fragonard reference in the first line. Though the effect is lost in translation, "The Procession of the Virgin" reveals further experimentation with the foreign word:

> Die Böschung Schauender umschliesst die Schiene,
> in der das alles stockt und rauscht und rollt:
> das Kommende, das Chriselephantine,
> aus dem sich zu Balkonen Baldachine
> aufbäumen, schwankend im Behang von Gold . . .

> The slope of spectators surrounds the path
> in which all these things stop, rustle and roll:
> from which rear canopies to balconies
> swaying in ornaments of gold . . .

The poem reproduces the exact effect the poet is trying to make through language. Each phrasing, each strophe suggests congestion, clumsy progress, the heaving of an excited mob. Not even the "leaping" canopies are a match for these weighted gold draperies. The use of the Greek compound in verse three, "chryselephantine," somehow recalling Eliot's "philoprogenetive of the Lord," drew from him one of his rarer technical comments: "The *chryselephantine* in the *Procession of the Virgin* signifies made-of-gold (*chrysos*, Greek) and ivory (*elephas*), and it is used of the statues of Phidias which were made of it, according to the texts. Here the expression is to help evoke suddenly, at a stroke, the white-gold aspect of the procession . . ."[57] While one may doubt whether any reader but a philologist would receive such an impression "at a stroke," the term does succeed in expressing clumsiness and heaviness, thoroughly in keeping with the poem.

Chiefly because of the formal aspect of *New Poems*, French critics and those with affinities for the Latinate tradition of the West have been enthusiastic about them. Thus Angelloz exaggerates to the extent of calling the collection "one of the summits of Rilke's poetry, not only of German poetry but of human poetry at large."[58] No doubt, as he further points out, the seventeenth-century classical tradition led French poets more and more away from romantic lyricism toward the impersonal form,[59] and Rilke is obviously indebted to France and its artistic models. Not for nothing did he dedicate the second part of *New Poems* to "mon grand ami: Auguste Rodin." Yet the *goût du réel* detected in this poetry is not the "reality" (*Wirklichkeit*) Rilke was ultimately heading for. His poetic nature was essentially musical, but his dread of the effects of music in poetry (after his painful early experiments) persuaded him to adapt his talent provisionally, and as a sort of discipline, to Western art forms. Hence his solution for obtaining significant form in the Paris poems is, in many ways, a synthetic and artificial one. His animals, flowers, statues, and vases come to life within their prescribed limits, but many of the poems seem more like wall frescoes or the ornamentations on a temple frieze. The study of so-called objective reality was not the task Rilke, more than any other modern poet, was called to perform. For this the Chartres Angel had first to descend from its niche before its Duino successor could mediate between the poet and his ultimate meaning. The great prose work, *The Notebooks of Malte Laurids Brigge*, is evidence of this need of a possible solution for it.

IV

o⅛ *The Autobiography of a Book*

IN *The Notebooks of Malte Laurids Brigge*, begun in 1904 and published in 1910, Rilke imaginatively records a poet's experience against the background of his culture. The work therefore provides a parallel to, and summary of, many aspects of *New Poems*, much in the same way as the Rodin essays accompany *The Book of Images*, or *Stories about God* complete *The Book of Hours*. It would be oversimplification to say that such parallelism falls into a neat pattern of question and response, though it does illuminate the dialectical play of Rilke's thinking, so fundamental in all he wrote. The *Notebooks* are a kind of inventory-taking, while serving at the same time as a springboard into the future. From now on there will merely be different arrangements and dispositions of the stock on hand, but nothing will be lost from the total inventory. Evidence of the importance of this stock-taking may be gathered from the fact that, with the exception of the *Elegies*, no other work drew from the author such abundant, and not altogether consistent, self-exegesis.

ORIGINS

Despite the many possible analogies this work is extremely difficult to place within a definite literary pattern or tradition. The fact that it is at the same time all things, and yet not strictly one, is tantamount to saying that it is not completely achieved as a work of art. The poet himself referred to its casual growth and lack of organization, at times labeling it a mere "mosaic" constructed of loose notes and letters lying in a bureau drawer.[1] Certain analogies to Proust are obvious, for both Rilke and Proust work through the agency of recall-patterns to explore the dark recesses of childhood, working out from the individual ego, breaking down conventional psychic structures and disregarding chronology. On the other hand, Proust's work is the result of a highly analytical, persistent mind and of an intellectual temper of a different order from Rilke's, which seems to be in flight toward the fantastic, the supernatural, plunging again and again into unknown depths. The *Notebooks* also recall some nineteenth-century diarists—Amiel, Maurice de Guérin—while lacking the complete personal revelation of self contained in these works. Dostoevsky's *Notes from the Underworld* and Gide's *Les Nourritures Terrestres* also come to mind, not to mention Kierkegaard's *Diary of a Seducer*. Surprising parallels may also be found in a modern work like Sartre's *Nausée*, which treats of similar themes and motifs. But such analogies do not bring us far toward exploring the essence of the work itself.

Because of the blending of autobiographical and aesthetic elements, the *Notebooks* serve both a psychological and artistic purpose. The author himself warned against a too literal, personal interpretation of his hero and his hero's destiny. But the fact remains, as Simenauer has explained on the basis of a psychoanalytic interpretation of the text, that the book grew out of infantile regressions of the childhood stage, and that the protagonist Malte is almost a classic example of a compulsive neurotic with aspects of paranoia and hypochondria.[2] The work was to have brought Rilke the adequate sublimation of all his troublesome repressions, but this it failed to do, as the sequel was to reveal. Yet his artistic tact enabled him to keep his project well within the bounds of art, though the overwhelming clinical evidence based on young René's life seems at times to imperil the organic unity.

Revelatory is the author's periodic commentary on the *Notebooks* during the various stages of writing and after completion. The earliest allusion (1904) indicates an artistic problem to be met and solved: the new book's "firm, close-grained prose is like a school and an advance that had to come so as to enable me, sometime later, to write

96

all the others." [3] And to Rodin, indirectly singling out the weakness of much of the Paris poetry: "You must know that in this prose I now know how to make men and women, children and old people. I have especially evoked women by carefully constructing everything that surrounds them." [4] The poet did not make much headway with his project during the next three years until, returning from Capri in 1907 to the "Paris that had consumed Malte" (the Baudelaire passage on "Une Charogne" had already been written), he sought to bring his subject into the focus of Cézanne's "factual expression." The revival of interest in the *Notebooks*, in fact, owes not a little to the sudden interest in Cézanne.

After publication he spoke somewhat apprehensively of what he had done: "I am a little horrified when I think of all the violence I put forth in *Malte*, how in my consequent desperation I plunged clean through to the back of things, behind death itself, so to speak, so that nothing more was possible, not even dying." [5] The sharpness of the tension between psychotherapy and artistic creation is clearly formulated in the lines that follow: "I do not think anybody has ever experienced more vividly to what extent art goes against Nature; it is the most passionate inversion of the world, the return journey from infinity on which you encounter all the honest earthly things." [6]

Doubts as to the efficacy of this catharsis were expressed after publication to Lou Andreas-Salomé (December 28, 1911):

Whether he, who is in part compounded of my own dangers, perishes in order to keep *me*, as it were, from perishing; or whether I have only now, with these notes, really got into the current that will sweep me away and dash me to pieces. Can you understand that this book has left me stranded like a survivor, my soul in a maze, with no occupation, never to be occupied again? The nearer I approached the end the more strongly did I feel that it would mean an indescribable cleavage, a high watershed, as I always told myself; but now it is clear that all water has flowed towards the old side and that I am going down into a parched land that grows no different. [7]

As late as midsummer of 1912 he could still refer to himself as convalescing from *Malte*, grimly adding a few days later that even the creative aridity of the present was better than another Malte Laurids Brigge. A note of warning is often blended, however, with one of self-justification. Difficulties inherent in the nature of the subject were likened to driftwood blocking the passage of a stream (here the psychological implications are clear).[8] Another correspondent is warned against a too literal interpretation of the *Notebooks*, whose effect might well be more seductive than beneficent. A book containing such elements of destruction was to be read, so to speak, "against the grain." [9] Here no immediate instruction was to be obtained as compared with *New Poems*, where the reader might follow "the determined and arduous transformation of an object into its unalloyed uniqueness." [10] Even toward the end of his life the poet was intent on keeping the references and figures of this work vague and merely indicated, as befitted a book "to be accepted, not taken in detail." [11] Only in the Hulewicz letter of November 10, 1925, to be quoted later, did the author appear with a more or less critical estimate of this most problematical work begun some twenty years before.

<h2 style="text-align:center">COMPOSITION AND STYLE</h2>

A certain amount of parallelism can be worked out between the first and second halves of the book. The Prodigal Son theme at the end is anticipated in Malte's Paris exile and recurrent nostalgia for home, the historical deaths balanced by the graphic description of the old Chamberlain's death. But a coherent pattern is nowhere worked out, and one is more aware of the dissimilarities between the two sections, beginning with the tapestry description of Our Lady of the Unicorn in the Castle of Boussac, which announces a conspicuous change in pace and style. The contrapuntal development of the first part is sharp and clean (in painting one would speak of impressionistic *pointilisme*). Not only is the diction forceful because of the author's firsthand experience of Paris scenes and his memories of Sweden and Prague; death, the master of the revels, actually engenders the laconic, thrusting style with its ironic understatements and various rhetorical devices. In complete reversal of the usual procedure, this most curious of prose works begins with dying and ends with rejection of possessive love. Whatever happens within these pages happens with and beyond death. Only on such a premise does Malte have the courage to start all over and make a clean breast of things, arraigning his age in a series of challenging questions that admit of but one answer:

Is it possible that despite discoveries and progress, despite culture, religion and world-wisdom, one has remained on the surface of life? Is it possible that one has even covered this surface, which might still have been something, with an incredibly uninteresting stuff which makes it look like the drawing-room furniture during summer holidays?
Yes, it is possible. . . .

Is it possible that all these people know with perfect accuracy a past that has never existed? Is it possible that all realities are nothing to them; that their life is running down, unconnected with anything, like a clock in an empty room—?
Yes, it is possible. . . .[12]

In the second part the distance of author from subject is greater; the protagonist is no longer *in* the events described but rather reflects back *on* them (witness the marginal notations toward the end). The episode of the newspaper vendor, for example, is handled quite differently from the St. Vitus victim and other destitutes in Part I. The historical deaths retold from Froissart seem remote and cold compared with the old Chamberlain's end. Time and place are less clearly focused as the central figure, drawing the summary of his experience, weaves the formerly isolated events into a personal philosophy. Abelone and the Prodigal Son are raised to the rank of the mythical.

Generically, the *Notebooks* present a variety of literary patterns and models, such as autobiography in the style of the older German *Bildungs-Roman*; the novel of education; real or imaginary correspondence and, finally, a daily record or journal. Yet if they actually fit into none of these categories, the main flaw lies in the author's conception of the titular hero. Here unity and clarity are not always achieved. Rilke's earliest plan for the work envisaged a central character participating (*à la* Gide) in a fictitious dialogue concerning a young Dane who had died, leaving behind a bundle of manuscripts. Quite in keeping with the "anonymous" quality of his poetic universe Rilke often had a flair, like the German romanticists and Kierkegaard, for the use of the pseudonym.[13] The first written entry, dated September 11, rue Toullier, reveals the planned dialogue become a monologue, and Rilke writing about himself, perhaps utilizing his recorded notes of Paris shortly after his arrival. Malte is conceived as a poet, but not until three years later, after a period of intense poetic experimentation and several travels, does the author get down to his conception of Malte as a person distinct from himself, a kind of mirror in which to see reflected the unbearable experience he was not yet strong enough to realize, in many ways a Malte realized through the medium of Cézanne. So absorbed did the author become with his character in the final stages of writing that the latter "grew beyond" the experiences to which he had predestined him, constraining his maker "to hold himself back" from new ones.[14] Malte becomes more and more detached from his creator; in dissatisfaction with his own fictitious living he seems to draw dangerously on the poet's own life. The old romantic *Doppelgänger* motif is largely at the bottom of Rilke's later description of Malte to his French translator as "the companion of so many nights, my friend and confidant. He accompanied me to Venice, he was myself as I wandered about in Paris streets, he stopped with me under the shade of the Allyscamps, together we met the shepherds in the Baux. In Kopenhagen, on the Langelinie, I saw him, we met each other in the Taxus avenues of Fredensborg, he still remembers the overly-sweet fragrance of phlox in summer, his youth was mine," but, as he significantly concludes, "he was my own ego and yet another."[15]

It is impossible to avoid mention of Goethe's *Werther* as a forerunner of the *Notebooks*, though the dissimilarities are greater than the likenesses. Both Werther and Malte are "scapegoats" loaded with their particular burden of sin. But whereas Goethe, as Butler points out, achieves "a relationship between art and autobiography, between confession and creation," with Rilke "poetry and truth, far from being inextricably mingled, relieve each other throughout the book whenever it suits the author."[16] Hence the emotions to be cast out—fear and love—still raise their problematical heads in the end. "He was my own ego and yet another," says Rilke; Goethe-Werther brings the two together. The "scapegoat" experiment was only partially successful[17]—the guilt plainly lingered on, he wrote Clara Rilke, as the reference to Dostoevsky suggests:

AUTOBIOGRAPHY OF A BOOK

The book of *Malte*, once it is written, will be nothing but the book of this knowledge, exemplified in one for whom it was too tremendous. Possibly he did triumph after all: for he wrote the death of the Chamberlain; but, like a Raskolnikov, he remained behind, consumed by his deed, ceasing to act at the very moment when action had to begin, so that his newly acquired freedom turned against him and destroyed him, the weaponless.[18]

On the work's actual method of composition Rilke himself, always keenly aware of poetry and prose as two different expressive media, is an acute commentator. In his poetry at its best he submitted his imaginative organization to an uncontrolled automatism. In prose his experience was quite otherwise, as he informed Maurice Betz when discussing the book with him toward the end of his life. The conversation is worth quoting in full as it throws much light on other aspects of the poet's work:

The requisite unity was no longer that of a poem, it was that of the individual personality which, from beginning to end, had to be brought to life in its infinite variety. It was a chopped-up, broken rhythm which just forced itself on me, and I was pulled in many directions I never foresaw. Now it was a question of youthful memories or Paris, again the atmosphere of Denmark or pictures which appeared to have no connection with my own self. Now I almost fused with Malte and again I lost him out of sight. A trip would remove him entirely from my range but when I returned, I found him again more actual than ever. Many pages I wrote at mere random. Some were letters, others notes, diary fragments, poems in prose. Despite the density of texture of this (for me) entirely new prose, it was a constant groping about, a march into darkness which seemed never to end. But finally it appeared that he was there after all, the companion of so many nights, my friend and confidant.[19]

Rilke is speaking, of course, long after the event, in ironic overtones and with some playfulness. But the passage accounts quite clearly for the fact that the now introspective, now retrospective character of Malte's entries imperil the book's organic form, setting up a kind of neutralization process that is reflected in the style itself. Through the protagonist's assimilation of the varied experiences of the past to his present mood they acquire the grey monotony and one-dimensional flatness of his present despair. Despite the variety and

101

multiplicity of impressions recorded, there is insufficient change of tone or depth to bring out the essential contours. And yet, with its brilliant flashes of intuition and unforgettably modeled scenes, the book contains some of the great prose passages of our time.

CHILDHOOD, LOVE, AND DEATH

Whatever real unity the *Notebooks* achieve is made possible by the interweaving of theme and motif that holds the loose structure together. Whether the locale be Paris or Denmark or a stylized Prague, the impinging present or the rediscovered past, separation in time and experience is actually no separation at all. Malte's childhood in retrospect and Malte's maturity in the present are so similar in quality and substance that a comparison of the Denmark-Prague-Paris motifs adds up to the same problem-clusters (Rilke will later speak of the great "question dynasties") of childhood, love, and death, all rooted in the dark soil of "dread." The Schulin and Mathilde Brahe episodes, for example, symbolize from one direction the same blending of real and unreal that is accomplished from another in the description of dismantled Paris houses.

Much in the book reverts to older levels of experience and feeling with their subjective and often sentimental overtones. The stories of Nikolaj Kusmitsch and the medical student—the "neighbor" motif— are in direct descendence from *Stories about God*. Jacobsen and Dostoevsky are still in the background, the former more often, so that it is reasonable to say with Butler that "by making his scapegoat an aristocratic young Dane, he proclaimed nis kinship with the north rather than with the east of Europe." [20] His contacts with Scandinavian lands through travels, friends, and the authors he read (Ellen Key, Hermann Bang, Sigborn Obstfelder, Jacobsen, Ibsen, Kierkegaard) were important to the genesis of the *Notebooks*, especially the latter two. Scholars are more or less in agreement that "Kierkegaard represents the decisive turning-point in Rilke's life," that "only in the meeting with Kierkegaard did Rilke find the path to himself," and that "Malte is in generous portions the adaptation of the demands set forth by Kierkegaard." [21] There is an obvious relatedness between the anxiety motif of the *Notebooks* and Kierkegaard's concept; be-

tween the latter's view of eternity and Rilke's of death.[22] One critic
has gone so far as to see, in Malte, Kierkegaard with his longing for
the "Knight of Faith." [23] The existentialist approach to Rilke, as with
Kafka, detects behind the concept of dread such factors as man's loss
of a personal center (*Zerstreutheit*) and his consequent imperilment
in a world of unconvincing or totally abeyant vital relationships. But
as in the similar case of Kafka again, while providing many valuable
critical insights, both the Freudian and existentialist interpretations
overstate their cases. All we know for certain in connection with the
Notebooks is Rilke's explanation that he made his hero a Dane "because only in the atmosphere of the Scandinavian countries does the
ghost appear ranged among the possible experiences and admitted." [24] Thus while the occasional occult episodes are in part re-
counted experiences of childhood in Prague, they are also in part
things experienced and overheard in Sweden.

The theme of childhood, the matrix from which all Rilkean conceptions of poetry spring, is not thoroughly assimilated and comprehended by the central character; indeed, it could hardly be otherwise
since he is caught in the unsolved conflict of truth with fiction, biog-
raphy with imaginative construction. In describing this past the author does indeed move between the two poles of dread and charm,
with inevitable forays into the sentimental and bathetic. Four years
after Malte's appearance Rilke was still writing of this "boundless
childhood" of which "so much will of course never accumulate again,
even if one were to have decades more to achieve under the most unspeakable sufferings and most incomprehensible blisses." [25] The
overwhelming burden of this past is succinctly stated in four lines,
after the lengthy anxiety manifestations of the preceding sections:
"I asked for my childhood and it has come back, and I feel that it is
just as difficult as it was before, and that it has been useless to grow
older." [26] And one recalls the famous birthday passage, a preliminary
draft of "The Death of a Boy" poem of 1915, with its caustic examples of adult obtuseness: "and one saw even at a distance that it was
a joy for somebody quite different, a totally alien joy." [27]

Childhood may be the beginning of wisdom, but the character
Malte begins with dying. At times within eyesight of the goal, his

strength is insufficient to the task and he becomes the passive victim, not the active hero. Not yet had Rilke discovered the formula to convert such defeat into the symbolic transcendence of the *Sonnets to Orpheus*:

Despite my fear I am yet like one standing before something great, and I remember that it was often like that in me before I began to write. But this time I shall be written. I am the impression that will change. Ah, but a little more, and I could understand all this and approve it. Only a step, and my deep misery would be beatitude. But I cannot take that step; I have fallen and cannot pick myself up again, because I am broken.[28]

Some light is thrown on this fearful hesitancy by Malte's heavy dependence on historical and literary references in his attempts to communicate the tensions existent between past and present, living and dying. His education and his experience of life were seemingly too indirect, too much derived from secondary sources. Hence his book is weighted with descriptions of *objets d'art*, memoirs of historic personages, and accounts of families that read like chronicles. The first and second parts nicely balance each other with a passage in each touching upon the relevance of literature to experience. Malte in Paris, after all human aid has failed, notes that he has "prayed," but, significantly, his prayers are fragments of Baudelaire and the Book of Job (we recall that *The Book of Hours* was originally conceived as "prayers"). The passage in the second part projects Malte as a young boy, and is concerned with the relationship of literature to life as seen from the childhood perspective. Here Rilke's often lamented ineptitude for systematic reading comes readily to mind. At Ulsgaard the boy Malte plunges into reading before he is quite ready for it. Suddenly he is confronted with the unsettling shocks of adolescence:

They were life-sized experiences that made themselves as heavy as they were. In the same degree, however, as I apprehended their actuality, my eyes opened also to the infinite reality of my childhood. I knew that it would not cease, any more than the other was only now beginning. I said to myself that everyone was naturally at liberty to make divisions, but they were artificial. And it appeared that I was too unskilled to think out any for myself. Every time I tried, life gave me to understand that it knew nothing of them. If, however, I persisted in thinking that my childhood was past, then in that same moment my whole future was also gone and there was left me only just so much as a lead soldier has beneath his feet to stand on.[29] The rhythm of life (actuality) is opposed to that of childhood (poetry), a dichotomy that finds full expression later in the antagonism of Destiny and Laurel (*Schicksal* and *Lorbeer*) in the opening lines of the Ninth Elegy; and the "too sharp distinctions" (between living and dead) we are accused of making in the First Elegy are presaged in the revealing "everyone was naturally at liberty to make divisions, but they were artificial." Malte is still faced with the predicament of "a lead soldier" with little to stand on, though many years later in the *Sonnets to Orpheus* Rilke will himself complete the Ring of Forms by raising a monument to a cousin who appears in the *Notebooks* and to all those "one-time sharers of childhood's treasure" who retained of *reality* "Only the balls" and "Their glorious curving."

References to death in the first half of the book are generally ironic, emphatic through pithy understatement, even spiced with sardonic humor. Indeed, the whole spiritual landscape of *The Magic Mountain* is compressed into one line: "In sanatoria, where people die so willingly and with so much gratitude to doctors and nurses, they die from one of the deaths attached to the institution; that is favorably regarded." Reflections on the theme in the second half are sober and branch off into metaphysics: "Sometimes I reflect on how heaven came to be and death: through our having distanced what is most precious to us, because there was still so much else to do beforehand and because it was not secure with us busy people . . ."

In *The Book of Hours* there is apprehension of physical death rooted in a more or less physical dread. In the *Notebooks*, along with many repulsive naturalistic details, the theme is handled much more expansively and subtly, set off against "something else" where it does not have to stand alone in a void. The *real* death of the Chamberlain not only requires feverish movement and a sense of space; it also involves the intimate aspects of an entire community's living: its daily occupations and births, its nights and animal world. What lends the subject a poignant force is its location in a definite social milieu, the twilight realm of Paris *misère*, and the equally twilight regions of history and family anecdote. From the hospitals with their prefabricated death it is only a step to the "bluish dregs in a coffee saucer" ("Der Tod," 1915) and to the gentle sarcasm of the Tenth Elegy six years later:

> Oh aber gleich darüber hinaus,
> hinter der letzten Planke, beklebt mit Plakaten
> des "Todlos,"
> jenes bitteren Biers, das den Trinkenden süss
> scheint,
> wenn sie immer dazu frische Zerstreuungen
> kaun . . .

> Oh, and then just outside,
> behind the last hoarding, plastered with
> placards for "Deathless,"
> that bitter beer that tastes quite sweet to its
> drinkers
> so long as they chew with it plenty of fresh
> distractions . . .

In the second half there is more integration between the themes of death and love, since the latter, for Rilke, can only be fully grasped if the death reference is included. By contrast with the earlier descriptions death is here raised to the plane of the mythical, the historical. The reconstructed "inner" destinies of the False Dmitri, Charles the Bold of Burgundy, and Charles VI of France are symbolical projections of Malte's own feelings into the turbulent lives he has read about, chiefly in Froissart. To the charge of obscurity Rilke later replied that factual "identification" was not necessary, that the reader would still derive enough from "the tension of these anonymities." [30] The resultant atmosphere is one of horror, wonder, and admiration, strained through reflection and meditation. He contrasts the immense and unsuspected potentialities of his characters' "inner realms" with what ordinarily passes for "objective" history. The Hulewicz letter already referred to, looking back through the vistas of *Elegies* and *Sonnets*, is a most revealing document. Here in a language charged with scientific metaphors, with its emphasis on Malte's "vowels of affliction" that go counter to the evidence of history and the distinctions of science until brought into focus with the "search-

AUTOBIOGRAPHY OF A BOOK

light of the heart," Rilke is his own best spokesman for one of the oddest books of the age:

> In *Malte* there can be no question of defining and substantiating the numerous allusions in it. The reader must communicate not with their historical or imaginary reality but, through them, with Malte's own experience: and even *he* was concerned with them only to the extent that a person may let a neighbour affect him, or a passer-by in the street. The connection lies in the fact that the people evoked exhibit the same 'frequency' of vital intensity as vibrates in Malte's being . . . And everything, no matter where experienced, has the same valuableness for him, the same duration and actuality. Not for nothing is Malte the grandchild of old Count Brahe who regards everything, past and future, as quite simply 'present', and in the same way Malte regards as present these reservoirs of his feeling . . . His own days of affliction and the great days of affliction of the Avignon Pontificate, when all the things that now strike *inwards* so grievously were projected *outwards*—are now put on an equal footing: it is of no consequence for us to know more of the figures conjured up than the searchlight of Malte's heart reveals. They are not historical figures or shapes of his own past, but *the vowels of his affliction*: hence one must bear with an occasional name which is not enunciated any further, as though it were a bird-note in this country where the minor lulls are more perilous than the storms.[31]

Upon the realm of death follows that of love, or rather both are interwoven. Since love, for Rilke, is a direction and not a goal, the passages dealing with this theme are necessarily symbolical projections, blueprints of the poetic imagination rather than of everyday reality. Whereas death, experienced to the hilt in Malte's early Paris days, is a fact, an already assimilated ingredient of what he lived through, love is a mystical possibility, a potentiality existing only in faint, fluttering outline. The wavering uncertainty again arises from the conflict between fiction and life, for surely personal guilt feelings are in some measure responsible for the "women-in-love" passage in the *Notebooks*:

> For centuries now, they [the women] have performed the whole of love; they have always played the full dialogue, both parts. For the man has only imitated them, and badly. And has made their learning difficult with his inattentiveness, with his negligence, with his jealousy, which was also a sort of negligence. And they have nevertheless

107

persevered day and night, and have increased in love and misery. And from among them, under the stress of endless needs, have gone forth those powerful lovers who, while they called him, surpassed their man; who grew beyond him when he did not return, like Gaspara Stampa or like the Portuguese nun, who never desisted until their torture turned into a bitter, icy splendor that was no longer to be restrained.[32]

Abelone, Malte's childhood friend, is a fictitious sister of these historical personages, and when she passes from the scene singing "because I never held you close, I hold you forever," she supplies us with a key to the Prodigal Son theme that follows. Malte wonders why Abelone "did not use the calories of her magnificent feeling on God," adding "but could her truthful heart be deceived about God's being only a direction of love, and not an object of love? Didn't she know that she need fear no return from him . . . ?"[33] Abelone and the Prodigal are in similar case. The Prodigal realizes that only One may love him, "but He was not yet willing."

The genesis of the Prodigal Son parable may be traced to the poet's personal conflicts in the early Prague years (cf. *Ewald Tragy*). "After scarcely a year," he informed a friend in 1897, "I tore myself away against the advice of everybody by an act of violence, and have, since that time, been declared a kind of Prodigal Son."[34] The conception of the False Dmitri in the *Notebooks* incidentally derives from a similar source, for his is "the strength of all those who have gone away."[35] In his own personal life, in his relations with others, Rilke more than once envisages variations of the Prodigal Son theme, as when he observes that "A togetherness between two people is an impossibility . . . But, once the realisation is accepted that even between the *closest* human beings infinite distances continue to exist, a wonderful living side by side can grow up, if they succeed in loving the distance between them . . ."[36] A personal confession, of course, is not to be confused with art creation like the *Notebooks* passage, though taken together, the two certainly admit of contradictions, a vicious circle of reasoning. The emphasis on "distance" at least points a finger in the direction of the Prodigal Son.

Thus Rilke was already attracted to the parable before he came across Gide's version (*Le Retour de l'Enfant Perdu*, 1907), which doubtless lent some impetus to his own interpretation. The two versions, however, have little in common, except here and there a tone, a certain quality of mind. Gide's work is built around a sequence of dramatic dialogues; Rilke treats the original Biblical story in the style of the historical vignettes that immediately precede it. Gide emphasizes the Prodigal's return as a result of failure, induced by despair and doubt, to go far enough to seize his freedom, which his younger brother may conquer in his stead. The return of Rilke's Prodigal is simply that of one "who did not want to be loved" and, confronted by his forgiving parents, had only "the gesture of supplication with which he threw himself at their feet, imploring them not to love." [37] It is, in fact, neither story, legend, nor parable, but a symbolic representation of the unrequited-love theme. In a marginal note to the Abelone passage Rilke states this theme with an aphoristic concision, which only loses its tense sharpness in some of the late poems: "To be loved means to be consumed. To love is to give light with inexhaustible oil. To be loved is to pass away, to love is to endure." [38]

SUPPORTING THEMES AND MOTIFS

Variations on the book's theme-clusters may be met at almost every stage in the prose and poetry from 1904 until 1926. Madame Lamort of the Seventh Elegy evolves from Malte's Madame Legrand, "brocanteuse in the Rue des Martyrs." The status of animals that "are self-aware and find each other and are content with this" is but more profoundly examined in the First and Eighth Elegies. Malte-Rilke's own life-theme is compressed into the few lines of Orpheus Sonnet I, 17. His threnody on the disappearance of the past's precious heritage is related to the "activity without an image" (*ein Tun ohne Bild*) of the Kalckreuth *Requiem* and, ultimately, to the transformation theme of the *Elegies* and their corresponding passages in the letters. The role played in childhood by the mother (Third Elegy) is already anticipated in "O mother: O you only who shut out all this stillness, long ago in childhood." Rilke is constantly refashioning old imagery and recombining used motifs until the images take on archetypal significance, many of them parallel to *New Poems* but also pointing ahead to the later poetry ("lace," "death mask," "mask," "face," "angel," "puppet," "mirrors," "outcasts," the "innocent ear" in connection with Beethoven's music which may ultimately find its willing listener in the desert of the Thebaid, in the "ear of earth" of one of the Orpheus Sonnets). The "dog" (cf. *New Poems*) is so much harped on in the *Notebooks*—a whole thread of meanings runs through "dog," "Cézanne," "the Solitary" and "the Saint"—that it becomes an archetypal symbol: the "A dog barks. What a relief! A dog!" bridging the years to the Tenth Elegy's "And dogs are following nature." One could proceed endlessly to enumerate correlations and cross references which would merely serve again to emphasize the extreme homogeneity of Rilke's thinking and practice.

We have already observed how his not altogether felicitous relationship with the theater was reflected in the early prose and poetry. Apart from the minor point that the *Notebooks* were originally conceived as a kind of dramatic dialogue, the subject of theater is introduced on at least four different occasions, not including the decidedly dramatic historical vignettes in the last section. Malte himself is the author of a bad tragedy, entitled *Marriage*, "which sets out to demonstrate something false by equivocal means." [39] Rilke's earlier ideas on theater are carried over into the sarcastic jibes directed at the unnecessary "third party" in modern plays (the eternal triangle), this indispensable screen and "pretext of nature" (*Vorwand der Natur*). What would happen, continues Malte, to modern drama, the public, and the playwrights with their rich villas, if the "third party" failed to appear or even missed his cue?

More important is the fervid tribute inspired by a performance of *The Wild Duck* in Paris, which disclosed an Ibsen who ventured "further in" among the "alembics of the firelight" than any dramatist had yet done. So novel, yet characteristic, is Rilke's appraisal of Ibsen's career that the following passage would hardly be intelligible without a commentary:

Your theater came into being. You could not wait until this life almost without dimension, condensed into drops by the centuries, should be discovered by the other arts and gradually made visible for single individuals, who little by little meet together in their insight and at last demand to see in common these august rumors confirmed in the parable of the scene thrown open before them. This you could not wait for; you were there, and that which is scarcely measurable . . . all this you had to determine and preserve; for in such processes life itself now was, our life, which had slipped into us, had withdrawn inward, so deeply that it was scarcely possible even to conjecture about it any more.

Given as you were to showing, a timelessly tragic poet, you had to translate this capillary action all at once into the most convincing gestures, into the most present things. Then you set about that unexampled act of violence in your own work, which ever more impatiently, ever more desperately, sought equivalents among the visible for the inwardly seen . . . Then you could do no more. The two extremities you had bent together sprang apart; your mad strength escaped from the flexible shaft, and your work was as nothing.[40]

Ibsen's search for "equivalents among the visible" stands midway between Rilke's earlier views on Rodin's sculpture, born into an age with no artistic public validity and only a fluid private form, and, on the other hand, the "invisible re-arising in us" of the Ninth Elegy. Rilke is merely formulating, in a fashion obscure because couched in the accumulating metaphors and rhythms of his own poetic thinking, what a modern critic, in reference to *Ghosts*, diagnoses as the Ibsen dilemma: the "photographically accurate parlor" and then the "empty but stimulating scene out of the window," the "cramped interiors" and then the "exhilarating wilderness." [41] This is what Rilke means by saying that the "two extremities sprang apart."

Fortunately, in the Hulewicz questionnaire, Rilke paraphrased for our better understanding the meaning of the Ibsen passage:

Life, *our* present life is scarcely possible of scenic representation, since it has withdrawn wholly into the invisible, the inner, imparting itself to us only through 'august rumors'; the dramatist, however, could not wait till it became showable; he had to use violence toward it, this not yet producible life; and for that reason too his work, like a wand too strongly bent, sprang from his hands and was as though not done.[42]

The "hopeless hyperbola" of Ibsen's career is only understandable in the light of Rilke's own demands of his evolving theory of poetry. He is speaking *pro domo* when Malte proceeds to define the factor

111

the dramatist could not wait for: "a feeling that mounted by half a degree; the angle of refraction, which you read off at close quarters, of a will burdened by almost nothing, the slightest cloudiness in a drop of longing and that barely perceptible color-change in an atom of confidence . . ." [43] This description of the workings of the "nuance," founded on the "long patience" of Rodin, should be read in conjunction with Malte's famous warning to the poet "to wait and gather sense and sweetness a whole life long, and a long life if possible, and then, quite at the end, one might perhaps be able to write ten lines that were good." [44] For an important level of meaning in the *Notebooks* is concerned with the function and purpose of poetry, of the poetic life, of creativeness in general. "He was a poet and hated the inexact (*das Ungefähre*)," records Malte of Felix Anvers, a French poet who died in 1850. The tortured style of the Ibsen passage is Rilke's own challenge to the "inexact" or "casual" in literary expression, in place of the "inevitable" and the "appropriate." Hence the figurative language, drawn largely from chemical science, describing the poet among the alembics "where the most secret chemistry of life goes on, its transformations and precipitations." Rilke's subtle use of scientific vocabulary when he wants to convey an important meaning in poetry, though never overdone, becomes more refined as he matures.

Just as the Ibsen tribute and Malte's own failure as a playwright follow and link up each other, so do the other chapters dealing with the theater at Orange and the actress Duse. The spiritual climate of the age is judged and condemned almost exclusively in metaphors of the theater:

Outside much has changed, I don't know how. But inside and before you, O my God, inside before you, spectator, are we not without action? We discover indeed that we do not know our part, we look for a mirror, we want to rub off the make-up and remove the counterfeit and be real. But somewhere a bit of mummery still sticks to us that we forget. A trace of exaggeration remains in our eyebrows, we do not notice that the corners of our lips are twisted. And thus we go about, a laughing-stock, a mere half-thing: neither existing, nor actors. [45]

The superhuman drama that Rilke conjures up from the past in the amphitheater at Orange hinges on the role played by an immense wall behind the stage, divided into three parts by its doors. This wall he employs as a symbol, comparing it to the icon wall in Russian churches, which served as focus for the concentration of feeling and thought. It is at this point that Malte accepts his permanent exclusion from the modern theater, "this same underdone reality that litters our streets and our houses, save that more of it collects there than can be put into one evening"—which sounds less like criticism of the theater and more like a description of the social milieu of the early Paris poetry.[46] His outburst "Let us be honest about it, then: we have no theater, any more than we have a God!" is a far cry from Lessing's criticism of the *Schauspielkunst* of his day. Even the tragic career of Eleonora Duse, though visualized against the backdrop of drama, is not strictly concerned with the theater proper but serves to embroider the theme of the unrequited lovers. All these factors are ingredients of the Rilkean aesthetic. Wherever he employs the motifs of theater or drama, with the allied motif of the mask, it is in support of his own poetic practice and his own poetic vision.

It is not until the critical years during the war that Rilke begins noticeably to take stock of himself and other writers in relation to literary traditions, but such an awareness is at least suggested in the *Notebooks*. Toward the end of the book he sketches in his own inimitable way the meaning of antiquity for Malte:

Now he instantaneously grasps the dynamic significance of that early world-unity, which was something like a new and simultaneous assumption of all human work. It does not trouble him that that consistent civilization, with its almost total visualization, seemed to many later eyes to form a whole, and that whole wholly past. There, it is true, the celestial half of life was really fitted against the half-round bowl of terrestrial existence, as two full hemispheres connect to form a perfect orb of gold. Yet scarcely had this occurred, when the spirits confined within it felt this utter realization to be no more than allegory; the massive star lost weight and rose into space, and in its golden sphere the sadness was reflected, hesitant, of that which could not yet be mastered.[47]

Rilke acknowledges the existence of an integral classical tradition but it is done rather on the sly, begrudgingly, with the same kind of negative strictures found in his criticism on the Renaissance. The qualifications "seemed," "almost," and "scarcely" suggest that the boasted organic unity of the ancient world, because of its numerous exclusions, had inevitably to pass from symbolism to allegory. To be sure, Malte accepts the heritage of the older world—"its meaning spreads through his blood"—yet remarks, taking an apple from a plate of fruit on the window-seat, "How my life stands around about this fruit. Around all that which is finished, that which still has to be done rises and takes increase." [48] The modern poet has released the spirits from their dungeon and given them over to the timeless and infinite. The same heuristic, futurist aesthetic, formulated in the early *Tuscan Diary*, accompanies Rilke until the end. Outlines of a futurist painting, premature by some years, may be found in Malte's description of Hieronymous Bosch's strange fifteenth-century illustrations of the "Temptations of St. Anthony." For Rilke was not only one of the first to introduce the stylistic dynamics of the later Expressionists into poetry, but actually anticipated many of the tricks of the Surrealists. The *Notebooks*, as a whole, in fact, draw appreciably on art values—Cézanne, Boussac tapestries, and ancestral portraits, for example. The imagery of the Bosch passage offers a singular contrast to the two hemispheres, the celestial half and "the half-round bowl of terrestrial existence," which together form the "perfect orb of gold":

How I understand now those strange pictures in which things meant for restricted and regular uses relax and wantonly touch and tempt one another in their curiosity, quivering with the random lechery of dissipation. These cauldrons that go about boiling, these pistons that hit upon ideas, and the useless funnels that squeeze themselves into holes for pleasure. And behold among them, too, thrown up by the jealous void, limbs and parts of limbs, and faces that warmly vomit into them, and windy buttocks offering them satisfaction. [49]

The *Notebooks* have frequently been supposed to conclude in tragedy, though Malte's death or even ultimate disaster is nowhere explicitly made clear. The tragedy is neither conclusive nor inevitable in the parable of the Prodigal Son. The poet himself, to a certain extent, fathered the sinister interpretation in a letter to his wife during the Cézanne phase: "For Cézanne is nothing else but the first primitive and bare achievement of that which in M. L. was not yet achieved. Brigge's death: that was Cézanne's life, the life of his last thirty years." [50] But this was in 1907, and we have seen how vacillating were his subsequent judgments of the work. At any rate, it can hardly be a question here of a literal death. Malte may "die" figuratively to his past, and we may even feel that he is incapable of ever coming to terms immediately with the forces of his immense solitude. Certainly it is no death implemented by a brace of pistols or even by the quiet disintegration of so many symbolists at the turn of the century. A critic like Angelloz reaps positive consolation from the book's conclusion: "Malte represents humanity on its march towards God, man in his realisations, his successive sublimations, and 'eternal return' whose goal is: to give birth to him who wishes to love. From death to love and from love to God, such appears to us to be the profound meaning of the *Notebooks*." [51]

Such a judgment errs too much in the other direction, though clearly the work is not merely a private record of a single artistic existence but that of an entire generation, the so-called *décadents* around 1900.[52] It should therefore be read not only as a psychological history of a weak descendant of an old Danish family, who may or may not perish, but also as a warning to the aesthetic types of the day to persist and thus rise above the impact of experience as a part of their artistic obligation. The Kalckreuth *Requiem*, written during these years, particularly emphasizes that not victory but surviving is everything. This is what Rilke meant later by saying that his book should be read "against the grain."

Butler's ingenious theory that Malte Laurids Brigge represents the failure of Rilke's hypothetical artist-god (cf. *The Book of Hours*) and a move in the direction of the transformation of life into art in an attempt to find an adequate substitute, while extremely interesting, does less than justice to its artistic importance.[53] Though no one would claim the *Notebooks* to be a completely achieved work of art, Malte's story nonetheless provides a valuable commentary on the Paris poetry and that yet to come, interpreting and enlarging still nuclear ideas. More than that, Malte allows us an inside view, as the poetry itself rarely does, into the poetic mind in process, with all its

115

variety and even confusion. It may well be that such interior exploration is the chief value of this most unusual novel. As Fritz Martini correctly points out in his recent close analysis of Rilke's method in the *Notebooks*, Rilke substitutes for the traditional novel form an associatively constructed sheaf of momentary impressions and fragmentary allusions, which seem almost to have been picked at random.[54] But Rilke's "impressions" are not arbitrarily selected, nor do they operate merely on the surface as in so much impressionistic writing; they are rigidly determined by the author's peculiarly individual experience and by the complex of themes and motifs that weave through all his work. [55] So far at times is Rilke from narrating objectively that, as in the case of some of the historical vignettes, for example, the problem of narration becomes itself the theme. Reflecting back upon himself, the author uses his material merely to probe into the still undivulged meanings of inner experience. As Martini phrases it, Rilke's language tends, as commonly since Nietzsche, toward expression as a means of aesthetic or ontological evaluation.[56]

But if confusion is undeniably there, it is because, in Malte's words, "Fate loves to invent patterns and designs. Its difficulty lies in complexity. But life itself is difficult because of its simplicity." [57] Without the *Notebooks* behind him, the poet would hardly have ventured to cross the Duino threshold in 1912.

V

○⚬ *The Critical Years*

A VERY good case could be made for assessing the period from 1910 to 1919, conveniently divided by a caesura with the onset of war in 1914, as perhaps the most important in Rilke's entire creative life. The significance of these years has usually been overlooked or treated with condescension.Too frequently the orientation has been taken from the fact that no major work appeared from 1910 to 1922. The emphasis only too readily has fallen on the factor of poetic sterility and intermittency of genius rather than on what actually went on in, or vitally contributed to, a second workshop much more important than the first. The real stress should fall on the inner concentration and emotional perseverance, even during months and years of stress and strain, that made possible the great work to come. Without the poet's spiritual resilience throughout this time we would have little guarantee that the final consummation of the *Elegies*, begun at Duino in 1912, would have been achieved. In its final form this work is the precipitation of not only what preceded the year 1912 but, to an eminent degree, of the restless travels and pathetic attempts at personal adjustment that followed. Even from the standpoint of productivity the critical years offer an astounding record in view of the circumstances: translations of Maurice de Guérin's *Centaur* (1911), Elizabeth Barrett Browning's *Sonnets from the Portuguese* (1911), Marianna Alcoforado's *Letters from the French* (1913), Michelangelo's *Sonnets* (begun in 1914), and Gide's *Le Retour de l'Enfant Perdu* (1914). New work includes the ten

THE RING OF FORMS

poems making up *The Life of the Virgin Mary* (1913), the *Five War Songs* (1914), as well as a number of prose essays and a vast correspondence. This record does not yet include the astonishing number of poems, either fragmentary or unpublished, which have recently been painstakingly collected and edited.¹ Nor does it make allowance for the fact that no less than eight of the ten *Elegies* were, if not completed, at least started or blocked out between 1912 and 1915 alone.

The real gains, however, of this period of distressing doubt and self-assessment, later referred to as *sécheresse d'âme*, cannot be computed quantitatively since they are primarily inner adjustments of a far-reaching psychological and aesthetic nature. To ignore these factors is to ignore the essential development of a poet's mind. With Rilke one is always forced to take into account the close interdependence of the poetic personality (not the *life*) and the poetry itself. These inner adjustments were basic and operative in at least four different areas: (1) the human, individual adjustment; (2) the religious factor; (3) awareness of the European, more specifically, German tradition; and (4) experience gained through travels.

As for the human adjustment, it would be difficult to find in all literature a more desperate record of psychic collapse and spiritual dislocation than Rilke's correspondence at this time reveals. The completion of the *Notebooks*, that "heavy, heavy book," destructive rather than beneficent, appeared to be a watershed on whose receding tides were swept away the middle Paris years when the disciple Rilke had humbled himself before Rodin's overwhelming personality and waxed enthusiastic over Cézanne, anxious to reach the core of art through the closest identification possible with the art-object. Now he had liberated himself completely from Rodin. "It doesn't seem to me," he wrote Lou Andreas-Salomé in 1914, "that a spiritual appropriation of the world, so completely at the service of vision, as was my case, could be any less dangerous to the plastic artist, just because he effects a more tangible composure in treating bodily factors" (cf. the poem "Wendung").² From the standpoint of the practice of poetry and its needs, Rodin no longer counts.

The completion of the *Notebooks*, it was now apparent, forced on him the choice of either continuing to create on the premise of pure

118

sensibility, and thus disappearing with Malte, or of establishing a new basis for his art. For a time Rilke thought of giving up writing altogether, but he could hardly have been aware at first of the magnitude of such a step: to retrace the road to humanity, to live for the first time with people and things in a normal, human context. The attempt naturally ended in a failure whose heartbreaking echoes may be heard in much of the correspondence of these years, the best of all Rilke letters despite stretches of hysteria and bathos, more sincere and humanly engaging than the somewhat canonical prose dispatched from Muzot some years later. He was a hollowed-out shell, the constant litany goes, and had stood so long at the service of objective things that his humanity had atrophied.[3] Or, again, he had so exaggerated the material impact of things that he ran the risk of becoming a caricature of his spiritual nature.[4] "Tell me, how does it come about that I spoil everything," he wrote to Lou Andreas-Salomé, "now it seems to me sometimes as if I were using too much violence toward impressions . . . I stay too long before them . . . au lieu de me pénétrer, les impressions me percent."[5] And again, to the same correspondent: "For I am no longer in doubt that I am ill and my illness has extended beyond itself and is inherent in what I previously called my work, so that from that direction there is for the moment no refuge."[6] The personal malaise, an aggravated symptom of *le malheur d'être un poète*, echoes over the years the plaint of Goethe's *Tasso*:

> Doch ach! je mehr ich horchte, mehr und mehr
> Versank ich vor mir selbst, ich fürchtete,
> Wie Echo an den Felsen zu verschwinden,
> Ein Widerhall, ein Nichts, mich zu verlieren . . .

From an all-devouring empathy Rilke turned to friends and acquaintances for advice and help: should he remove from Paris to settle in a small country-town, preferably a university town where, at the age of thirty-five, he might study medicine, for example, and thus reinstate himself among the normal human functions? Or should he submit to psychoanalytic treatment to come at the root of a suspected neurosis? Neither alternative was adopted; he changed one country estate for another, Paris for Germany, Italy and Spain for a short flyer to Egypt, always haunted by a spiritual isolation he was not ready calmly to confront. As for the finally rejected psychoanalysis, a very penetrating insight into the heart of his poetic purpose is revealed, especially in the parenthesis section, in a comment of July 4, 1914: "To bring this body of mine, riddled with troublesomeness, and my false relation to it to a doctor: that will probably be the only way out eventually. But not to a psychoanalyst who starts off from the Original Sin (for to meet this Original Sin with counter-magic is actually my innermost profession and the cause of my whole artistic attitude towards life)." [7]

By the end of 1913, however, he had apparently accepted, and become reconciled to, a most terrifying fact, even for a poet. He who had boasted that he was always on the way back from God to humanity confessed that, in by-passing the human, he could no longer hope for a return. He might, indeed, wave to mankind in a vision, as from a distance, cheerfully and without bitterness, but over an insurmountable barrier. [8] Even the Benvenuta episode, a venture to find satisfaction in the love relationship, resulted on the contrary in anxiety as to whether he were not betraying his poetic mission. [9]

One can hardly avoid mentioning Keats, again, in this connection. The psychic structure of the two is similarly grounded in an unusual degree of empathic reaction to experience which determined the kind of poetry they wrote. The Keats letter passage, defining the poet as the most unpoetic thing in existence because he had no identity but was always open to invasion from without, fairly reproduces Rilke's dilemma of these years. [10] Even for the man of action, not to mention the poet, he wrote to Gide, it was at times necessary to suspend understanding ("ne pas comprendre quelquechose parfois"). [11]

As for another important adjustment, the religious factor, the critical years further clarified a misconception bordering on delusion and kept alive by feminine admirers and messiah-hunters who had beset his path from the beginning. Already he had taken the measure of, and denounced, orthodox Christianity with its mediator, the "warmed-over stew of Protestants and American Christians" with their "telephone Christ into which one calls: who is there, and nobody answers." [12] But the problem of sanctity—the saint as an existential possibility of life, like the hero or poet—was still much in his thoughts, a logical sequel of *The Book of Hours* and *Stories about God*, as well as of the mystical atmosphere of the intelligentsia of prewar Europe. We tend to forget that just as readily as posterity, to the utter confusion of criticism, will seize on the heroic element in the artist (Byron), it will also seize on the "religious" or "saintly" aspect.

During the critical years, abetted probably by conversations with his friend Kassner, Rilke implied his disqualification for the saintly life on grounds of physical insufficiencies, the inability to suffer as saints are reputed to suffer, and, at the same time, perform the functions of living. To the distinction between "saint" and "poet," he himself gave mordant expression in the already mentioned autobiographical fragment of 1913: "Had he been a saint, he would have derived from this condition a cheerful sense of freedom . . . but he had not removed himself cleanly from the shell, had torn himself out of himself, giving away pieces of the shell in the process." [13] This brand of religiosity simply functions as a mask to conceal artistic gropings and is only of concern for the poetry insofar as a metaphorical shift slowly takes place in the use of a term, like *God* to *gods*, a *god*, and, finally, *the god* of the later *Sonnets*. As a symptom of the antitranscendental, anti-Christian tendencies inherent in modern literature (Rilke, Yeats, Lawrence) the subject is an integral part of the history of the modern mind.

Some mention should be made of the poet's travels from 1910 to 1914, and of the significance of the landscapes met in these travels.[14] The short trip to Egypt left traceable effects on Rilke, evident both in his poetry and his ensuing interest in the archaeology of that country. The very landscape of the *Elegies* is often a reflection of the Nile country, "where life was but a preparation for death," particularly in the matter of imagery ("Nile potter," "startled bat," "Karnak pylon," "vale of lamentation").[15] The four-month sojourn in Spain reacted more profoundly on the poetry then and to come, as we shall see. Even in Switzerland, after the war years, his affiliation with Spain remains unbroken. Duino, finally, on the rock-ribbed Adriatic, aside from personal associations and his friendship with the Princess

121

Marie, was not only the birthplace of the first two *Elegies* but in a way prepared the poet, with its forbidding isolation, for his more stringent retirement at Muzot ten years later. Psychological, social, or biographical factors attending these travels are of little concern for our purpose, but those aspects which an impressionable mind stored away to become incorporated later into the general landscape and metaphors of his poetry are by no means negligible.

LITERARY TRADITIONS

Of considerable importance for Rilke's poetic growth during this period was his confrontation not only with the German but the wider European tradition. His knowledge of literature had always been eclectic and unsystematic, particularly in the earlier years (the knowledge of the amateur, the *Feinschmecker* like Malte, reading against anxiety in the Bibliothèque Nationale). Previously the accent had fallen more on the French classics and the Nordic literature of Jacobsen and Kierkegaard. With the onset of the critical years new contacts, travels, and his forced stay in Germany directed his reading into other channels. After the completion of the *Notebooks*, personal relations with Verhaeren and Gide opened up new vistas. The old eclecticism still prevails, as the following strange galaxy of authors reveals: "I am slowly reading in your Bergson and can follow from time to time; am reading Stefan George's strange new book (*The Star of the Covenant*),—passed an afternoon recently with Maeterlinck's essay on the Elberfeld horses." [16] Still, in 1911, he was writing Gide of "toutes les harangues de charlatans dont l'Allemagne en ce moment surabonde." [17] Now forced back on the German scene for a continuous period because of the war, he came to know and measure himself for the first time in relation to the authors of his day and to German literature as a whole. His correspondence lists the names of authors like Worringer, Werfel, Trakl, Hofmannsthal, Strindberg, and later, Spengler, Otto zur Linde, Lernet-Holenia, Annette Kolb.

Particularly his interest in three classical writers was awakened: Goethe, Kleist, Hölderlin. Here, again, Rilke proceeded at first eclectically, selecting authors or aspects of authors to conform with the needs of the moment rather than with any critical objective in mind.

Aroused for the first time to the life-size dimensions of Goethe's art, he at first betrayed his own bias in dwelling on the theme of isolation and nonconformity underlying such a work as "The Harz Journey in Winter." From Goethe it was but a step to the early German romanticists: the Schlegels—Caroline in her delightful letters—and Bettina von Arnim. In his youth he had shied away from Goethe, repelled by his alleged impassivity. Later he had thrown himself into the arms of the plastic arts precisely because he judged it dangerous to follow another poet—especially one like Goethe. His drawing closer to Goethe at this time is a sign of a broadening interest in the direction of world literature, and we may well owe to this impact his turning more and more toward the "mythical" element in poetry or what has been called "the generally representative and symbolical aspects of antiquity." [18]

In the case of Kleist his interest was similarly motivated by a feeling of kinship with the most spiritually isolated genius of his age, next to Hölderlin. As early as 1898 he had written verses on the dramatist after visiting his winter-solitary grave in Wannsee:

> None of us is clearer, none is blinder,
> all of us are searchers, as you know,
> and perhaps you thus became the finder,
> somber and impatient Kleist.[19]

The Kleist references during the critical years are sparse, yet sufficient to evidence his strong appeal. It was Hölderlin, however, and the "starlike lofty immediacy" of Hölderlin's poetic idiom that transcended mere personal preference, shaping to an incalculable extent Rilke's evolution as a poet.

The first mention of Hölderlin dates from letters immediately preceding the outbreak of war, though it would be gratifying to know if Rilke had not, in fact, become familiar with him earlier. He had just written the poem "Wendung," usually accepted as the "turning point" in his poetic development, a poem that displays some familiarity with Hölderlin's work. His interest in the earlier poet had been actually stimulated by the recent Hellingrath edition of the Pindar translations (1910), which left an impression "vast and magnanimous." [20] Particularly the hymns and longer poems weighed heavily at this time, and to the impact of Hölderlin was suddenly added that of the war-god, producing that curious by-product of his poetry, the *Five War Songs* of 1914, which clearly show a structural indebtedness.

Quite noticeably in the *Elegies*, for example, Rilke's handling of dactyl and pentameter and his syntactical arrangement (end-words, disjunctions) are suggestive of Hölderlin, though the characteristic of the latter's verse is generally a mounting rhythm while Rilke's almost invariably descends, in the elegiac mode. This difference in tone is due to a fundamentally different attitude to the life-problem. In the last analysis, both poets were struggling to create a consonance between image (*Bild*) and activity (*Tun*), the one by means of a synthetic myth, the other by a transformation of reality through art into the invisible resources of the heart. Yet for all his sadness and despair Hölderlin found consolation and hope in the communal activities of man, an aspect completely closed to Rilke.[21] Hölderlin's childlike innocence operated, as Beissner nicely puts it, as though he took for granted that his cosmos might actually be existent, before the public eye, like a toy left in the "gentle grass" by certain divine children after play, belonging to no one and for everybody's use.[22] For the modern poet, however, the "objects" are bent inward, in narcissistic refraction, and the toys are not for public use.

Rilke's Hölderlin poem is revealing structurally and ideologically. Slowly evolving his world of inner-space, with Hölderlin's cosmos before him, Rilke derived both comfort and clarification. The opening lines continue one of the basic motifs of the First Elegy ("For staying is nowhere"), though again the tone is different from Hölderlin's:

> Verweilung, auch am Vertrautesten nicht,
> ist uns gegeben; aus den erfüllten
> Bildern stürzt der Geist zu plötzlich zu füllenden; Seen
> sind erst im Ewigen . . .

>> Tarrying, even where we are most intimate,
>> is not our lot; from images replete
>> the spirit plunges to those that need refilling; lakes
>> are the matter of eternity . . .

Now and again in the *Elegies* one detects echoes of Hölderlin, and lines like the following from the latter's "Homecoming" poem inevitably suggest a connection with the Duino angel; for closely related in the thinking of both poets is the need imputed to divine agencies of the feeling heart of man for their acknowledgment and perpetuation:

Much did I say to him, for no matter, what poets think
or sing is mostly for angels and him. . . .

THE VIRGIN AND SPAIN
Especially plentiful for the years 1913–14, the yield of scattered and posthumously published poems tapers off sharply until the end of 1915, followed by a brief creative spurt that persists only to 1919. A lapse into virtual inactivity then sets in until 1922. Most of this poetry is fragmentary or lacks organic finish. "I would prefer to keep them in my desk," he writes in true Malte fashion, "and wait to see whether time will contribute to their correction, relation and intensity." [23] Yet themal consistency continues, homogeneity of motifs and images remains practically unaltered. What is new is the emotional plane on which all these elements are organized. What emerges as a whole is the variety and, at times, tragic intensity of the poet's experimentation as he gropes for new directions.

Not all the poetry of these years can be assigned to the new trend. *The Life of the Virgin*, a collection of thirteen poems depicting conventional episodes treated in Western art (Dürer's Virgin cycle, for example), was written in a short time, in January 1912, though the original idea of providing poems on this theme for illustrations by Heinrich Vogeler can be traced back to 1900. But Rilke was no longer the thrall of his early impressionism. Only under pressure from Vogeler was he able to finish the task with no high opinion of its merit, and critics have been more or less prone to concede it, perhaps unnecessarily, a secondary place in his production. [24] The result is a tribute to his artistic conscience. He might have attempted to rework an old phase of experience in terms of his new insights and discoveries, still in the seminal stage and beyond the scope of Vogeler's designs. This would have inevitably flawed the organic style of the

125

cycle. Instead he cast *The Life of the Virgin* in the formal dress and modes of his earlier poetry, using chiefly the old rhythms and meters of *The Book of Images* and *New Poems.*

The cyclical pattern parallels that of the *Cornet,* permitting the poet to treat as a sequence some of his favorite themes.[25] The theological implications are of a non-Christian order, presenting rather "a human fresco glorifying womanhood" than "a divine legend glorifying God." [26] The cycle has been aptly called an "expanded thing-poem" or *Dinggedicht* (the "Presentation of Mary" and "Pietà," for example, carrying back to *New Poems).*[27] Spender has even likened this poetry to "a series of variations in words on themes by painters." [28] Yet unmistakable earmarks point ahead (the cycle is dated from Duino) to the *Elegies,* in whose "fore-and-after vibrations," as Rilke later put it, the collection was written.[29] These angels, birds, and winds have already acquired a new dimension in the rarified atmosphere of *Weltinnenraum*:

> Glut und Regen spricht,
> der Vögel Zug, der Wind und was ihr seid,
> keins überwiegt und wächst zur Eitelkeit
> sich mästend an. Ihr haltet nicht
> die Dinge auf im Zwischenraum der Brust,
> um sie zu quälen. So wie seine Lust
> durch einen Engel strömt, so treibt durch euch
> das Irdische. . . .

> The fire and rain speak,
> passage of birds, the wind, what you may be—
> none prevails and grows to vanity,
> glutting itself. You don't hold back
> things within the intervals of the breast
> in order to torment them. Just as his ecstasies
> stream through an angel, thoughts of the earth
> rush through you. . . .

"Passage of birds," "intervals of the breast," "ecstasies" that "stream through an angel," "thoughts of earth": all are metaphorical configurations of the elegiac landscape. Even the elegy meter is undisguised in a poem like "The Birth of Mary." In "The Consolation of Mary with the Risen Christ," the only free-verse poem in the collection, there is more than a hint of the "restrained gesture" motif of the Second Elegy, composed less than a month later.[30] An excellent example of the unceasing expansion of motif and imagery, the thought is further developed in a letter of the same period (Jan. 10, 1912): "I believe I have sometimes reached the pitch where I could express the entire urgency of my heart . . . by softly laying my hand on someone's shoulder." [31] And that is not all. In a late poem (1922) the Attic steles of the Second Elegy are put to still further use, and much more subtly developed:

> Mehr nicht sollst du wissen als die Stele
> und im reinen Stein das milde Bild
> beinah heiter, nur so leicht, als fehle
> ihr die Mühe, die auf Erden gilt. . . .

> > Seek no graver knowledge than the pillar,
> > than the gentle image on the stone,
> > knowing serenely, seem to breathe a stiller,
> > lighter air than we have ever known. . . .

The reader of *The Book of Hours* will already have been reminded of the artist-monk in relation to Browning's "Fra Lippo Lippi," the one in pursuit of the artist-god, the other of "simple beauty and nought else." Apropos of *The Life of the Virgin* Spender considers the comparison of Rilke with Browning interesting because of the "Rilkean virtues and vices" which correspond to the same qualities in Browning. On these he enlarges with considerable discernment:

The virtues are aesthetic and moral raptures which, while not always seeming quite natural, are nevertheless lyrically ecstatic. The vices, exaggerations of a style of thinking which has become removed at some points from nature, with the result that there is often a facility in attaining the timeless, the nameless, the infinite, the inexpressible, etc. which gives the reader the feeling that the poet's very highmindedness can betray him into a kind of spiritual opportunism. The poetry is best . . . when it is simplest, as in *Visitation of the Virgin* and the immensely moving *Before the Passion* . . .[32]

Another poem-cluster of this period is associated with Spanish experiences. In November 1912, Rilke was writing of Toledo as " 'a city of heaven and earth,' for it is really in both, it goes right through all existence." [33] This unmistakable idiom of the *Elegies* is further expanded in two letters to the same correspondent:

THE RING OF FORMS

What it is *like* here, that, dear friend, I shall never be able to say (it would be the language of angels, their use of it among men), but *that* it is, that it *is*, you will just have to believe me. One can describe it to no one, it is full of law, yes, I understand at this moment the legend that when on the fourth day of Creation God took the sun and set it, he established it right over Toledo: so very star-ish is the nature of this extraordinarily laid out estate, so outward, so into space—, I have already got all around, have imprinted everything on my mind as though tomorrow I had to know it forever, the bridges, both bridges, this river and, shifted over beyond it, this open abundance of landscape, surveyable, like something that is still being worked on. . . .[34]

And again:

I tried recently to make this intelligible in one sentence to P. by saying that it is there in equal measure for the eyes of the dead, the living and the angels,—yes, here is an object that might be accessible to all three of those so widely different visions, over it, one feels, they could come together and have one and the same impression.[35]

Important here is not only the imagery used (bridges, landscape, language of angels, star-ish) but the very emphasis and position of the italics. The vision of the three realms is a rehearsal for the final angelic drama.

The poems that are considerably indebted to Spain, structurally and emotionally ("The Harrowing of Hell," "The Awakening of Lazarus," "The Death of Moses," "Saint Christopher," "Lamentation," "To the Angel," "Spanish Trilogy," etc.), are all projected against the Spanish landscape, as indeed Rilke's best poetry expresses human values in terms of landscape.[36] Places like Toledo, Ronda, and later the Valais countryside of Muzot, provided him with that "spiritual atmosphere" (he is writing of Les Baux in Provence) in which "the especial relationship of things to each other, entirely as in Spain, at certain hours seems to display that tension which we think to identify among the stars of a constellation (*Sternbild*)."[37] It was not so much a Toledo proper as a Toledo seen through El Greco's eyes that evoked the illuminations and tensions of this atmosphere. Compared with almost any El Greco painting, "The Harrowing of Hell" reveals a "similar passion, power, and intensity of color, the same shadows and nuances," not to overlook the same linear rhythms upwards and downwards that "seem to strain the framework of the conception to its uttermost." [38] The poem's language is almost violently made to conform to the tensions and dynamics of a figure rocketing through space with the aid of unexpected word-and-syllable combinations as well as syntactical arrangements. There is hardly another modern poem, with the exception of Hopkins' "Wreck of the Deutschland," whose rhythms and tempi succeed so well in building up to the desired climax: a Christ plunged into and out of Hell, standing *breathless* (not *panting*) "on his unrailinged tower of endurance," some pinnacle-point outside of time, in strange contrast to the elevation of the Christ of the Apostles' Creed. "The Harrowing of Hell" is not an apocryphal gloss but an artist's inferno.

Likewise redolent of El Greco's countryside is "The Spanish Trilogy," an uneven poem consisting of variations on the subject of poetry and what Rilke expected of it. The iambs of the first section begin majestically with a series of subordinate constructions that start to soar into the cosmos but are brought gently back, anchored in the subjective reference (*und mir*). The pattern is repeated until the poet's concern is articulated in an agonized, almost hysterical demand:

> Das Ding zu machen, Herr Herr Herr, das Ding,
> das welthaft-irdisch wie ein Meteor
> in seiner Schwere nur die Summe Flugs
> zusammennimmt: nichts wiegend als die Ankunft.

> To make the thing, Lord, Lord, Lord, Lord, the thing,
> that cosmic-earthly, like a meteor,
> only includes within its heaviness
> the sum of flight, weighing nothing but arrival.

The significant modification of the *Ding*-correlative of *New Poems* is no longer the object viewed in isolation but in cosmic perspective, in the expanded dimensions of the cosmo-earthly. The second section of the "Trilogy" repeats in a different key, and with different breathing, the actual query of the opening lines of the Ninth Elegy, written about the same time:

> Warum muss einer gehen und fremde Dinge
> so auf sich nehmen, wie vielleicht der Träger
> den fremdlings mehr und mehr gefüllten Marktkorb . . .?

129

> Why must one always go about assuming
> the burden of strange things, like a poor porter,
> heaving a more and more remotely filled
> basket from stall to stall . . .?

The poetic experience lies somewhere between the two poles of "space full of process" and the "tree in the landscape." The appearance, in the third section, of the verbal substantive *standing* introduces the motif classically formulated ten years later in the Fifth Elegy as "the great initial letter of Thereness" (*das Dastehens grosser Anfangsbuchstabe*).

Even the *Five War Songs* of August 1914, not of the highest literary merit, are interesting for the effect produced by imposing the genuine emotional patterns of the *Elegies* on a subject that ran directly counter to them. The "most distant, incredible war-god," hailed with an impulse of release, was too pat a solution, a premature choice for election to the elegy hierarchies; yet tone, imagery, and underlying conception of these poems, like many unfinished fragment-clusters of these years, clearly belong to their *Umkreis*. Not only thematically but in the very phrasing the first two anticipate the Third and Sixth Elegies, taken together.[39] The Fourth Elegy's "Outstript and late/we suddenly thrust into the wind, and fall/into unfeeling ponds" is reproduced in "The summer/tarries behind outstript among the meadow games." Here are ingredients of Rilke's mature poetry: the metaphorical mirrors and trees, the motifs of death and lamentation, praise and rejoicing, and the theater-symbol of the Fourth Elegy ("A long time has the drama not been true"). The *Five War Songs* once for all disprove the charge that the poet remained untouched by the crucial struggles of his day. But they just as emphatically impart that the poetic solution was not to be derived from the events of August 1914:

> Dennoch es heult bei Nacht wie die Sirenen der Schiffe
> in mir das Fragende, heult nach dem Weg, dem
> Weg . . .

> > And yet in the night, like ship sirens wailing,
> > in me a questioning wails for the path, the
> > path . . .

THE CRITICAL YEARS

Though the same themes recur during this period (love, death, and life seeking anchorage in both), we naturally expect from a state of spiritual crisis a transformation and deepening of earlier conceptions. The emphasis during these years on translations from other languages is itself a residue of Malte's search for an existence-pattern (*Existenzmöglichkeit*) centered in love. Rilke's activity as a translator was never a casual enterprise but a deliberate part of his creative program; first, as discipline in the language of poetry; second, as a source of nourishment for the development of congenial themes. The very titles of most of the translations actually point to the love theme: *Sonnets of Louise Labé, Sonnets from the Portuguese, Letters of Marianna Alcoforado, The Love of the Magdalene.*

Two poems especially testify to the dominant importance of this theme, forming termini between which the poet's emotions played. The poem "One must die for knowing her," fugal variations on a theme from an Egyptian papyrus, adopts the Malte standpoint of the unattainable beloved ("Oh, how distant they are!") and betrays perhaps emotional experiences he was then undergoing. If the youth may sing of the perilous beloved who advances over the "summits of his feeling," the man is warned to silence, shaken, wandering in the "night of the mountain," feeling like the seasoned sailor, the overcome terrors "at play in him as in trembling cages." Yet only a few months later Rilke will pit the incomprehensible terror and renunciation of the earlier poem against the wistfully accepted (perhaps better accepted because unaccounted for) *sancta simplicitas* of earthly fact:

> Immer wieder, ob wir der Liebe Landschaft auch
> kennen
> und den kleinen Kirchhof mit seinen klagenden
> Namen
> und die furchtbar verschweigende Schlucht, in
> welcher die andern
> enden: immer wieder gehn wir zu zweien hinaus
> unter die alten Bäume, lagern uns immer wieder
> zwischen die Blumen, gegenüber dem Himmel.

> Again and again, however well we know
> the landscape of love,

> and the little church-yard with its mourn-
> ful names,
> and the frightfully silent ravine in which
> the others
> end: again and again we go out two to-
> gether,
> under the old trees, lie down again and
> again
> among the flowers, face to face with the
> sky.

The "configurated" landscape is similar to that of the Tenth Elegy. One is tempted to interpret the point of this poem (one of the most quietly winning and conciliatory of this period) as a contrast of figures opposing each other: the metaphorical "landscape of love," "little church-yard," and "frightfully silent ravine" in a losing battle with the simple images of "trees," "flowers," and "sky."

In those years of mass-dying without and of spiritual aridity within, no one could have avoided preoccupation with the theme of death. The four *Requiems* beautifully arch the early poetry and that of the present, the requiem form itself pointing ahead to further developments in both *Sonnets* and *Elegies* ("Requiem for Clara Rilke" in *The Book of Images* of 1901, the Kalckreuth and Modersohn requiems of 1908 in *New Poems*, and, finally, the "Requiem on the Death of a Boy" of 1915). Starting with the Jacobsen conception of the "individual death" in the first and proceeding to emphasize the conflict between life and art in the next two ("For somewhere there is an old enmity/between life and the great work"), in the last the problem is considerably condensed and at the same time deepened.[40] Here the dead boy himself is spokesman as he tries to distinguish between things that once *lived* (fruits, dogs, toys, etc.) and people who did *not* live, as judged from the perspective of the dead:

> Ihr spracht, ihr lachtet, dennoch war ein jeder
> im Sprechen nicht und nicht im Lachen. Nein.
> So wie ihr alle schwanktet, schwankte weder
> die Zuckerdose, noch das Glas voll Wein.
>
> > You spoke, you laughed, and yet not one of you
> > was in the speech and in the laughter. No.

And as you swayed unsteadily swayed neither
the sugar bowl nor the glass of wine.

Kohlschmidt justly concludes his study of this requiem by saying that
"death is for Rilke for the first time a means of serving as a radical
existential criticism of human life." [41] The atmosphere of the elegies
is closely approximated in the last line: "Still have I not seen those
who drink us . . ."

Yet the refractoriness of the death theme is apparent when taken
in conjunction with another short poem ("Death"), described as
"one of the most unmusical and 'unloveliest' of all Rilke's poems, irregular in rhythm and in the scheme of the harsh lines," though these
aspects are considered to lend it "an element of ruthless strength." [42]
The poet himself referred to it as "grotesque." [43] The cynicism, heav-
ier, more corrosive than Malte's vision of dying in Paris, is hardly
typical. The "objective correlative" in this case Rilke traced to a
vision of a hand before his eyes one day in a Munich park, and a cup
resting on the back of the hand:

> Da steht der Tod, ein bläulicher Absud
> in einer Tasse ohne Untersatz.
> Ein wunderlicher Platz für eine Tasse:
> Steht auf dem Rücken einer Hand. Ganz gut
> erkennt man noch an dem glasierten Schwung
> den Bruch des Henkels. Staubig. *Hoff-nung*
> an ihrem Bug in aufgebrauchter Schrift . . .

> There stands death, a bluish extract
> in a cup without a saucer.
> A remarkable place for a cup:
> standing on the back of a hand. Very clearly
> you recognize still on the polished curve
> the handle's jointure. Dusty. And 'Hope'
> on rounded front in faded lettering . . .

The tone of indignation is due to human failure to come to grips with
"real" death. The opposite picture is shown in the allegory of the
child-death (*Kindertod*) at the end of the Fourth Elegy, written only
two weeks later, but more magnificently in the three-line coda of the
poem itself. Here Rilke utilized components of his Spanish experience, commenting on the matter at some length in his correspond-

ence.[44] Thus even a less favored poem may be a good illustration of the almost chemical concretion-process of his poetry:

O Sternenfall,
von einer Brücke einmal eingesehn—:
Dich nicht vergessen. Stehen!

O fall of stars,
beheld once from a bridge,
O not to forget you. Only stand!

TURNING POINT

Bassermann and others have made careful studies of the three transitional poems of the critical years ("Forest Pond," "Turning Point," and "Lament"), and given particular attention to the personal and psychological adjustments that the poet was struggling to achieve.[45] Both "Turning Point" and "Lament" reveal a Rilke experimenting with free rhythms, a combination of his elegy rhythms and those of Hölderlin, interspersed with expressionistic devices. The sustaining figure of "Lament" is the "slow tree of rejoicing" that has now reached the point of "breaking in the storm," a figure that bridges the years from the introductory poem of *The Book of Images* to the triumphant opening of the first Orpheus Sonnet: "A tree ascending there. O pure transcension!" Over-didactic and unimaginative, "Turning Point" has chiefly psychological and theoretical value. The poet advises himself (the vocative forms are beginning to creep in) to seek his *Ding-object* not in isolated things but in the object's meaning for human feeling, human living—*heartwork*, therefore, and not *eyework*. We have already heard him deplore the violence done to the world of impressions; in answer, this poem is the expression of a need to recreate outer experience in invisible inwardness.

But the true dilemma of the modern artist, the problem of the "language of poetry" in an age of dissociation, is incomparably voiced in the poem "Exposed on the Hills of the Heart" (1914), the very apogee of anxiety and despair. It recalls Hopkins' sonnet "No worse, there is none. Pitched past pitch of grief," and a very interesting study could be made of their respective imagery, tone, ideological premises, and their "landscaping" ("in-scaping"):

Ausgesetzt auf den Bergen des Herzens. Siehe,
   wie klein dort,
siehe: die letzte Ortschaft der Worte, und höher,
aber wie klein auch, noch ein letztes
Gehöft von Gefühl. Erkennst du's?
Ausgesetzt auf den Bergen des Herzens. Steingrund
unter den Händen. Hier blüht wohl
einiges auf; aus stummen Absturz
blüht ein unwissendes Kraut singend hervor.
Aber der Wissende? Ach, der zu wissen begann
und schweigt nun, ausgesetzt auf den Bergen des
   Herzens.
Da geht wohl, heilen Bewusstseins,
manches umher, manches gesicherte Bergtier,
wechselt und weilt. Und der grosse geborgene
   Vogel
kreist um der Gipfel reine Verweigerung.—Aber
ungeborgen, hier auf den Bergen des Herzens . . .

Exposed on the hills of the heart. Look,
   how small there!
look, the last hamlet of words, and,
   higher,
(but still how small) yet one remaining
farmstead of feeling: d'you see it?
Exposed on the hills of the heart. Bare rock
under the hands. Though even here
something blooms: from the dumb precipice
an unknowing plant blooms singing into
   the air.
But what of the knower? Ah, he began
   to know,
and now, exposed on the hills of the
   heart, is silent.
While, with undivided mind,
many, maybe, many well-assured mountain-beasts,
pause and pass on. And the mighty, sheltered bird
circles the summit's pure refusal.—But,
   oh,
unsheltered here on the hills of the
   heart . . .

The ultimate intent of the poem is again aesthetic ("last hamlet of words"): the nigh impossibility of finding exact verbal equivalents for ultimate feelings ("Higher . . . yet one remaining farmstead of feeling"). The exposure "on the hills of the heart" is accentuated by reference to "precipice," "plant," "mountain-beasts," "mighty bird," "summit's refusal," which are respectively paired (as the poet-knower is not) with such unifying, undivisive epithets as "dumb," "unknowing," "well-assured," "sheltered," "pure."

Rilke's poetry, from the inception of the *Elegies* in 1912, was indeed developing with remarkable rapidity in the direction of "inwardness," "heartwork." A forward step was his realization that, from the creative standpoint, psychological correlatives such as states of mind or aspects of personality are just as valid materials for poetry as literal, concrete objects, and much closer to hand. Instead of panthers, heliotropes, and rococo staircases he deals more and more with "smiles," "tears," "music," "night," and the like. Two good examples of this type are "Soul in Space" (1917) and "The Spirit Ariel" (1913), written after reading Shakespeare's *The Tempest*. His interpretation of the Prospero-Ariel relationship, incidentally, illustrates his habit of always reading out of a work of art his own meaning. The poem derives entirely from the *ambiance* of the *Elegies* and would probably baffle the orthodox Shakespeare scholar.

DRAMA AND MUSIC

The topical interest in drama and the plastic arts continues as before. "I must assume," he wrote in 1917, "that our experiences are shifting always further into the invisible, into the bacillary and microscopic: and thus it is possible to understand the absurd violence with which painting, like the stage, comes to display its magnified and wrenched-out objects. What violence here too, how little Nature, how little peace." [46] The letter then picks up these interests following the Cézanne year in Paris, acknowledging a feeling for Franz Marc and Picasso, though El Greco is strangely omitted. There are no more enthusiastic outpourings like the Cézanne letters. While allowing modern art to carry "a certain strength and conviction," he is equally as skeptical as to the number of artists creating "within the law" (the law of his own poetic growth).[47] No doubt he encountered and absorbed certain aspects of the expressionistic revolution, but several letter passages dissociate him completely from the movement as such:

. . . how cramplike is the 'new' asserted only because it's new, and how quickly practised frivolity closes over it again. Nothing, Nothing, Nothing. . . . Now I will take a good look at Kokoschka and see if I can get to hear some Schönberg music. How squandered is it all here, in this atmosphere—where is it really? (And yet Beethoven was here [Vienna]) . . .[48]

In 1919 he was caustic about the Expressionist, this explosive innerman, "who pours the lava of his boiling mood over all things."[49] More and more he manifests his independence of the plastic arts and all future interest in that direction was dictated more or less by motives of personal friendship or regard.

Less negative was his response at the time to another of the arts. If Malte had definitely bid farewell to the stage as a vehicle of art-expression, Rilke's own interest continued to elicit further comment, especially in correspondence. In October 1913 he was writing to Gide of the pleasure derived from the new performances of Copeau's *Theatre du Vieux Colombier*, and the year previous he seems to have been deeply impressed by Strindberg, the father of German Expressionism, particularly by his chamber plays. One correspondent's attention is called (July 1915) to a performance of Strindberg's *Ghost Sonata*, while Büchner's *Wozzek* is described as "incomparable drama . . . real theater . . . what a real theater might be."[50] Again, on December 22, 1918, reporting a performance of a Norwegian play starring a contemporary German actress, he described himself as "little up to date" in matters of the theater but gave it as his opinion that in an ensemble directed by Stanislavsky the artist might have attained to unknown heights.[51] As late as August 1920, toward the end of the critical period, the Princess Marie received his enthusiastic impressions of Pitoeff's Russian performances in Geneva, in which Rilke had collaborated with the director as adviser and scriptwriter. Yet one perceives immediately that his interest was after all directed not toward the stage proper but toward symbolic representation, the *mise en scène* projected from his own thinking about poetry as in his early days. This "theater-in-poetry" is evident in several poems of the critical years ("Pearls slip from the thread," and others).

More complex and fascinating than the theater connection is his relation to music. Rilke was always explicit as to his consistent distrust of music. Music, Malte had complained, never set him down where it had once picked him up, but rather a range below, in the diffuse and unformed.[52] Yet Rilke's early poetry seems to be at times almost perilously swamped in music, while the later best is conceived under the sign of the god of the lyre. The question is how a poet of a distinctly "visual" order came to employ musical figures and to anticipate musical solutions in support of a symbolic musical myth (Orpheus). The contradiction is only apparent, one of the many woven into the structure of his personality without destroying its unity. In Rilke the Western plastic form-sense had always to confront an innate Slavic musicality. The visual plastic and the indeterminate musical are throughout alternating terminals in an unceasing dialectic. One could plot a curve showing the predominance of one or the other, beginning with *The Book of Hours* through *New Poems* to the later work. Yet here, as at all times, it is impossible to demarcate phases and set up inorganic divisions. If during the critical years the approach to musical understanding seems closest, it is not owing to personal and private considerations alone. For the orphic mission itself had already been foreshadowed in a long, shapeless poem of 1890, whose imagery is provocative in the light of the later Benvenuta episode ("Pearls rolled away . . ."). Here music, a constructive principle, the "beginning" and "soul" of song, is played off against the diffusion of earthly experience:

> Music! Music! Orderer of dissonances,
> take what is scattered in the large hour,
> entice on strings the pearls that rolled away . . .

Music, the player-performer of the world, preparing the way for the singing god, is invited to open the door of every object in which the unavowed, timid experience lies captive. Rilke's Paris apprenticeship, a precautionary damper, still withheld the key. But the poem

138

of the agitated years 1913–14, "Shatter me, music, with rhythmical fury!" again picks up, in ruffled Hölderlin rhythms, the vaulted arches awaiting to receive the new "vibrations," out of which will later issue the "antennae feeling the antennae" of the *Sonnets*. A few years afterward an attempt is made in "Music, Breathing of Statues" (1918) to relate the art to the language of poetry. The original constructive principle ("orderer of noises") had not changed appreciably, though immensely refined, after eighteen years:

> Musik: Atem der Statuen, vielleicht:
> Stille der Bilder. Du Sprache, wo Sprachen
> enden, du Zeit,
> die senkrecht steht auf der Richtung vergehender
> Herzen . . .

>> Music! Breathing of statues, perhaps:
>> stillness of pictures! You speech, where
>> speeches
>> end, you time
>> vertical on the direction of vanishing
>> hearts! . . .

Music, for Rilke, was at least as much speculatively as personally conditioned (it has even been suggested that he may have been intrigued by a reference to a "musical silence" in a curious eighteenth-century esoteric, Fabre d'Olivet).[53] At least he seems no longer to be impressionistically afraid of it, but ready to bring it into harmony with forming views of poetry. For example, in the last quotation music is defined as an *ultima Thule* of language, a language where all languages end—in short, "the last hamlet of words." No longer subject to "rhythmical anger" or vague "vibrations," it is "audible landscape," "weaned heart-space," still beyond our reach, capable of definition only in the paradoxes of the inner-space world:

> als geübteste Ferne, als andre
> Seite der Luft,
> rein,
> riesig,
> nicht mehr bewohnbar.

>> as practised horizon, as other
>> side of the air,

pure,
gigantic,
no longer lived in.

From here to the reconciliation of music and poetry in the threshold figure of Orpheus is but a step ("Once and for all,/it's Orpheus when there's song . . ."), and another step to a late poem ("Music," 1925), written as a dedication in a copy of the *Elegies*. Hardly anywhere has a Romantic carried through so consistently the doctrine of correspondences with all its implications of synaesthesia and generic overlappings. What this full orchestration may mean for the ear *here* is *elsewhere* intended for the eye ("Somewhere *stands* music"), just as light may be said to penetrate the ear with distant clangor. To post-Cartesian rationalism Rilke opposes a mathematico-physical cosmos of invisible numbers, atomic frequencies, and sound radiations, undivided and untouched by human distinctions:

> Musik; du Wasser unsres Brunnenbeckens,
> du Strahl der fällt, du Ton der spiegelt, du
> selig Erwachte unterm Griff des Weckens
> du durch den Zufluss rein ergänzte Ruh,
> du mehr als wir . . . von jeglichem Wozu
> befreit . . .

> Music: water of our fountain basin,
> you ray that falls, you tone that mirrors, you
> blissfully wakened by the grip of waking,
> you rest purely refilled by the afflux,
> you more than ourselves . . . from every goal
> freed . . .

NARCISSUS

If one major critical theme of these years has been left to the end, it is not because of its secondary importance. On the contrary, it is one of the purest symbols not only of Rilke's poetic mind but of the structure of much modern poetry. The term "narcissism" is so pathologically and clinically tainted these days that it would be well to call attention to its wider philosophical and human relevance. "Man seeks to find his own reflection in another human countenance, in the Thou," writes Berdyaev. "This longing to be truly reflected is inherent in personality and its 'image'. This latter seeks a faithful mirror. In a certain sense it implies narcissism. Love, the lover's image, is such a faithful mirror, the desired communion." [54]

Rilke's two Narcissus poems of April 1913 have led some critics to examine exhaustively the Freudian implications of the "mirrors" (*Spiegelschau*) in his poetry and their connection with such weighty images as Narcissus and the Duino angel.[55] It is mainly of anthropological interest that the poet's psyche seems to have been deeply rooted in a substratal folklore (the ancient taboo of mirror-gazing from which derives the artist's projection of self into other surfaces, both as a means of overcoming his personal inhibitions as well as creating his ideal, often in a form in opposition to socially accepted norms).[56] The circular movement of Rilke's poetry, always revolving about its own center, is rather a concern of aesthetics than of psychology. Its homogeneity may be compared, to use a figure of speech, with what happens when a pebble is dropped in a still pool: the ripples expanding concentrically always flow back to the same center. In its broadest sense, the "mirror" is perhaps the basic Rilkean image to which all the others are, in one way or another, linked. Whether it be "Music: Water of our Fountain Basin" or "Narcissus released into lucency" (Orpheus Sonnet II, 3), all have to do with the reflective vehicle of the artist's projection of his world.

Prawer has stated that Rilke was obsessed with two cardinal figures: Narcissus who loved only himself and St. Francis who loved only the "little flowers" of the world—two extremes which, toward the end, seem to "coalesce" in the Duino angel: "Loving this world like St. Francis was to be only a first step: we must come to have a transformed world *in ourselves,* our own hearts, our own minds, like Narcissus, like the 'angel' of the *Duino Elegies.*" [57] This is putting the best construction on what many have considered the basic weakness of Rilke's cosmos: its self-centeredness and denial of the loved one (in Berdyaev's sense). "Indeed," writes Holthusen, "those of his poems in which the figure of Narcissus appears show to what extremes Rilke is prepared to go in his way of thinking. St. Francis and Narcissus are the antitheses of a dialectic of feeling which is not concerned with the value of love as reflected in its object, but which is fully spent within its own, self-contained activity . . . In both instances the perfection of feeling leads to a suspension or dissolving of personal being."[58] Here are two contradictory statements, both plausible, both very evidently starting out from different premises and envisaging different goals.

Putting aside for the moment the human implications of Rilke's myth-symbol, let us examine its application in his poetry. His very absorption with a theme which has exercised on the French an irresistible fascination is another proof of his affinity with Western thought. Yet we need but compare his Narcissus versions with Gide's *Le Traité du Narcisse* of 1891, and again with Valéry's three *Fragments du Narcisse* (which Rilke was translating in the last year of his life), to see how differently the treatment is managed. In Gide's prose treatise the accent falls on the fusion of the moral and aesthetic natures into a new principle of art as the pure, static Platonic Forms disintegrate in the flowing river of time.[59] Valéry's figure, an image of introspective mind bent on preserving its integrity from worldly fragmentation, is to point out, as the author himself puts it, "the opposition of the whole to one of its parts and the kind of tragedy that results from this inconceivable union," in which Narcissus is doomed.[60] Rilke's variants are narrowed down and intensified to convey the poet's undivided concern with the "World of Inner Space" in which Narcissus is the poet and, at the same time, the symbol. Narcissus, angel, and Orpheus are but different names for the same experience.

Part I is Narcissus' own version of the experience, told in seven stanzas of four verses each. Part II is an objective two-stanza commentary on what poetic experience has meant to the poet Rilke (a kind of documentary of poetic evolution like the earlier "Death of a Poet"—certain lines are almost identical). In adhering to his ideal, the poet's personality dissolves, he is involuntarily dissipated into space; as in the poem "Soul in Space" (which belongs to the same theme-cluster) all his contours have broken away. The real image is there, "trembling upwards in the ciphers of tears," not where one might expect it, in the heart of a woman or in any other human occasion. The old opposition between life and art is Narcissus' essential tragedy:

142

THE CRITICAL YEARS

Dort ist er nicht geliebt. Dort drunten drin
ist nichts als Gleichmut überstürzter Steine,
und ich kann sehen, wie ich traurig bin.
War dies mein Bild in ihrem Augenscheine . . .?

> There is no lover for him there. Down below
> is but the calm of toppled-over stones,
> and I can see the sadness I present.
> Was this my image in the light of her eyes . . .?

The eight lines of Part II are more compactly structured, less diffuse than the preceding section. If the latter contained interrogation and ominous doubt, expressed in the first person of the subject, the final section in the third-person is objective and placid, and clarifies the meaning of the Narcissus mission. The discrediting of the individual in the human situation is absorbed into a philosophy of art in which the individual no longer matters: the cancellation of actuality has restored the fullness of all figures, the Ring of Forms, in which the poet is all-contained. The opening phrase "Narcissus perished" picks up neatly where the foregoing section had ended on a query:

Er liebte, was ihm ausging, wieder ein
und war nicht mehr im offenen Wind enthalten
und schloss entzückt den Umkreis der Gestalten
und hob sich auf und konnte nicht mehr sein.

> All that went from him he loved back again,
> no longer in the open wind contained,
> he closed in ecstasy the ring of forms,
> cancelled himself and could no longer be.

The Narcissus poems are formulations of a kind of poetic process, of the poet's growing demand for "Inwardness" (*Innerlichkeit*), an objectivity in excess of Cézanne's as Rilke understood it, now playing with the much larger freedoms of the inner landscape. The line "cancelled himself and could no longer be" relates back to the "last hamlet of words" and forward to a later Narcissus poem (1922) that falls within the thought-patterns of Orpheus: "Oh for a mouth, a mouth,/some one to speak and sing . . ./just to hear something, without/being the thing . . ." Thus Rilke's Ring of Forms is held together by the seemingly impossible paradox of a drama without spoken word, of song where silence is, of a language of fish where

143

nothing is articulated. This is only a more drastic formulation of what Eliot is saying in the fifth section of *Burnt Norton*:

> Words move, music moves
> Only in time; but that which is only living
> Can only die. Words, after speech, reach
> Into the silence. . . .

The tensions set up by these paradoxes are present in Rilke's poetry from beginning to end, and reproduce, I believe, in aesthetic conversion the dialectical and chiliastic movements of Christianity which he never completely rid himself of. For the Ring of Forms contains the realms of both life and death, the here and hereafter, the one implicit in the other. We shall soon find Rilke's Orpheus, preceded by Narcissus and the angel, re-enacting in an aesthetic setting the drama of the Incarnation.

VI

o⚬ *Angel*

T H E various attempts to interpret the *Duino Elegies*
on the part of Rilke critics have helped to clear up many obscure
problems. Yet none has been entirely successful since the poetry
itself is made up of a number of blended elements which, when dis-
entangled, may be made to serve the critics' special bias. Again, it is
almost impossible to treat the *Elegies* and *Sonnets* as a whole without
in some measure falling back on paraphrase, for in no other modern
poetry are "expression" (*Ausdruck*) and "statement" (*Aussage*), to
use Guardini's terms, so closely interwoven.[1] In his later poetry, in
fact, Rilke assumed more and more the role of a prophet who, having
taken the measure of an age that was dying, reached out to give utterance to the future. Accordingly those critics who argue that his statements should not be judged as mere aesthetic *aperçus*, but as value
judgments as to their truth or untruth, have some foundation to rest
on. A study of some of the essential themes and motifs perhaps serves
best to preserve the poetry's original integrity, without at the same
time ignoring the ideas and thoughts which the poet was explicitly
concerned to bring before his reader's attention.

GENESIS OF A SYMBOL

Bassermann has carefully examined the chronological genesis of
the *Elegies* in relation to the *Sonnets*. The former are bedded between
the two sonnet sequences in point of time, yet since the latter as a
whole form an antiphonal response to the poet's integrated elegy

145

themes (as *sursum corda* to the *de profundis* or, as Rilke himself so aptly put it, "the small rust-colored sail of the Sonnets" to "the gigantic white sail-cloth of the Elegies"), these will be considered first.[2] Again we confront the extreme functional consistency of his thinking. At least half of them, we have seen, were either started at Duino in 1912, resumed either in Germany or Spain before and during the critical years, and finished, along with two completely new ones, at Muzot in 1922. Yet temporal distinctions help less than in the case of most poets, because of this very homogeneous organization. In this crystallization process the particles come silently and imperceptibly together, form patterns, and solidify. But if the solution be shaken at any stage in the process (as during the poet's war years, for example), the patterns may be destroyed or the precipitation retarded.

On the other hand, the almost chemical concretion of Rilke's poetic thinking will account for many hesitations and difficulties encountered in understanding his work. He himself was subsequently astonished at his inability to understand much of his later creation (hence as a medial personality-type he was able to speak of what was "enjoined" or "dictated" to him). A Muzot letter described the "infinite, unavoidable difficulties which these verses present, not so much because of their obscurity but because the point of departure is often concealed, like roots in the ground."[3] And a few lines further: "It is hardly possible to indicate to what degree one is capable of transposing himself into the artistic concentrated texture of those elegies and individual sonnets, frequently it is strange for the producer's situation to feel close by, on the thinner days of life (how many), such essence of one's own existence in its indescribable preponderance."[4] Rilke himself quite clearly stated the scope and major themes of this collection:

But it lies in the nature of these poems, in their condensation and abbreviation (in the way they frequently state lyric totals instead of listing the figures that were necessary for the result) that they seem more designed to be grasped in general by means of the inspiration of those of like direction than by what one calls 'understanding'. Two inmost experiences were decisive for their production: the resolve that grew up more and more in my spirit to hold life open toward

death, and, on the other side, the spiritual need to situate the transformations of love in this wider whole differently than was possible
in the narrower orbit of life (which simply shut out death as the
Other). Here, so to speak, would be the place to look for the 'plot' of
these poems, and now and then it stands, I believe, simply and
strongly in the foreground. . . .[5]

The *Elegies* are more accessible to the auditory than to the visual
sense; the *Gestalt* of the language must be really listened to, with an
ear attuned to its distant vibrations, if it is to be felt. The intimate
union of sound (*Klang*) and meaning (*Sinn*) is the result of emotion
or feeling flowing directly out of the word. The language is symbolic,
suggestive, but never rhetorically affirmative. As for the style, analogies have been sought in the feverish intensity of Keats and the
abrupt, forceful rhythm of Browning, without doing justice to the
peculiarly Rilkean accents and cadences. The metrics vary, from
dactyls in lines of varying length to iambic pentameter; the arrangement is loose, and modulates according to the particular emotion to
be expressed. The elegy usually opens in the form of interrogation or
exhortation, a conditional or optative statement. Upon the symbolic
illustration or demonstration follows the bare proposition (in the case
of the First Elegy, "For staying is nowhere"), the procedure of geom-
etry reversed. The development itself is contrapuntal: a theme is
dropped and picked up again later; even different meanings of a
single word (*brauchen*—"to use," "to need," in the First Elegy) are
woven into the complexity of pattern.

In what sense may these poems be called *elegies*? Recent investigations on this point may here be reproduced in condensed form.[6]
In the modern sense, the term is about as elastic as that of *ode*, and
indeed Rilke may be said to have contributed in good measure to
the vogue of the elegy in contemporary poetry. In classical times the
elegy was characterized by its peculiar meter rather than by its subject matter. In Greek literature elegies were usually poems of lament,
in Latin literature frequently love poems. Goethe's *Roman Elegies*,
for example, are in the Latin tradition. Later the term came to designate a poem of lament, either for a particular person, or, as in Rilke's
case, expressing a more general sorrow. The tone of the *Duino Elegies*, however, is not confined solely to lamentation. As in *Lycidas*

and *Adonais*, the mood shifts several times, from lamentation to rapturous joy, but unlike these two poems, they are not pastoral nor indeed essentially lyrical in character, but rather dramatic monologues of inner debate, variously interrupted flashes of heightened insight and revelation.[7]

Much has been written about the angel of the *Elegies*. Confusion has arisen because the temptation lay near to confuse religious and aesthetic categories, morals with art. Except insofar as Rilke's entire poetics is shot through with moral implications, the Duino angel has no religious significance whatever. The poet himself warned against a Christian interpretation (though the absolute validity of his statement is open to debate): "The 'angel' of the elegies has nothing to do with the angel of the Christian heaven (rather with the angelic forms of Islam) . . ."[8] And Nora Purtscher-Wydenbruck has pointed out certain analogies, possibly unconscious, between the angel hierarchies and the Jewish mysticism of the Cabala.[9] A rather fruitless attempt has also been made to relate the figure to the effort made by German Expressionists (with whom Rilke had only peripheral connections) to reconcile the Finite and Infinite (angel and Orpheus establishing a link between conflicting worlds).[10] These speculations do not carry us far, for of all Rilke's symbols his angels can be least "explained." The angel develops its own definition (the ideal fullness of existence as seen and justified through the poetic process itself) as the various poems are written. Thus the unspeakable, unreachable angel of the First Elegy condescends at least, in the Tenth, to listen, after having been warned off at the conclusion of the Seventh. The poet himself defined the angel, in connection with the transformation theme of the Ninth Elegy, as "that being committed to the recognition of a higher order of reality in the invisible" rather than in the visible.[11]

The angel symbol itself we have seen to reach far back into the poet's early Prague days (*Schutzengel*). The wayside Madonnas of the early poems are still religious figurines, but with "L'Ange du Méridien" of *New Poems* other spiritual dimensions open up:

Lächelnder Engel, fühlende Figur . . .
Was weisst du, Steinerner, von unserem Sein?

Und hältst du mit noch seligerm Gesichte
vielleicht die Tafel in die Nacht hinein?

O smiling angel, sympathetic stone,
with mouth as from a hundred mouths distilled:
do you not mark how, from your ever-filled
sundial, our hours are gliding one by one?

This angel is still contained within our human perspective, directing his glance, with ours, toward the eternal mystery, yet the blissful realization is, after all, his, not ours. The figure is more clearly adumbrated in another angel-figure of *New Poems*, where both the bridgeless distance and the "open hand" of warning point unequivocally to its Duino counterpart:

Gib seinen leichten Händen nichts zu halten
aus deinen lastenden. Sie kämen denn

bei Nacht zu dir, dich ringender zu prüfen,
und gingen wie Erzürnte durch das Haus
und griffen dich, als ob sie dich erschüfen,
und brächen dich aus deiner Form heraus.

Put nothing in his light unfettered hands
from all that burdens yours. Unless indeed

those hands should come by night to prize and rate you,
and fill your house with fury and with storm
and grasp at you as they would new-create you,
and strike at you and break you from your form.

Another step in the genesis is the part played by Hölderlin's angel, already a symbol of poetic experience, a private concern of the heart, restricted and not readily accessible. The Duino figure is the tenor, in varying degree, of all these implications. What neither the neighbor-god of *The Book of Hours* nor his objective surrogate in *New Poems* had been able to perform is now imputed to a mediator too remote from the concerns of man to be more than the unattainable yet constantly sought goal of his longing (longing being at the same time a part of the creative ideal, in a restricted sense, and the concern of modern man, at large). Man's position in the universe is peripheral, hypothetical, endorsed, if at all, by the limited and often esoteric symbols that occur throughout the work. An almost geo-

149

metrical patterning of this situation is provided by one of the *Late Poems*, "To the Angel" (1913):

> Starker, stiller, an den Rand gestellter
> Leuchter: oben wird die Nacht genau.
> Wir vergeben uns in unerhellter
> Zögerung an deinem Unterbau. . . .

>> Strong, still light upon the verge of Being,
>> burning out into nocturnal space,
>> while we spend ourselves in dimly-seeing
>> hesitation round about your base. . . .

The beacon light thrown by the angel from his eminence extends downwards with decreasing clarity until it reaches the borderline of human obscurity. The paradox ensues that, from the poet's vantage-point, the night above is clearer than our day below. He appeals to his symbol to throw more light lest he forfeit all assurance of existence. The concerns of pure being are thus linked up with cosmic forces visualized in a setting reminiscent of El Greco, as the poem concludes:

> Dass ich lärme, wird an dir nicht lauter,
> wenn du mich nicht fühltest, weil ich *bin*,
> Leuchte, leuchte! Mach mich angeschauter
> bei den Sternen. Denn ich schwinde hin.

>> You I'll never reach with lamentations
>> if my heart-beats cannot make you hear,
>> shine upon me! Let the constellations
>> look at me before I disappear!

THE FIRST ELEGY

A more careful analysis of the First Elegy, which was the first written in full and has been well compared to an overture where all the main themes of the subsequent work are touched on, may perhaps clarify the understanding of the sequence as a whole.

> Wer, wenn ich schriee, hörte mich denn aus der
>> Engel
> Ordnungen? Und gesetzt selbst, es nähme
> einer mich plötzlich ans Herz: ich verginge von
>> seinem
> stärkeren Dasein. . . .

ANGEL

> Who, if I cried, would hear me among the
> angelic
> orders? And even if one of them sud-
> denly
> pressed me against his heart, I should
> fade in the strength of his
> stronger existence. ...

If the angel is the ultimate court of appeal from experience, the symbolic goal of the artist's striving, the introductory verses inform us of his inaccessibility, illustrated by the grammatical structure and the rising curve in the interrogation from a low-level *wer, wenn* to a high, clear upper-level *Ordnungen*. The word of sharpest contour (*schriee*) appears, incidentally, not in a statement but as a condition. What does the scattered human voice have to offset a power self-contained, admittedly stronger and more controlled (*Ordnungen*)? Even the simple approach by the path of the heart rather than of the intellect spells disaster. The broken sentence-structure, with overlapping lines and abrupt caesuras, is intended to convey the impression of breathless consternation, pulling up short in the sharp conclusion, itself a supposition ("I should fade in the strength of his stronger existence").

> Denn das Schöne ist nichts
> als des Schrecklichen Anfang, den wir noch
> grade ertragen,
> und wir bewundern es so, weil es gelassen ver-
> schmäht,
> uns zu zerstören. Ein jeder Engel ist schreck-
> lich. ...

> For Beauty's nothing
> but beginning of Terror we're still just
> able to bear,
> and why we adore it so is because it
> serenely
> disdains to destroy us. Each single angel
> is terrible. ...

The frigid exclusiveness of the angel is conditioned by the absolute existential vulnerability of man, and his terror, defined aesthetically, is closely associated with the poet's ideas on the nature of

151

beauty—more akin to Dmitri Karamazov's sodomic beauty ("The
awful thing is that beauty is mysterious as well as terrible") than to
Schiller's classical harmony:

> Was wir als Schönheit hier empfunden,
> wird einst als Wahrheit uns entgegen gehn.[12]

Here Rilke deliberately points away from the "beautiful" angels of
art and religious imagination,[13] for the "beautiful" is merely the
outside turned toward us; any attempt to get closer "in" would only
reveal the angel's tolerance in sparing us what we cannot yet endure: the unfractured reality and the full Ring of Forms. The *Elegies*
as a whole, it has well been said, "set out to search for man, not for
the life-devouring beauty, for beauty is no longer the ultimate and
absolute end," as it was for nineteenth-century *fin de siècle* poets.[14]
Nor is the "terrible" here the dark and uncanny *libido* of the Third
Elegy, but rather the sublime and incomprehensible, *fascinosum et
tremendum*, just as the appearance of angels in the Old Testament is
usually heralded with the words: Be not afraid![15] In himself the
angel is neither cruel nor horrendous but indifferent, as befits a symbol extending beyond and above human experience.

> Und so verhalt ich mich denn und verschlucke
>   den Lockruf
> dunkelen Schluchzens. Ach, wen vermögen
> wir denn zu brauchen, Engel nicht, Menschen
>   nicht,
> und die findigen Tiere merken es schon,
> dass wir nicht sehr verlässlich zu Haus sind
> in der gedeuteten Welt. . . .

> And so I keep down my heart, and swal-
>   low the call-note
> of depth-dark sobbing. Alas, who is there
> we can make use of? Not angels, not men;
> and already the knowing brutes are aware
> that we don't seem very securely at home
> within our interpreted world. . . .

Apart from the usual mastery of alliteration and assonance (the
sch and *v* sounds of the introductory verses combining to suggest
hushed sobbing), the lines are characteristic of the elegy style, with

its interweaving of long and short sentences and its expanded statement followed by a rhetorical question or exhortation. The use of
the word "call-note" (*Lockruf*), in the first line quoted above, stands
in relation to "cried" (*schriee*) in this elegy's opening sentence. We
suddenly learn that the poet's voice is not merely a cry of distress but
also one of longing, of wooing (an important themal link to the Seventh Elegy). For the first time the first-person plural is used instead
of the singular as the poet identifies himself with the common spiritual dilemma, thus introducing the first "lament" (*Klage*) motif. The
function of ambiguity centers on the verb *brauchen*, here meaning "use," as one uses a utensil, while later (line 70), in its substantive
form, it comes to mean "customs," "manners," and again (line 86),
"to need."

The structure of human experience, in relation to consciousness,
may be regarded as divided into three realms.[16] On the angelic level
there is the embodiment of the full creative consciousness; on another plane the unconscious world is represented by instances taken
from the plant and animal kingdoms. Both the angelic and naturalistic levels share this in common, that their harmony with nature is
without fissure where all is unity and undividedness of being. Midway between the two categories falls the split human being, both unconscious and conscious at the wrong times, never really at ease in
his environment (note the variations on this theme in the Fourth and
Sixth Elegies). If the angelic hierarchy is too far beyond man's reach,
man is likewise suspect in the eyes of primitive, undifferentiated being. The animal-consciousness theme or motif is recurrent throughout the *Elegies* (especially the Fourth and Eighth), where it is further
expanded. We are then told that the integral animal-consciousness
is attained only in the embryonic stage; grown-up animals apparently
already display some signs of man's divided condition. On the other
hand, not all humans are fragmented, troubled by death-anxiety or
uncertainty as to the meaning of life—children, for example, and
perhaps the hero. This theme of man's wholeness of being, or rather
his lacking it, is presented from various angles: in the Fifth Elegy as
determined by human treacheries and transiencies; in the Sixth by
the unequivocal status of the hero. Now and again one overhears

echoes of primitivistic cults popular during the first quarter of our
century: D. H. Lawrence's earth-spirit, Klage's cosmogonic Eros,
Montherlant's athletic types.

The question next posed is, logically: Which realm or level can
we make use of?

> Es bleibt uns vielleicht
> irgend ein Baum an dem Abhang, das wir ihn
> täglich
> wiedersähen; es bleibt uns die Strasse von gestern
> und das verzogene Treusein einer Gewohnheit,
> der es bei uns gefiel, und so blieb sie und ging
> nicht. . . .

> There remains, perhaps,
> some tree on a slope, to be looked at day
> after day,
> there remains for us yesterday's walk and
> the cupboard-love loyalty
> of a habit that liked us and stayed and
> never gave notice. . . .

Humble, marginal artifacts of everyday living are selected to frame
our experience, as though the age of technocracy and material progress had quite vanished away: the streets of yesterday, an old, in-
veterate habit, the tree on the slope (which we probably would not
notice until it were chopped down). Their simple unpretentiousness
is intended to point up the degree of human distress. The uniniti-
ated Rilke reader is at first nonplused by the fact that positive human
qualities are frequently assigned, as in this case, to practically every
other component of the poetry but the human being himself: it is
not *we* who have the habit but the *habit* which has us. The spiritual
poverty of such an "at home" is clearly evident in the bald monosyllabic statement with ironic overtones: "and stayed and never gave
notice."

> O und die Nacht, die Nacht, wenn der Wind
> voller Weltraum
> uns am Angesicht zehrt—, wem bliebe sie nicht,
> die ersehnte,
> sanft enttäuschende, welche dem einzelnen
> Herzen

mühsam bevorsteht. Ist sie den Liebenden
leichter?
Ach, sie verdecken sich nur mit einander ihr
Los. . . .

    Oh, and there's Night, there's Night,
      when wind full of cosmic space
    feeds on our faces: for whom would she
      not remain,
    longed for, mild disenchantress, pain-
      fully there
    for the lonely heart to achieve? Is she
      lighter for lovers?
    Alas, with each other they only conceal
      their lot! . . .

Rilke's arraignment of modern love harks back to the "night longing" motif of the old German romanticism. The tone of the first verse, with its cadenced repetitions, starts like a romantic night-hymn, serving to render the shock of disillusionment all the more poignant. All five lines are built up around antitheses of heavy and light, open and closed sounds (*Wind voller Weltraum . . . verdecken sich nur mit einander ihr Los*). Yet for the lonely the night lies still "painfully" ahead, still to be endured. Is it any easier for lovers? The elegiac "Alas" merely confirms the poet's basic conviction that conventional love is itself unable to give a sense of stability and permanence. The One is always intruding on the Other, a theme taken up again in the next three elegies, though the whole idea had, of course, been previously stated in Malte's *Notebooks* and elsewhere.

    Weisst du's *noch* nicht? Wirf aus den Armen die
      Leere
    zu den Räumen hinzu, die wir atmen; vielleicht,
      dass die Vögel
    die erweiterte Luft fühlen mit innigerm Flug. . . .

    Don't you know *yet*?—Fling the empti-
      ness out of your arms
      into the spaces we breathe—maybe the
      birds
      will feel the extended air in more inti-
      mate flight. . . .

THE RING OF FORMS

Taken in conjunction with the preceding lines, the impatient "not yet" suggests casting such abortive love to the wide spaces we daily inhale, and there is irony in the thought that "perhaps" the birds will feel this aggregate emptiness in their delicate flights. (Here, as elsewhere in the later poetry, the precise use of italics, as well as such qualifying adverbs as "perhaps" or "maybe" or "almost," is to be given substantial weight in the interpretation.) We are not to visualize such space, however, as something physical outside ourselves, but as imaginative "inner-space," the landscape of all Rilke's mature poetry, activated by such simple substances as "arms," "trees," "air," "flight," "birds." The bird motif, indeed, is frequently linked with "inner-space" in *Late Poems*:

> Durch den sich Vögel werfen ist nicht der
> vertraute Raum, der die Gestalt dir steigert.
> (Im Freien, dorten, bist du dir verweigert
> und schwindest weiter ohne Wiederkehr) . . .

> The one birds plunge through's not the intimate space
> where each confided form is magnified.
> (Out in the open there you're self-denied,
> and go on vanishing without a trace) . . .

More than a century before, Blake had formulated a similar thought in his comment on the Ratio of the Five Senses: "How do you know but every bird that cuts the airy way/Is an immense world of delight, clos'd by your senses five?" [17]

But to return to the First Elegy and the Poet's attempt to answer the question stated in the introductory lines of section two:

> Ja, die Frühlinge brauchten dich wohl. Es mu-
> teten manche
> Sterne dir zu, dass du sie spürtest. Es hob
> sich eine Woge heran im Vergangenen, oder
> da du vorüberkamst am geöffneten Fenster,
> gab eine Geige sich hin. Das alles war Auftrag.
> Aber bewältigtest du's? Warst du nicht immer
> noch von Erwartung zerstreut, als kündigte sich
> alles
> eine Geliebte dir an? (Wo willst du sie bergen,
> da doch die grossen fremden Gedanken bei dir
> aus und eingehn und öfters bleiben bei Nacht.)

ANGEL

Yes, the springs had need of you. Many
  a star
was waiting for you to espy it. Many a
  wave
would rise on the past towards you; or,
  else, perhaps,
as you went by an open window, a violin
would be giving itself to someone. All
  this was a trust.
But were you equal to it? Were you not
  always
distracted by expectation, as though all
  this
were announcing someone to love? (As
  if you could hope
to conceal her, with all those great
  strange thoughts
going in and out and often staying over-
  night!)

Through indifference and callousness we miss the really major, accessible aspects of experience. Springtime, memories, violin music
from an open window: such give themselves, needing us as lovers
do, but we evade the assignment. The concept of "heaviness"
(*Schwere*) is carried over from its seed-germ in *The Book of Images*
into the term "managed" (*bewältigtest*) some ten years later. Man's
typical distraction is seen as a search for a love-dream. The parenthesis ("What time would you have for her anyway with all your
other concerns?") is characteristic of Rilke's grave, unsmiling, and
underplayed irony.

The following lines leading to the close of section two present
further variations on the love-theme, carried over from previous
works:

Sehnt es dich aber, so singe die Liebenden, lange
noch nicht unsterblich genug ist ihr berühmtes
  Gefühl.
Jene, du neidest sie fast, Verlassenen, die du
so viel liebender fandst als die Gestillten. Beginn
immer von neuem die nie zu erreichende Preisung;

157

denk: es erhält sich der Held, selbst der Untergang war ihm
nur ein Vorwand zu sein: seine letzte Geburt.
Aber die Liebenden nimmt die erschöpfte Natur
in sich zurück, als wären nicht zweimal die Kräfte,
dieses zu leisten. Hast du der Gaspara Stampa
denn genügend gedacht, dass irgend ein Mädchen,
dem der Geliebte entging, am gesteigerten Beispiel
dieser Liebenden fühlt: dass ich würde wie sie?
Sollen nicht endlich uns diese ältesten Schmerzen
fruchtbarer werden? Ist es nicht Zeit, dass wir liebend
uns vom Geliebten befrein und es bebend bestehn:
wie der Pfeil die Sehne besteht, um gesammelt im Absprung
mehr zu sein als er selbst. Denn Bleiben ist nirgends. . . .

> No, when longing comes over you, sing
> the great lovers: the fame
> of all they can feel is far from immortal
> enough.
> Those whom you almost envied, those
> forsaken, you found
> so far beyond the requited in loving. Begin
> ever anew their never attainable praise.
> Consider: the Hero continues, even his fall
> was a pretext for further existence, an
> ultimate birth.
> But lovers are taken back by exhausted Nature
> into herself, as though such creative force
> could never be re-exerted. Have you so
> fully remembranced
> Gaspara Stampa, that any girl, whose
> beloved's

eluded her, may feel, from that far in-
tenser
example of loving: 'If I could become
like her!'
Ought not these oldest sufferings of ours
to be yielding
more fruit by now? Is it not time that, in
loving,
we freed ourselves from the loved one,
and, quivering, endured:
as the arrow endured the string, to become in the gathering out-leap
something more than itself? For staying
is nowhere. . . .

Compared with earlier statements these variations on the love
theme are deeper in tone and syntactically more complex, due primarily to the dialogic reference. Interlinked with this theme is that
of the hero with its Hölderlin echoes. The meaning is that the hero's
existence is already guaranteed and predicated on his eventual destruction; he is committed to mortality from the beginning and his
real career begins after death, a theme elaborated in more detail in
the Sixth Elegy. But the lovers in the restricted Rilkean sense have no
such guarantee; they are a loan from nature and, having once committed themselves, have nothing left when nature welcomes them
back into her exhausted system. It becomes almost obligatory for
the poet to praise them. Unrequited lovers serve further a pedagogic
purpose, as examples to others of the use to which genuine suffering
may be put. The association of suffering with growth and fruitful-
ness is to be met with at various stages in Rilke's work, from the
Requiems through the *War Songs* to the vision of the Mountain of
Primal Pain in the Tenth Elegy. The last four quoted lines contain a
metaphor frequently discussed in Rilke criticism. Rilke has already
told us that the lover's object escaped (*entging*) her concern, without apparent protest or complaint. Isn't it time, he asks, that genuine
love be put to the test, that it evaluate renunciation more in the
direction of felicity—just as the arrow gathers a certain strength
from the tense bow-chord beyond the measure of its own force? And

then, as so often, Rilke concludes the interrogative steps of his syllogism with his main premise last: "For staying is nowhere."

His later poetry consistently elevates singulars into universals, simple images into cosmic or cultural symbols (the reference to Gaspara Stampa is a good example). The recurring phrase "the lovers" (*die Liebenden*), embedded in successive clusters of liquid sounds, enhances the musical effect, while the alliteration and assonance of old Germanic verse, united with a closer regard for vowel tone in sequence, play an important role (*berühmtes Gefühl, erreichende Preisung, bebend bestehen*). The increasing use of verbal substantives not only removes emphasis from the concrete person or thing to the generic type, but accentuates living function, the very process of being.

> Stimmen, Stimmen. Höre, mein Herz, wie sonst
> nur
> Heilige hörten: dass sie der riesige Ruf
> aufhob vom Boden; sie aber knieten,
> unmögliche, weiter und achtetens nicht:
> so waren sie hörend. . . .

> Voices, voices. Hear O my heart, as only
> saints have heard: heard till the giant-
> call
> lifted them off the ground; yet they went
> impossibly
> on with their kneeling, in undistracted
> attention:
> so inherently hearers. . . .

Change of rhythm and tone is made possible by invocation substituted for interrogation. The successive repetition of "voices" prepares us for the new theme of the young dead, at the same time discharging an acoustic effect of something soft and far away. The exhortation is addressed to the poet himself and, in this case, the appeal is launched into a figure derived, characteristically, from the fine arts. The psychological situation itself is compressed in paradoxical statement between the double colons. The glimpse of kneeling saints, as in the foreground of Renaissance paintings of the Adoration, is another form of the paradox presented by the "unicorn" sonnet (II, 4), as well as by the earlier "Donor" (*New Poems*): the supernatural call whose whirlwind sweeps saints *up* from the ground leaves them just as they were, still *kneeling*, lost in concentration. Their unwittingness, in fact, is the very condition of their hearing at all, just as the unicorn in the sonnet existed by virtue of a loving belief on the part of others in its existence ("Not there, because they loved it, it behaved/as though it were . . .").

         Nicht dass du Gottes ertrügest
die Stimme, bei weitem. Aber das Wehende
  höre,
die ununterbrochene Nachricht, die aus Stille
  sich bildet.
Es rauscht jetzt von jenen jungen Toten zu dir.
Wo immer du eintratst, redete nicht in Kirchen
zu Rom und Neapel ruhig ihr Schicksal dich an?
Oder es trug eine Inschrift sich erhaben dir auf,
wie neulich die Tafel in Santa Maria Formosa.
Was sie mir wollen? Leise soll ich des Unrechts
Anschein abtun, der ihrer Geister
reine Bewegung manchmal ein wenig behindert.

        Not that you could endure
  the voice of God—far from it. But hark
    to the suspiration,
  the uninterrupted news that grows out of
    silence,
  rustling towards you now from those
    youthfully-dead.
  Whenever you entered a church in Rome
    or in Naples
  were you not being always quietly ad-
    dressed by their fate?
  Or else an inscription sublimely imposed
    itself on you,
  as, lately, the tablet in Santa Maria For-
    mosa.
  What they require of me? I must gently
    remove the appearance
  of suffered injustice, that hinders
  a little, at times, their purely-proceeding
    spirits. . . .

The third repetition of "voice" recalls the original invocation; we are now to learn its source: not as utterance of god or angel, beyond human endurance like Goethe's Earth Spirit, but as a message accruing from silence.[18] The word "suspiration" (*das Wehende*) is, with Rilke, replete with connotations. The long-familiar paradox of an awareness conveyed through silence serves to introduce the third major theme of the early dead. And since most of the *Elegies* commemorate, at least once, some moment in the history of Western art and seek to transform it, as Rilke urged, into coefficients of the spirit, so the unruffled status of the early dead is conveyed by another figure from the fine arts, an inscription on a tomb in a Venice church. How the venerable phrasing of the epitaph must have appealed to him: *Vixi aliis dum vita fuit/post funera tandem/Non perii, at gelido/in marmore vivo mihi. . .* ! Moreover, the word *erhaben* has a double meaning: as relief lettering standing out from the stone, and as "majestic" or "sublime" in regard to the inscription's meaning. The last three verses contain the charge to the poet, here as elsewhere, to compensate the early dead for the blow dealt them by fate (an "injustice" from the human viewpoint) by invoking them in appropriate verse.

From the early dead to the consideration of death as a whole is a mere step:

> Freilich ist es seltsam, die Erde nicht mehr zu
> bewohnen,
> kaum erlernte Gebräuche nicht mehr zu üben,
> Rosen, und andern eigens versprechenden Ding-
> en
> nicht die Bedeutung menschlicher Zukunft zu
> geben;
> das, was man war in unendlich ängstlichen
> Händen,
> nicht mehr zu sein, und selbst den eigenen
> Namen
> wegzulassen, wie ein zerbrochenes Spielzeug.
> Seltsam, die Wünsche nicht weiter zu wünschen.
> Seltsam,
> alles, was sich bezog, so lose im Raume
> flattern zu sehen. Und das Totsein ist mühsam

und voller Nachholn, dass man allmählich ein
   wenig
Ewigkeit spürt. . . .

      True, it is strange to inhabit the earth no
         longer,
      to use no longer customs scarcely ac-
         quired,
      not to interpret roses, and other things
      that promise so much, in terms of a hu-
         man future;
      to be no longer at all that one used to be
      in endlessly anxious hands, and to lay
         aside
      even one's proper name like a broken
         toy.
      Strange, not to go on wishing one's
         wishes. Strange,
      to see all that was once in relation so
         loosely fluttering
      hither and thither in space. And it's hard,
         being dead,
      and full of retrieving before one begins to
         espy
      a trace of eternity. . . .

Almost imperceptibly the viewpoint is shifted; we are no longer
viewing the experience from the human angle but from that of the
early departed (the aspect of "strangeness" is three times repeated).
The argument from here to the end consists of three moments: (1)
the human standpoint regarding death; (2) the human error of distinguishing too sharply between the two realms; (3) the final status
of the dead, who do not need us but whom we need. Rilke selects his
images carefully to suggest this delicate transition from life (roses,
customs, toys, human attachments) to the death-reference ("so
loosely fluttering hither and thither in space"). The difficulty of
"being dead" (because supposedly the life that was missed will
have to be "retrieved," "made-up") is an assertion made from the
human standpoint and will shortly be retracted:

              Aber Lebendige machen
    alle den Fehler, dass sie zu stark unterscheiden.

Engel (sagt man) wüssten oft nicht, ob sie unter
Lebenden gehn oder Toten. Die ewige Strömung
reisst durch beide Bereiche alle Alter
immer mit sich und übertönt sie in beiden. . . .
          Yes, but all of the living
    make the mistake of drawing too sharp
    distinctions.
    Angels (they say) are often unable to tell
    whether they move among living or dead.
    The eternal
    torrent whirls all the ages through either
    realm
    for ever, and sounds above their voices
    in both. . . .

The angel-figure is again picked up, along with one of the cardinal
ideas of the *Sonnets to Orpheus*, written some twelve years later
("Does he belong here? No, his spreading/nature, from either do-
main has sprung"). The Orpheus figure is prepared for by the
angels, who (the parenthesis relegates the statement to the realm
of rumor and legend) make no distinctions between young and old,
living and dead. (A startling philosophical parallel to this thought
may be found in Vaihinger's critique of our conceptual classificatory
systems as based on abstractions of the most one-sided nature (*The
Philosophy of As If*), where "light and darkness, black and white,
life and death are merely the artificial products of rationalistic abstractions, fictions necessary for purposes of reference, but to be
used with caution.")[19] Here the poet's statement about normal consciousness inhabiting merely the apex of a pyramid comes to mind,
as well as Leishman's remark that "no view of life could be less
anthropocentric than Rilke's."[20]

The expression "torrent" (*Strömung*) suggests an invisible element, like an ether current, recalling the "suspiration" mentioned a
few verses back. A tactile image is associated with an acoustic one.
A prose variant of such imagery, with its partly scientific, partly
romantic atmosphere, is suggested in a letter of November 13, 1925:
"The true figure of life extends through *both* spheres, the blood of
the mightiest circulation flows through *both*."[21]

Schliesslich brauchen sie uns nicht mehr, die
    Frühentrückten,
man entwöhnt sich des Irdischen sanft, wie man
    den Brüsten
milde der Mutter entwächst. Aber wir, die so
    grosse
Geheimnisse brauchen, denen aus Trauer so oft
seliger Fortschritt entspringt—: könnten wir
    sein ohne sie? . . .

    They've finally no more need of us, the
        early-departed,
    one's gently weaned from terrestrial
        things as one mildly
    outgrows the breasts of a mother. But
        we, that have need of
    such mighty secrets, we, for whom sor-
        row's so often
    source of blessedest progress, could we
        exist without them? . . .

This passage picks up and answers—from the inverse point of
view—the "need" expressed in the elegy's opening lines. The process of severing from life is stressed in the threefold repetition of the
verbal prefix (*ent-*), while the last three lines, if placed in normal
order, state two ideas. If the opening lines had implied that we cannot "use" angels, animals, or men, the early dead are proposed as
an exception; for though they do not "need" us, without experience of them we should not fully exist, since sublime mysteries are
essential to life.[22] The second idea emphasized here is a favorite one
that Rilke never tires of repeating: the advent of progress through
sorrow.

    Ist dìe Sage unsonst, dass einst in der Klage um
        Linos
    wagende erste Musik dürre Erstarrung durch-
        drang,
    dass erst im erschrockenen Raum, dem ein bei-
        nah göttlicher Jüngling
    plötzlich für immer enttrat, das Leere in jene
    Schwingung geriet, die uns jetzt hinreisst und
        tröstet und hilft?

> Is the story in vain, how once, in the
> mourning for Linos,
> venturing earliest music pierced barren
> numbness, and how,
> in the horrified space an almost deified
> youth
> suddenly quitted forever, emptiness first
> felt the vibration that now charms us and
> comforts and helps?

The coda-like conclusion—a summation of theme in a mythological or imaginative "scene"—is rather typical of most of the *Elegies*. Since Linos, whose name is a personification of lament, is mentioned in Homer and belongs to the orphic legend-cycle, it is clear that as far back as 1912 the seed of the later *Sonnets* was already sprouting in the poet's mind. Just as sorrow for the youthful dead may, for us, be a source of "blessedest progress," musical lamentation (or the art of poetry) creates those vibrations of consolation for the stoniness of grief. Rilke's careful craftsmanship carries through to the end, in the wording, syntax, and pace of the final verse. The "vibration" rounds off the organic chain of the preceding sections ("suspiration" and "torrent"), while the decrescendo caused by the final three verbs, with copula, issues on a note of solace and silence.

THE SECOND ELEGY

The First Elegy has been discussed in some detail because it is the main stock, one may say, from which throughout the next eleven years other shoots put forth, all acknowledging their derivation from the parent stem. The *Elegies* are all related in parts, yet certain groupings are indicated. The First, Second, Seventh, and Ninth Elegies, for example, are concerned with man's existential vulnerability, implied by their supporting themes: the unrequited lovers, the early dead, the potentialities of the death-realm, the apotheosis and transformation of the visible world into the invisible. The "chthonic" Elegies, the Third, Sixth, and Seventh, are thematically related in dealing with the subconscious world of human sex and animal biology, the Dark God of D. H. Lawrence, and its complementary theme, the hero. The Fourth, Fifth, and Tenth Elegies are unified

ANGEL

around the motif of "symbolic theater." The Fifth and Tenth, finally, are also the most richly organized and motivated of the series,
forming two arches that support the entire sequence.

What immensely enhances the effectiveness of these poems is the
use in each of a historical symbol (mythological, literary, aesthetic)
as a kind of hub for the rapidly moving spokes of Rilke's cosmic
wheel. The symbol serves a twofold purpose. It links an intangible
Innenraum with specific landmarks of the European tradition: Linos
(First Elegy), Tobias and the Attic steles (Second), the blood's
Neptune (Third), August the Strong of Saxony and the Sphinx (Seventh), the soul of the Etruscans (Eighth), the corder of Rome and
the Nile potter (Ninth), and the sybils, Sphinx, and matriarchal symbols of the zodiac in the Tenth. Rilke's incorporation of the tradition,
comprising largely pre-Socratic, Egyptian, Hebrew, medieval and
modern *Lebensphilosophie* elements, may be interestingly compared
with the exploitation of its other components as selected by Eliot, for
example, or by George in the synthetic arrangements of his early
verse.

Originating at the same time as the First Elegy, the Second is
closely related thematically. Despite the terror inspired by the angel,
the poet in anguish here persists in his appeal. If, for him, the angel-
types are "almost mortal birds of the soul," in Biblical times it was
quite otherwise, when communication between divine and earthly
orders was taken for granted. The reference to the "days of Tobias"
from the Apocrypha recalls an analogue to Milton's

    . . . God or Angel Guest
With Man, as with his Friend, familiar us'd
To sit indulgent . . .[23]

The first two sections have, in addition, their own particular structural interest:

    Träte der Erzengel jetzt, der gefährliche, hinter
        den Sternen
    eines Schrittes nur nieder und herwärts: hoch-
        auf-
    schlagend erschlüg uns das eigene Herz. Wer
        seid ihr? . . .

167

THE RING OF FORMS

> Let the archangel perilous now, from be-
> hind the stars,
> step but a step down hitherwards: high-
> upbeating,
> our heart would out-beat us. Who are
> you? . . .

The conditional is effectively carried over from the opening lines of the First Elegy: "Who, if I cried . . .?" The immense complacency of the angel's single step in our direction is suggested by the majestic stride of the sentence to the colon. In contrast, the emotional confusion on the receiving end is expressed in the final apodosis in several ways—first by distribution of the multiple-compound participle in a run-on line, so that between each syllabic element there is a pause, a catching of breath, to indicate the shock of confrontation; further, by the increasing Rilkean use of the same word stem in juxtaposition (*hochauf-schlagend erschlüg*) with different meanings and connotations. The basic rhythm of all three lines is sustained by a tension of opposites, an upward and a downward pull. The climax is reached at the colon, where the poet's desperate predicament, with his back to the wall, is panted forth in the abrupt and brief interrogation: "Who are you?" Rilke would hardly have had any knowledge of Hopkins, but the rhythmical impact of these lines suggests "The swoon of a heart that the sweep and the hurl of thee trod/Hard down with a horror of Height."

Parallels between German *Literaturbarock* and Rilke's later poetry have been suggested, especially in reference to section two of this elegy with its intensity and exuberant expansiveness, its piling up of personifications, exaggerated metaphors, and seemingly incongruous linkages. Yet a moment's reflection suffices to show that he has really transcended the baroque. The word elements are not indiscriminately strung out in sheer zest of color or motion or other sensational effects; and the imagery is selected with care, first from the world of nature, then from the supernatural with its orders and hierarchies blended of Christian and pagan elements:

> Frühe Geglückte, ihr Verwöhnten der Schöpfung,
> Höhenzüge, morgenrötliche Grate

aller Erschaffung,—Pollen der blühenden Gottheit,
Gelenke des Lichtes, Gänge, Treppen, Throne,
Räume aus Wesen, Schilde aus Wonne, Tumulte
stürmisch entzückten Gefühls und plötzlich, einzeln,
Spiegel: die die entströmte eigene Schönheit
wiederschöpfen zurück in das eigene Antlitz. . . .

Early successes, Creation's pampered darlings,
ranges, summits, dawn-red ridges
of all beginning,—pollen of blossoming godhead,
hinges of light, corridors, stairways, thrones,
spaces of being, shields of felicity, tumults
of stormily rapturous feeling, and suddenly, separate,
mirrors, drawing up their own
outstreamed beauty into their faces again. . . .

The profusion of clamorous sounds in the opening verses subsides
in the pauses after "suddenly" and "separate," as if a waterfall were
quietly to ripple out on the smooth surface of a pool. Again, as in the
preceding section, the essence of angelic freedom is contained between two extremes of feeling. The invocative imagery is organic,
not rhetorical, and the scale of values ascends from the earthly to
the heavenly orders, where the "thrones" suggest the angel choruses
of the Bible or Dionysius Aeropagita or even some of the Church
liturgies. The series of apostrophes, each with its special connota-
tion, terminates quietly in a Rilkean key-symbol, "mirrors," reflecting back on the Narcissus poems and forward to Orpheus Sonnet II,
22, written a decade later.

Three ensuing verses of the Second Elegy help to ascertain how
Rilke sometimes obtains subtle effects with his imagery. Mortal
transience, even that of beauty, requires an unusual imagery if it is
to avoid ringing changes on rather trite themes:

Like dew from the morning grass
exhales from us that which is ours, like heat
from a smoking dish . . .

Here the combination of a romantic with a banal simile achieves just
the right effect of ironic contrast and distance. The Fourth Elegy
offers a similar example where, between angel and puppet, the bourgeois actor "passes through the kitchen into his dwelling." The con-

clusion, finally, picks up a distinctly modern note: the absence of suitable and compelling images or myths as vehicles of poetic thought and feeling.

TRANSFORMATION

A brief review of the remaining *Elegies* will reveal their kinship with the ones already discussed as well as with other poetry. The Third Elegy, on first sight, seems to run counter to the thought-pattern of the others. Often called a Freudian elegy, as though a therapeutic technique were synonymous with the organic growth of a poem or explained it (though Rilke was acquainted with Freud's work and probably with that of Jung), it treats of the submerged sex-force in all its primitive rawness and terror. If it seems more atypical of the poet than the other elegies, it is because we forget at times the polarity in his thinking (those perpetual "contradictions" that were never to hear of each other, like "the tree of rejoicing" contrasted with "the strings of lamentation" or, in historical perspective, the Dionysian aspect of poetry as opposed to its Apollonian serenity).[24] Important is the "inner landscape," not "the luxuriant forest primeval, but a landscape of a quite different, more naked and colder type." A comparison of the imagery with that of an earlier poem ("Tombs of the Heterae," *New Poems*) and, again, with that of the Tenth Elegy, points to a consistency of poetic pattern. It is true, however, that among the poet's many references to love, this poem alone presents the case of the man instead of the woman, though the range is narrower and less indicative of Rilke's entire work.

The Eighth, which he referred to as the "quiet" one, is the only elegy besides the Fifth to bear a dedication; indeed, one might with more assurance claim that it was influenced in some degree by association with Kassner than that the Third Elegy was indebted to Freud. The epithet "quiet" may be owing to the regular flow of the pentameters and to the fact that, of the entire series, it is the most didactic and the least dramatic. Again Rilke offers a variation on the death theme, conceived from the standpoint of the lesser creation and contrasted with the human situation. Before man lies always the barrier of death, but

> . . . das freie Tier
> hat seinen Untergang stets hinter sich
> und vor sich Gott, und wenn es geht, so gehts
> in Ewigkeit, so wie die Brunnen gehen. . . .

> . . . the free animal
> has its decease perpetually behind it
> and God in front, and when it moves, it moves
> into eternity, like running springs. . . .

In contrast to the animal's unity-in-death, the human situation is again one of "oppositeness" (*Gegenüber*), which permits the poem to terminate on the familiar theme of human impermanence and symbolic departure. Certain effects are also achieved by the use of repetitions in a colloquial setting (*und wenn es geht, so gehts/in Ewigkeit, so wie die Brunnen gehen*).

The Sixth Elegy, more than the Seventh, serves as a variation on the Third, whose "youth" reappears, in the fig tree metaphor, as the "hero." The fig tree leaps into fruit without concern for its hidden blossom while "we linger, alas, we glory in flowering; already betrayed/we reach the retarded core of our ultimate fruit." Rilke works up to his main theme at line twenty-one through a profusion of metaphors:

> Feigenbaum, seit wie lange schon ists mir be-
>   deutend,
> wie du die Blüte beinah ganz überschlägst
> und hinein in die zeitig entschlossene Frucht,
> ungerühmt, drängst dein reines Geheimnis.
> Wie der Fontäne Rohr treibt dein gebogenes
>   Gezweig
> abwärts den Saft und hinan: und er springt aus
>   dem Schlaf,
> fast nicht erwachend, ins Glück seiner süssesten
>   Leistung.
> Sieh: wie der Gott in den Schwan. . . .

> Fig tree, how long it's been full meaning
>   for me,
> the way you almost entirely omit to
>   flower
> and into the seasonably-resolute fruit

> uncelebratedly thrust your purest secret.
> Like the tube of a fountain, your bent
>   bough drives the sap
> downwards and up: and it leaps from its
>   sleep, scarce waking,
> into the joy of its sweetest achievement.
>   Look,
> like Jupiter into the swan. . . .

The major metaphor is the directly addressed fig tree, bearing fruit before the blossoms are visible. To carry through the idea of quick pulsation into fruit, a simile is combined with the tree-metaphor: bent boughs are compared to the communicating pipes of a fountain whose accumulating pressures jet suddenly into graceful arcs. As if this were not enough, a second mythological simile, also with erotic implications, is superadded to the first. Then the development contrasts the human predicament, where showy blossoming is bought at the expense of the fruit. To only a few—namely, heroes and the early dead—is it vouchsafed to "glow in the fulness of heart." (Heroes *perhaps*, qualifies Rilke, while the case of the early dead is indisputable.) Verse 17 links up two of the initial figures in the image of the "gardener death" (cf. *Tuscan Diary*) who, in the case of these fortunate ones, has "bent their veins differently" (as the water pipes are bent). The Leda figure in the middle section is now balanced and concluded by a simile from ancient Egypt, the Karnak reliefs, "mild" and "hollowed out" to go with "smiling," where the steeds seem perpetually to outdistance the victorious king in his chariot. All figures are interrelated, there is nothing haphazard about them, and they occur, as elsewhere, in two carefully timed sequences: the personal-individual and the mythological-historical. It has never been sufficiently emphasized how much the Rilkean art-work, beyond its extraordinary personal imagery, owes to such traditional moments as these for its simultaneous range and concentration of experience.

The Seventh and Ninth Elegies mention for the first time the transformation theme, which lies at the core of Rilke's aesthetic; for the first time a positive program is offered in counterbalance to the unreachable angel hierarchies:

Nirgends, Geliebte, wird Welt sein, als innen.
Unser
Leben geht hin mit Verwandlung. Und immer
geringer
schwindet das Aussen. . . .

> Nowhere, beloved, can world exist but
> within.
> Life passes in transformation. And, ever
> diminishing,
> vanishes what's outside. . . .

We have spoken of the wavering relationship of the poet to his angel-symbol throughout. In the Seventh Elegy this relationship is particularly ambiguous, for if the tone of the introductory sections is radiant and almost ecstatic, that of the end is aggressive and defiant. Despite the initial deprecation ("Not wooing, no longer shall wooing, voice that's outgrown it,/be now the form of your cry . . ."), the poet is throughout torn between the urge to "woo" (*werben*) and, at the same time, to assert his human prerogative. All the subsidiary themes and motifs—lovers and childhood, birds and fountains—are marshaled again to support the jubilant message: "Life here's glorious" (*Hiersein ist herrlich*). After the spiritual debacles so poignantly depicted in the Fourth, Fifth, and Seventh Elegies, the angel is now to be shown the human credit-side of the ledger. However small the sum, music and art, Chartres and Sphinx, and all other symbols of creative energy "stood once among men" in the great vast and abysm of time. The partly coaxing, partly challenging tone employed to solicit the angel's attention to these factors abruptly breaks off seven lines from the end; added later, these reverse the former relationship and introduce the one somber note of discord in the sequence: the image of the poet with outstretched, "upwardly open hand," signaling warning and resistance. The tension between the two forces could hardly be better conveyed than in the final three words (*unfasslicher, weit auf*) with their heavy accents and too ominous pauses.

In the Ninth Elegy are placed on display the major issues of the angelic struggle (love, death, art; suffering, childhood, nature), subsumed in a blanket affirmation:

> Erde, ist es nicht dies, was du willst: *unsichtbar*
> in uns erstehn?—Ist es dein Traum nicht,
> einmal unsichtbar zu sein?—Erde! unsichtbar!
> Was, wenn Verwandlung nicht, ist dein drängen-
> der Auftrag?

> Earth, isn't this what you want: an in-
> visible
> re-arising in us? Is it not your dream
> to be one day invisible? Earth! invisible!
> What is your urgent command, if not
> transformation?

There are two distinct movements in this conception. First, the affirmation of earth's splendor, taken over from the Seventh Elegy, is sustained in the second section by the repetition of "only once" (*einmal*) no less than six times; and then we are urged to establish contact with the higher life (angel) by calling his attention to the simple facts of our earth. No geographical or metaphysical conception, Rilke's "earth" is the realm of the homely, isolated *Dinge* that sprawled sentimentally in the early poetry, were artfully dominated in the Paris period, and are now refined into "laral" values. The title of his first volume of verse, we recall, was *Household Gods* (*lares*, tutelary gods or spirits associated with particular localities in the Roman religion). The artifacts of this "earth" were already enumerated in the Seventh Elegy: culture, thought, creative productivity, Chartres and Sphinx (as opposed to American gadgets and prefabricated homes with their "imageless activity").[25] One may, if one wishes, interpret the final section in sociological, metaphysical, or even ethical terms, but Rilke's concern is primarily a creative one. The emphasis is on experience that is "tellable" (*sagbar*) and places in the foreground the priority of poetic interpretation. The magnificent stroke of irony derives from the imputation of the salvation of these "perishable" things to the "most perishable" agencies of all, namely ourselves, until the poet comes to the rescue.

Rilke's transformation theme is of old romantic heritage. Even Coleridge, in the wake of Schelling's "activation of nature" and "equating of nature and spirit," had modulated on it in his *Biographia Literaria*:

174

The highest perfection of natural philosophy would consist in the perfect spiritualization of all laws of nature into the laws of intuition and intellect. The *phenomena (the Material)* must wholly disappear, and the laws alone *(the formal)* must remain. Thence it comes that in nature itself the more the principle or law break forth, the more does the husk drop off, the *phenomena* themselves become more spiritual and at length cease altogether in our consciousness.[26]

More in harmony with Rilke's purpose than Coleridge, perhaps, is the thought of another great romantic, Novalis, who likens the inner world to "the gold and silver in the inward parts of the earth, and the poet is the miner who is spirited down into the depths and rejoices in all that he sees." [27]

THE DRAMATIC ELEGIES

It has been remarked that the Fifth and Tenth Elegies are the most richly composed and lengthy of the sequence. Written but a few days apart (February 1922), in equal periods of concentration, they sustain like columns the structure of the remaining eight. But they stand out from the others for more than formal reasons. Rilke's lyric is at its best in a dramatic setting, in a particular "landscape." Picasso's "Saltimbanques" in Hertha Koenig's Munich apartment, as well as the poet's earlier Paris impressions of Père Rollin and his troupe of strolling acrobats, merely sets the scene for the Fifth Elegy. Nor is this inconsistent with his warning in 1922 not to use other art forms as the starting point of a new inspiration, the method of second or third hand relying upon appropriation rather than invention.[28] The painting may have been a *motif* (in the strict sense), but not the starting point of a theme which had always been there from the start. The stage is set for presenting the vulnerability of the human dilemma, projected in concrete symbols of drama. Whether it be Parisian acrobats with their spring from "the pure too little" to the "empty too much," or the *Jahrmarkt* adjoining the City of Suffering, the presence of "theater," its movements, crises, and denouements, is always suggested. The director behind the scenes is, perhaps, death, that unseen power whom the acrobats struggle and strain to satisfy, personified toward the end in Madame Lamort with her bourgeois millinery (the "winds and binds" of her motions corresponding ex-

175

actly to the unnamed power in the opening lines that "keeps on
wringing them, bending them, slinging them, swinging them, throw-
ing them and catching them back"). The acrobats' questionable relation to reality is expressed in a panorama of clearly articulated imagery: first, the world's threadbare carpet, like a "plaster laid on a
wound"; in the second section the "rose of onlooking," with all the
implications of the rose in Rilke's poetry; in section three the flowers'
perishing petals that expand into the figure of the negative fertiliza-
tion of pistils and stamens, organized around the repetition of a dis-
affected *u* sound—all derogatory sexual references, picked up again
later in section eight where the mummers' antics are likened to the
copulation of ill-mated animals. The figure in section four, describing the young man as "the son of a broad-back and a nun," is a
characteristic Rilkean catechresis where the metaphorical discrep-
ancy wins force through exaggeration, resulting in a kind of grim
humor. Had Rilke dropped the figure there, its use would seem arbitrary and adventitious. Its justification is provided further along,
after the colon, where the "broad-back" (*Nacken*) carries forward
to "muscles," the "nun" to "simplicity."

For a brief moment we are given a glimpse of the real human gesture before it is brutally blanked out: the tender smile that the boy-
acrobat tries to send to his "seldomly tender mother" before it is
repressed in the hurlyburly of the show:

> . . . und eh dir
> jemals ein Schmerz deutlicher wird in der Nähe
> des immer
> trabenden Herzens, kommt das Brennen der
> Fuss-sohln
> ihm, seinem Ursprung, zuvor mit ein paar dir
> rasch in die Augen gejagten leiblichen Tränen.
> Und dennoch, blindlings,
> das Lächeln. . . .

> . . . and before
> a single pain has got within range of your
> ever-
> galloping heart, comes the tingling
> in the soles of your feet, ahead of the
> spring that it springs from,

ANGEL

        chasing into your eyes a few physical
        tears.
        And, spite of all, blindly,
        your smile. . . .

From a suburban sideshow with its straggly spectators and mechanical clowns we are transferred to the angelic realm where the
figurations of the heart may conceivably win real authenticity in a
performance before an audience of the countless dead. Though the
achievement may be only a supposition ("*suppose* they could man-
age it there" and "Angel: *suppose* there's a place"), it is strong
enough to permit of reconciling the possibilities of new life in re-
pudiation of the inference contained in the elegy's opening lines.
The carefully wrought rhythm, sensitive to the effects of breathing,
spacing and tempo, together with the elliptical syntax, brings the
elegy to a conclusion. The piling up of epithets, often participial, the
relative employed as epithet before the antecedent, above all the
use of insignificant words, like pronominal forms, in both initial and
end position, reveal the elegy style at its best. The innate assurance
of the vision flows unbrokenly and rhythmically, coming to a halt in
the last two words, "quietened/carpet" in emphatic position—the restored counterpart of the discredited carpet figure in the opening
section:

        Würfen die dann ihre letzten, immer ersparten,
        immer verbogenen, die wir nicht kennen, ewig
        gültigen Münzen des Glücks vor das endlich
        wahrhaft lächelnde Paar auf gestilltem
        Teppich?

                Would not the dead then fling their last,
                    their forever reserved,
                ever-concealed, unknown to us, ever-
                    valid
                coins of happiness down before the at
                    last
                truthfully smiling pair on the quietened
                carpet?

Only the coin of the dead is valid and hence hoarded and preserved.
Taken literally, this would mean that beyond life, and only in death,

                                            177

are real values restored. But this is to forget the main aesthetic orientation. It is more reasonable to suppose that Rilke, like Hofmannsthal and other romanticists, regarded regeneration not as a literal death but transformation to more effective levels of living. It is also to forget the First Elegy's warning that "the living make the mistake of drawing too sharp distinctions."

Coming after the jubilant earth-hymn of the Ninth, the Tenth and final Elegy brings the dirge and lament which justify the title of the collection. It synthesizes the tone of the First and Ninth (despair and jubilation) into one which derives perfected happiness from the wellsprings of sorrow. After finishing the *Elegies* the reader is struck by their unmistakable musical structure, with its intricate variations and constant recrossing of theme and motif. The musical arrangement is akin to the multileveled modern forms of poetry and has little in common with the older German romantic indulgence in musical analogies. Thus "How an angel would tread beyond trace their market of comfort" is a variation on the Second Elegy—"Let the archangel perilous now, from behind the stars,/step but a little step hitherwards"—in a different context. The Hills of Primal Pain modulate on the "fathers, resting like mountain-ruins within our depths" of the Third Elegy; the metaphor of "the clear-struck heart-hammers" recalls the Ninth Elegy's "Between the hammers lives our heart." The planet-figures are old friends, one of them ("The Rider") reappearing in the *Sonnets to Orpheus*. The cross references are numerous and point to the organic density of the pattern. The introductory invocation to Suffering ("our winter foliage") picks up a theme expressed many times in both the poetry and prose.

The Tenth Elegy particularly conjures up its own peculiar landscape, the landscape of death, whose pageantry is carefully designed for this Rilkean Pilgrim's Progress. At times, in fact, the treatment comes close to abstract allegory.[29] From the City of Pain (the artificial *décor*, perhaps, of a southern European cemetery),[30] through its outer fringes occupied by a country fair (*Jahrmarkt*) symbolizing all the empty frivolity and sordid materialism of modern civilization, we are led, step by step, into the Landscape of Sorrows (*Landschaft der Klagen*), the death-realm where true being exists in purity, resting on the foundations of suffering. This landscape recalls certain features of early German romanticism, of Tieck and Novalis. Santayana is almost describing it when he speaks of "numinous objects, like giant trees or migratory birds, leaving a certain personality":[31]

> . . . und manchmal
> schreckt ein Vogel und zieht, flach ihnen fliegend
> durchs Aufschaun,
> weithin das schriftliche Bild seines vereinsamten
> Schreis.

> . . . and, at times,
> a startled bird, flying straight through
> their field of vision,
> scrawls the far-stretching screed of its
> lonely cry.

The more the dead youth is led outward (*hinaus*) by the personified girl-lamentation into the death-realm, to vanish at length alone into the Mountains of Primal Pain, the more eerie the landscape becomes. The trees, plants, animals, meadows, and ravines are those we know in real life, only they hang suspended in other dimensions of being, in projections of "inner landscape" where the barriers of sense break down, acoustic and visual interchanges take place (cf. Rilke's essay *Urgeräusch*, "Primitive Sound," for his interest in this extreme form of synaesthesia).

When the great monument rises up in the moonlight (brother to the Egyptian Sphinx), Egyptian ceremonies of the dead come to mind. The Hulewicz letter of 1925 again clarifies this thought as it speaks, at the same time, for the *Elegies* as a whole. In setting up the *"more actual and invisible* within us" as the "norm of existence," the *Elegies*, Rilke continues, "cautiously relate to its origins, claiming primeval traditions and rumors of traditions as support for this conjecture, invoking even in the Egyptian cult of the dead a foreknowledge of such relationships. (Although the *Lament-Land*, through which the elder 'Lament' guides the dead youth, is not to be identified with Egypt, but only to be regarded as a kind of reflection of the Nile country into the desert-clarity of the dead's consciousness.)"[32] In keeping with this atmosphere the elegy is almost entirely organized around the dark vowels *u, o, ö* (*Jubel* and *Ruhm* start it off and it finishes on *Urleid, Dunkel, Glück, Rührung*). This pilgrimage to the realm of the dead is quite unlike Dante's *Inferno*, which it calls to mind. Where Dante's projections are framed in a definite system of tradition and in a specific historical perspective, Rilke's are hyper-individualistic and fade out in the silence of solitude.[33] Could Dante's Beatrice have less in common with the girl-lamentation who conducts the dead youth toward the Mountain of Primal Pain?

The victory belongs to the "endlessly" dead who, to give us a like-ness, would point "to the catkins, hanging from empty hazels" or to "the rain that falls on the dark earth in early spring." Whether or not one agrees with Rilke's debatable thesis of death's seeming priority over life, the issue may be narrowed to the theory and practice of poetry. Paradox is the stabilizer of its tensions, and its statement is prepared in the final verses, set off by themselves in the poet's own italics to serve, from the perspective of the timeless dead, as *l'envoi* to the whole series. Warp and woof, falling and rising, systole and diastole, life and death, the dual nature of the human equation, the contradiction from beginning to end, bring the *Elegies* to a close in a hush of four trimeters, the shortest lines of all:

> Und wir, die an *steigendes* Glück
> denken, empfänden die Rührung
> die uns beinah bestürzt,
> wenn ein Glückliches *fällt*.

> And we, who have always thought
> of happiness *climbing*, would feel
> the emotion that almost startles
> when happiness *falls*.

VII

o͞o Orpheus

I F W E had only the *Elegies*—particularly drawing upon the Tenth, with its unreverberating footfalls from the Hills of Primal Pain—we should, as Rilke informs us, have only a partial picture of the possibilities of the human spirit for achieving self-realization.[1] We may, if we will, accept such critical estimates that the *Elegies* merely express despair without interpreting it, or that they are more concerned with problem and process—the *Sonnets to Orpheus*, on the other hand, with implication and result.[2] Such abstractions, when applied to Rilke, are misleading once they leave the ground where the key symbols, metaphors, and other artistic devices actually operate.

In his correspondence he went to some pains to explain the relationship of the two sequences. The "Elegies and Sonnets support each other constantly";[3] the "Tree of Rejoicing" (*Jubelbaum*) that had seemed broken during the critical years stands erect in the very first sonnet, its orphic music containing and ordering the dissonances of the "Strings of Lamentation" (*Klagesaiten*). With the close of the *Elegies* there is no certainty that the poet's plea is heard, and he can only hope, with Donne's stubbornness:

> O that some day, at the end of this grim vision,
> my voice were joy and praise to assenting angels . . .

The plea is still a fear that is finally resolved in the *Sonnets*, the "natural overflow of so much abundance."[4] Rilke here achieves what the unfortunate eighteenth century poet, Christian Günther, had vainly hoped for in one of his *Klagelieder*:

181

THE RING OF FORMS

Dass nach Klageliedern bald
Auch ein Halleluja schallt.

NATURE OF THE SYMBOL

If the Duino angel is existential fullness, a goad to human striving but at the same time a measure of human insufficiency ("Shine
upon me! Let the constellations/look at me before I disappear"),
Orpheus is the instrument by which the potentialities of earthly existence may be realized, as outlined in the Ninth Elegy: "Being here
is splendid." The magic powers of the god Orpheus provide a positive key to the transcending of the human situation, as compared
with the negative exclusiveness of the angel hierarchies. Orpheus
does what the angel cannot do. There is a point where the terrible
aspect of life, only provisionally too overwhelming for our strength,
passes over into bliss—a step which Malte had foreseen but was unable to take.[5] To offset the angel stands the figure of Orpheus, whose
body was cut up and scattered throughout the universe until the very
trees and stones were his singing. To be mystically open in every
pore to this animated world of ours means, for Rilke, to glorify it,
and glorification is art. The *Sonnets* are an endless laudation (*Rühm-
en*) of such kind that not only is earth glorified but, through the
mediation of the god, the earth glorifies itself. Rilke would have
subscribed to his friend Verhaeren's "Il faut aimer pour découvrir
avec genie," but he goes much further in erecting on this foundation
a most singular poetic credo.

In Greek mythology, Orpheus, the son of Apollo, was first the
master magician, able to activate inanimate nature with his song.
The legend of his dismemberment by Thracian women introduced
a second phase when Orpheus became the religious center of a
Dionysian sect and presided, in his magical godhead, over the ancient religious mysteries of Greece. It is this second (magical) aspect
of the god to which the title and underlying reference of the *Sonnets*
is referred, though the mutations undergone by this divinity hardly
admit a kinship with that primitive orphic world.[6]

Rilke's Orpheus symbol is a composite of a whole line of themes
and motifs dating back to his earliest period: St. Francis, the Russian

monk, Keats, Baudelaire, Hölderlin, Malte, Narcissus, as well as the
Duino angel. (The "Orpheus. Eurydice. Hermes" poem of 1914 will
be considered later.) These manifestations and metamorphoses now
coalesce into one figure—the singing god, *der Gott der Vollzähligkeit*
—who redeems out of time into space and whose function immediately links him with the *Elegies* through the principle of transformation (Sonnet I, 5):

> Errichtet keinen Denkstein. Lasst die Rose
> nur jedes Jahr zu seinen Gunsten blühn.
> Denn Orpheus ists. Seine Metamorphose
> in dem und dem. Wir sollen uns nicht mühn
>
> um andre Namen. Ein für alle Male
> ists Orpheus, wenn es singt. Er kommt und geht. . . .

> > Raise no commemorating stone. The roses
> > shall blossom every summer for his sake.
> > For this is Orpheus. His metamorphosis
> > in this one and in that. We should not take
> >
> > thought about other names. Once and for all,
> > it's Orpheus when there's song. He comes and goes. . . .

Another feature of this divinity is the most surprising of all, in view
of the poet's notorious anti-Christian prejudice. Despite all his efforts to eliminate the Christian paraclete, Rilke merely succeeds in
substituting a symbol which, in function and attribute, is in many
ways modeled after the Christ of the Gospels. Unconsciously or
otherwise, his most inclusive symbol no more belies his strong Christian heritage than Nietzsche's paganism did in his case. Sometimes
he seems to pose as a pagan *post Christum natum*,[7] in the wake of
Nietzsche and Bachofen, yet betrays his tradition at every step. What
has happened, as with many modern poets, is a radical shift in, a
"theologizing" of, the concept of the poet, a kind of *Mythisierung
des Dichters*.[8] Christian dogma is secularized, and the artist-god,
another facet of Dostoevsky's man-god, becomes the fulfiller of the
prophets and saints. One critical statement, in fact, refers to Rilke's
late poetry as a kind of "transformed *Book of Hours*," *horae canonicae*, in the service of the redeemer and savior Orpheus.[9] The use of
the word *heil* coupled with *heiter*, contrasted wtih words like *zer-*

schlugen and *aufgerissen*, in reference to the legend, clearly indicates the redemption pattern. The death of Orpheus is a sacrificial Christian idea (I, 26):

> O du verlorener Gott! Du unendliche Spur!
> Nur weil dich reissend zuletzt die Feindschaft verteilte,
> sind wir die Hörenden jetzt und ein Mund der Natur.

>> O you god that has vanished! You infinite track!
>> Only because dismembering hatred dispersed you
>> are we hearers today and a mouth which else Nature would lack.

The Christian dualism is further enlarged in the twofold function of Orpheus, a symbol of both kingdoms, of the living and of the dead. But contrary to Christian belief, where death is a humiliation for man and an atonement for sin, there is no death for the Singing One. God of the threshold, he issues from the other realm, "always abiding," giving form to ours and reflecting it back again (I, 7):

> Er ist einer der bleibenden Boten,
> der noch weit in die Türen der Toten
> Schalen mit rühmlichen Früchten hält.

>> He is a messenger, always attendant,
>> reaching far through their gates resplendent
>> dishes of fruit for the dead to praise.

We have said that Orpheus redeems out of time into space, out of change into permanency (or, in terms of Rilke's own work, from the time-anxiety of *The Book of Hours* to the space-composure of the *Sonnets*). Having undergone, furthermore, the sacrificial death, Orpheus becomes pure song which, combined with the space-concept, accounts for the numerous spatial and acoustic metaphors ("Baum im Ohr," "Gott des Ohres," "ein Ohr der Erde," etc.). To sum up, the two main attributes of the Orpheus symbol are openness toward all experience, a fullness whose *Innenraum* includes both life and death, to such an extent that Rilke refers to it as an "overflowing" (*Überschuss*); and, secondly, the ordering or forming of this experience through music, i.e., art, poetry.[10] To a greater degree than in the *Elegies* it is possible here, as has been pointed out, to speak of musical counterpoint, for "music is order and precept, though not the music of traditional romantic or dramatic art, but spatial music, the sister of architecture in Valéry's sense."[11] The apotheosis of music as the final court of appeal, after suffering, love, and death have individually failed to yield up their secret, is canonically declared in Sonnet I, 19:

> Nicht sind die Leiden erkannt,
> nicht ist die Liebe gelernt,
> und was im Tod uns entfernt,
>
> ist nicht entschleiert.
> Einzig das Lied überm Land
> heiligt und feiert.

> Sorrow we misunderstand,
> love we still have to begin,
> death and what's hidden therein
>
> await unveiling.
> Song alone circles the land,
> hallowing and hailing.

Orpheus is Rilke's answer to the condition of the modern poet: "Exposed on the hills of the heart." But to get at the core of this symbol, one must study its refractions and relationships as they develop in the *Sonnets* as a whole.

STYLE AND STRUCTURE

It is as impossible to give a complete résumé of the *Sonnets* as of the *Elegies*; their symbolical fullness is not reducible, unless we murder to dissect. This poetry is, as Pongs has said, "not a lyric of the heart but of revelation," not fragments of a great confession, as with Goethe, but esoteric doctrine and teaching.[12] But whether the *Sonnets* deal with praise of the world of objects and the rejection of machine civilization, or with constancy in the abiding aspects of living and with transformation of the imprisoned ego, all themes and motifs come home to rest in the orphic purpose.

The poet himself lent a few helpful hints as to certain individual interpretations. Thus the "unicorn" sonnet was not to be taken as a Christ-parallel but as love for the intangible, unproven validity of belief (a Rilkean disguise for the Pauline definition of faith as the substance of things hoped for, the evidence of things not seen). The "dog" sonnet, a correspondent is informed, had nothing to do with the migration of souls but with the inclusion of the animal ("almost like Esau") in the full scope of the human equation. To secure this inclusion Rilke intentionally refrains from mentioning the animal by name in the poem, though his query as to whether the reader would answer the riddle for himself apparently raised some doubt in his mind. What he particularly rejected was any approach to the poems by way of allusion-hunting: "I believe that no poem in the *Sonnets* means anything that is not completely articulated (*ausgeschrieben*) in them, often of course with its most reticent names. Anything in the nature of 'allusion' contradicts, for my feeling, the poem's indescribable There-ness." [13] There is some equivocation here, for he also admitted, while claiming that both love and death were the plot of the *Elegies* and *Sonnets*, that "a knowledge of certain assumptions" might be requisite to the comprehension of the latter.[14] With the *Sonnets*, at any rate, he seems to have been more than usually sensitive to the subject of "audience reaction."

As for their general structure and arrangement, the fact that he claimed that they were dictated to him implies that their first law is rhythm. Compared with the solemnly-pacing rhythms of the *Elegies* or the rigid immobility of *New Poems*, the sonnet verses trip and soar with a winged lightness. A certain lack of "gravity" and density about these poems is refreshingly new and singular (e.g., Sonnet II, 25). "Some of this newly acquired lightness," writes Belmore, "must be credited to the influence of Valéry" where "the short-lined sonnet occurs several times in his *Poesies*," though it is "not this form alone that contributed to Rilke's style," but rather "the spirit of Valéry's language . . . a kind of intellectual, rational ecstasy we discern in the exalted, lucid language of the *Sonnets*." [15]

For specific details as to the structure of the poems one is referred to Holthusen's penetrating analyses, which are here reproduced in abbreviated form.[16] Considering Rilke's development over the years, one may note a definite progression in the conception of the objective correlative according to the following pattern: (1) the object (*Ding*), neutral and inorganic, of the early poetry; (2) the art-object (*Kunst-ding*) of the Paris period; and (3) the increasing resort to the naturized object (*Naturding*) of the final poems. We have found Rilke referring to the "laral" values of his poems, and in both *Sonnets* and *Elegies* images often transcend their literal nature and manifest themselves in cosmic or planetary symbols. The word assumes a mythic import, and the language as a whole becomes the expression of an orphic attitude. There is, accordingly, a certain flexibility in the use of the pronominal address forms. The *Sonnets* speak of "we," "you," and "I" interchangeably, and are thus directed toward no particular person but to humanity at large (exceptions are the two Wera Knoop sonnets—I, 25 and II, 28—Sonnet II, 23 addressed to the reader, and II, 29 to a friend of Wera's). A certain reserve is maintained by the sparing use of the first-person pronoun.[17]

The cycle is loosely grouped according to content and rhythmic effects. Part II differs from Part I in the greater independence from the orphic legend proper, just as parallels between the two parts do not issue from a symmetrical arrangement but from a more or less unconscious inclination to mythic correspondences, conditioned by the return of a specific motif-cluster.[18] The Rilkean sonnet usually begins with the naming of a specific phenomenon (tree, girl, spring, apple, horse) and ends with its sublimation in the orphic context (II, 21):

> Welchem der Bilder du auch im Innern geeint
> bist
> (sei es selbst ein Moment aus dem Leben der
> Pein),
> fühl, dass der ganze, der rühmliche Teppich ge-
> meint ist.

> > Feel, with what pattern soever you're in-
> > wardly blended
> > (even a scene from the story of Agony),
> > feel that the whole, the praisable, car-
> > pet's intended.

Rhythm and meter work interdependently, the former often creating its own meter.[19] Thus, in formal dactylic tetrameter, the scansion in the first verse is practically forgotten in the suspended pauses of listening occasioned by the marked syncopation (II, 25):

> Schon, horch, hörst du der ersten Harken
> Arbeit; wieder den menschlichen Takt
> in der verhaltenen Stille der Starken
> Vorfrühlingserde. . . .

> Hark, the earliest harrows striving
> already; the rhythm of man once more
> breaks the tense stillness around reviving
> pre-vernal earth. . . .

Though the *Sonnets* cannot be arranged in any unified metrical scheme, Rilke still adheres to a thoroughly symmetrical sonnet composition, with divisions into quatrains and tercets, while the individual metrics are flexibly varied. He himself was quite aware of the "free" treatment accorded to this "so quiet and stable form." It was, indeed, a kind of challenge to modify the sonnet form while at the same time not destroying it altogether.[20] The iambic pentameter of the Paris poems reappears less often as trochaic and dactylic meters take its place. The meters become increasingly antique as the cycle progresses, beginning with iambic pentameter and shading more and more into dactylic forms. Without violence words of original dactylic structure are mixed with those of undactylic nature.[21]

Noticeable is the new use of rhyme as compared with the earlier poetry, where it determined the entire poem, its strophic and stanzaic development. The sonnet rhyme is "unmusical" and has even been called "mathematical rhyme." [22] Generally there is little relationship in sense between the rhymed pairs, the connection lying rather in phonetic arrangement: nouns rhyme with adjective endings, conjunctions with nouns, pronouns with verbs, while even contractions are used for phonetic unity.

The word being the all-important element, what devices are employed to bring out its substance? One is the employment of repetitions in successive lines, as in Sonnet I, 4 (my italics):

> Fürchtet euch nicht zu leiden, die *Schwere*,
> gebt sie zurück an der Erde Gewicht;
> *schwer* sind die Berge, *schwer* sind die Meere.

> Be not afraid of suffering, render
> heaviness back to the earth again;
> mountains are heavy and seas . . .

and much more emphatically in II, 13:

> Sei allem Abschied voran, als wäre er hinter
> dir wie der *Winter*, der eben geht.
> Denn unter *Wintern* ist einer so endlos *Winter*,
> dass, *überwinternd*, dein Herz *über*haupt *über*steht.

> Anticipate all farewells, as were they behind you
> now, like the winter going past.
> For through some winter you feel such wintriness
> bind you,
> your then out-wintering heart will always outlast.

Another device is the use of cognate forms in the same line ("Sie sprechen nicht die Sprache nur des Jahres"), or, again, the word's active sense may be modulated passively and vice versa ("Wer sich als Quelle ergiesst, den erkennt die Erkennung"). Temporal succession is transformed into an associative present by substituting infinitive or participle for the verb form proper. The presentation of the object is generally in the vocative, for magic appellation is both statement as well as exclamation.[23] Demonstratives are frequently used to evoke this or that object, frequently italicized, for Rilke's experiments to make the word actually "convey" the object's essence are essentially dramatic.

The most important device employed to bring out his "felt" meaning is, of course, the metaphor. Critics speak of a "sound magic" (*Lautmagie*), sounds that evoke the objects they represent, a kind of object exorcism.[24] Through metaphorical paraphrase the object "horse," for example, is designated as "this pride of earth," the "unicorn" and "animal which is not," etc. In the cases of Keats and D. G. Rossetti, wrote Kassner, the "metaphors are like printed red Sundays or holidays in the calendar; with Rilke, however, everything is more or less printed red, with no longer any distance between word and image, word-space and image-space."[25] A kind of metaphorical primitivism may account for the apparent simplicity, grammatical and otherwise, of most of the *Sonnets*.[26] More and more in the later poetry words are used as signs, as sign language, often in Hölderlin's cosmic sense (*Sternbild*, "planet"; *Figur*, "configuration"). More and more the images become "points," "mathematical integers," "cosmic "configurations," much in the sense understood by modern *Gestalt* theories.[27] Indeed, Rilke's mature language eminently strives to create design, as if one had before one a nighttime diagram of the heavens with lines connecting the various constellations "as one connects up the features of a face, the stars of a planetary system, the points of a mathematical diagram." [28] Only in such a pattern, endorsed by Orpheus, can *Vollzähligkeit* or the totality of Forms be preserved, no longer seen in isolation but adapted to the requirements of a universal myth.

THE ORPHEUS SONNETS PROPER

Presupposing much that has gone before, the *Sonnets* reveal the interplay of old themes and motifs, transposed to a new key and adapted to other reaches of the spirit. Both sections form a cycle, with parallelisms Rilke himself wished noted.[29] One cannot, of course, set up a rigid formula, themal or chronological, to get at the core of such purpose. At best one may note certain loose groupings, as to position and theme, as Geering has done,[30] and propose a rough classification: (1) the Orpheus sonnets, strictly speaking; (2) sonnets incorporating poetic memories (mnemonic); (3) sonnets of a didactic, reflective nature.

Approximately a dozen poems deal with the orphic legend in the closer sense (all from Part I, except II, 26). Sonnets 1, 7, and 26 of Part I contain the main elements of the Orpheus theme which opens the series and, as the circle widens to include other motifs, gradually drops out, to appear one last time in Part II, Sonnet 26. The initial sonnet of Part I is interesting on many counts:

> Da stieg ein Baum. O reine Übersteigung!
> O Orpheus singt! O hoher Baum im Ohr!
> Und alles schwieg. Doch selbst in der Verschweigung
> ging neuer Anfang, Wink und Wandlung vor.
>
> Tiere aus Stille drangen aus dem klaren
> gelösten Wald von Lager und Genist;
> und da ergab sich, dass sie nicht aus List
> und nicht aus Angst in sich so leise waren,

sondern aus Hören. Brüllen, Schrei, Geröhr
schien klein in ihren Herzen. Und wo eben
kaum eine Hütte war, dies zu empfangen,

ein Unterschlupf aus dunkelstem Verlangen
mit einem Zugang, dessen Pfosten beben,—
da schufst du ihnen Tempel im Gehör.

A tree ascending there. O pure transcension!
O Orpheus sings! O tall tree in the ear!
All noise suspended, yet in that suspension
what new beginning, beckoning, change, appear!

Creatures of silence pressing through the clear
disintricated wood from lair and nest;
and neither cunning, it grew manifest,
had made them breathe so quietly, nor fear,

but only hearing. Roar, cry, bell they found
within their hearts too small. And where before
less than a hut had harbored what came thronging,

a refuge tunneled out of simplest longing
with lowly entrance through a quivering door,
you built them temples in their sense of sound.

This is pure myth-making: at the beginning of the world (or of the poet's art-consciousness) stands Orpheus, whose music instilled life into trees and stones, thus breaking down the rigid forms of nature, lending them new rhythms and dimensions. In the first half-verse we are presented with creation *in actu*. But why *tree*, we ask, and why its location in the *ear*? "Orpheus, the ideal poet," Leishman rightly explains, "does not merely sing *of* a tree or *about* a tree, he *sings a tree*, and, as he sings, by a 'pure transcension', the visible ascends into invisibility, while a temple (or shrine) to receive it rises in the ear."[31] True to "correspondence" theories of art and the blending of various sense perceptions, Rilke, here as frequently elsewhere, interchanges acoustic and visual sensory functions. Space and music, we have seen, are the concomitants of orphic song.

The tree-symbol, furthermore, like that of the rose, is an old property of his poetry, and it would be an interesting assignment to trace their respective evolutions from mere signs to metaphorical

images and symbols. Almost a quarter of a century before the inception of the *Sonnets* he had written, for *The Book of Images*, the
poem "Prelude" (*Eingang*):

> Mit seinen Augen, welche müde kaum
> von der verbrauchten Schwelle sich befrein,
> hebst du ganz langsam einen schwarzen Baum
> und stellst ihn vor den Himmel: schlank, allein . . .
> und hast die Welt gemacht. Und sie ist gross
> und wie ein Wort, das noch im Schweigen reift . . .

>> With your eyes, which wearily
>> scarce from the much-worn threshold free themselves,
>> you lift quite slowly a black tree
>> and place it against the sky: slender, alone.
>> And you have made the world. And it is large
>> and like a word that yet in silence ripens . . .

Here Rilke, the young poet, imbued with theories of the autonomy
of art, is looking at the object "tree" in a real landscape (Worpswede): the individual poet creates the world as an isolated event. In
the first sonnet, however, the individual has been absorbed into the
universal symbol of Orpheus. One may marvel at the exceptional
tenacity of Rilke's thought over so many years, for the conception
of the artist's autonomy is carried over from the earlier to the later
poem, without rift or break, down to the very elements of "silence"
and "house." What has changed, or better, what has been transformed, is the relation between sign and symbol, the literal and cosmic, a single idea and a general world-view. In the sonnet, music has
replaced language, so to speak; the solitary act (*allein*) now becomes
general participation (*und alles schwieg*). The tree is no longer par-
ticularized ("black"), rather it is cosmically defined as "high," in
keeping with the repeated emphasis on "mounting" in the preceding
lines (the fitting epithet for the object is therefore "light," "clear").
We are no longer among the Worpswede studios, but at the timeless
beginning of creation. The fleeting arbitrariness of the earlier perception, ending in disjunction, is in the Orpheus sonnet a never-
ending process: permanence in change. The "tree" becomes a fixed
symbol, contributing, as a modern critic puts it, to achieving ob-
liquity. ("When the symbol has been established, the mere naming

of it will present obliquely the whole body of associations it has collected. Moreover, by repetition, you mitigate the dangers of overextensiveness; for every fresh context limits *some* of the possible vagaries to which the isolated symbol might lead.")[32] In further comparing the earlier with the later poem we detect a slight shifting of accent, best observed through the texture of Rilke's language. The soft, pastel qualities of the earlier poem's vowels, indiscriminately placed, give way to hardness and precision. As Rilke's mastery of idiom grows, there occurs a subtle vocalic arrangement, generally around the principle of antithesis, a grouping of dark and light, closed and open sounds. Compare strophe two of the first sonnet, for example, with its repeated *a* vowels, with strophe one dominated by *ei* and *ie*, and both series with the salient *u*'s and *o*'s of the two tercets. Rilke is a master in the manipulation of subtle verbal elements, with prefixal variants unknown or rarely used before in the German language. Finally, in the *Sonnets* particularly, the use of paradox, antithesis, underplayed irony, and ambiguity support admirably the condensation of the meaning. Thus in the last strophe the antithesis is sharply drawn between the fragility of the bestial lair and the marble temples created by the god of song.

The functions of Orpheus in relation to the poet's world are expressed in the key sonnet, I, 7. Orpheus is the poet's surrogate, alone able to cross the threshold and, by virtue of his adherence to both realms, praise the evidences of earth before the "soundless dead" (cf. the Fifth Elegy):

> Rühmen, das ists! Ein zum Rühmen Bestellter,
> ging er hervor wie das Erz aus des Steins
> Schweigen. Sein Herz, o vergängliche Kelter
> eines den Menschen unendlichen Weins.
>
> Nie versagt ihm die Stimme am Staube,
> wenn ihn das göttliche Beispiel ergreift.
> Alles wird Weinberg, alles wird Traube,
> in seinem fühlendem Süden gereift.
>
> Nicht in den Grüften der Könige Moder
> straft ihn die Rühmung Lügen, oder
> dass von den Göttern ein Schatten fällt.

> Er ist einer der bleibenden Boten,
> der noch weit in die Türen der Toten
> Schalen mit rühmlichen Früchten hält.

> Praising, that's it! As a praiser and blesser
> he came like the ore from the taciturn mine.
> Came with his heart, oh, transient presser,
> for men, of a never-exhaustible wine.

> Voice never fails him for things lacking lustre,
> sacred example will open his mouth.
> All becomes vineyard, all becomes cluster,
> warmed by his sympathy's ripening south.

> Crypts and the mouldering kings who lie there
> do not belie his praising, neither
> doubt, when a shadow obscures our days.

> He is a messenger, always attendant,
> reaching far through their gates resplendent
> dishes of fruit for the dead to praise.

Actually the poet identifies himself with his symbol and they become one. First of all, the creative process operates within the paradox of silence and song, perishable and imperishable. Again, it is visualized as landscape, the warm vineyards of the south, for whose infinite wine the poet's heart is the perishable winepress. The effect of the first tercet is enhanced not only by the vocalic change from the two quatrains but by the enjambment in verse ten, pivoting on the insignificant conjunction "or" (*oder*).

Praise is only one function of Orpheus' song; the chord of lamentation is its complement. Sonnet I, 8 is therefore related to the Tenth Elegy, where lamentation is more or less personified and acted out. The personification is continued in the sonnet: Sorrow, the youngest sister of Rejoicing (who *knows*) and Longing (who *confesses*)— Sorrow still young enough to learn from grief-stricken nights and yet, in abrupt reversal and by virtue of that very experience, able to represent the human status among the constellations.

Sonnet I, 6 further defines the orphic double-nature with the aid of nature symbols. In the second quartet Rilke draws most effectively on old anthropological lore, folk customs, and superstitions hardly extinct today with regard to the spirits of the dead:

Geht ihr zu Bette, so lasst auf dem Tische
Brot nicht und Milch nicht; die Toten ziehts—.
Aber er, der Beschwörende, mische
unter der Milde des Augenlids

ihre Erscheinung in alles Geschaute;
und der Zauber von Erdrauch und Raute
sei ihm so wahr wie der klarste Bezug . . .

> Going to bed, never leave on the table
> bread or milk, forcing the dead to rise.
> He shall invoke them, he who is able
> to mingle in mildness of closing eyes
>
> their appearance with all that we view;
> he for whom magic of earth-smoke and rue
> shall be clear as the clearest link between things . . .

To the crudity of superstition Rilke opposes the gentle knowledge and memory of the dead in all our actions. Only he who has eaten poppies with the dead (I, 9) can register the full scale of orphic praise. Sonnet I, 3 contrasts the divine art of the god with human inadequacy resulting from man's split nature. The great phrase *Gesang ist Dasein* ("Song is being") offsets our non-Being, our unrelatedness to earth and stars. After the antithesis (*aufsangst-verrinnt*) the *real* definition of poetry, its stability and inevitableness, concludes the final tercet:

In Wahrheit singen ist ein andrer Hauch.
Ein Hauch um Nichts. Ein Wehn im Gott. Ein Wind.

> Far other is the breath of real singing.
> An aimless breath. A stirring in the god. A breeze.

Antithesis in the form of paradox results from the contrast between unreal sound and real silence (real in the orphic sense) as the basis for authentic poetry. The foregoing poem, again, leads logically to Sonnet I, 4, introducing the theme of the lovers, to whom are applied the orphic attributes (*O ihr Seligen, o ihr Heilen*). The dancing tone derives from the incantatory effect of the rhythm, remarkable in view of the fact that the accent falls upon such weighty words as "suffering" and "heaviness."

195

THE RING OF FORMS

MEMORIES

With the basic orphic myth once established, some twenty-eight sonnets incorporating poetic memories explore the variegated materials of Rilke's art-world and are revealing on several counts. These roses, mirrors, dancings, and breathings: what are they but their counterparts in *New Poems*, one step transformed from intended objectivity into the "closed circle of legends" (*geschlossener Sagenkreis*, I, 20)? And what could be more revealing of the quality of his work than the mnemonic faculty, which preserved over the years the highly specialized instances of his experience? Here is symbolism as understood by Mallarmé and Valéry, yet where these two often produce only complex abstractions, with Rilke we are still within the human, perhaps all-too-human realm. Indeed, the greatness of his best poetry lies in the fact that each isolated subject or theme, while seemingly bearing only aesthetic implications, exposes a highly sensitive nerve of modern living.

The tone of the "mnemonic" sonnets also differs from that of the orphic group proper. Rilke is not here proclaiming the decalogue of his myth but reverently and affectionately recalling the little events or occasions, all related in some way to the collection's key symbol (memories of an antique sarcophagus, I, 10; a dog, I, 16; the Russian horse, I, 20; the unicorn, II, 4; and the flowers "whom we lend fate from the borders of fate," II, 14). On the other hand, the approach to these poems is in some ways more difficult than in the case of those of the other two groups since they rely less on mythical or didactic aids. For some of them Rilke even appended brief notes as a guide to the reader, and on others there are helpful comments in the correspondence of these years.

The embodied memories lead to a new kind of *Dinglichkeit*, distinct from that of the Paris poems and centering more and more upon intangible states of feeling that transcend concrete terms of expression. A good illustration is Sonnet I, 13:

> Voller Apfel, Birne und Banane,
> Stachelbeere . . . Alles dieses spricht
> Tod und Leben in den Mund. Ich ahne . . .
> Lest es einem Kind vom Angesicht,

Wenn es sie erschmeckt. Dies kommt von weit.
Wird euch langsam namenlos im Munde?
Wo sonst Worte waren, fliessen Funde,
aus dem Fruchtfleisch überrascht befreit.

Wagt zu sagen, was ihr Apfel nennt.
Diese Süsse, die sich erst verdichtet,
um, im Schmecken leise aufgerichtet,

klar zu werden, wach und transparent,
doppeldeutig, sonnig, erdig, hiesig—:
O Erfahrung, Fühlung, Freude—, riesig!

> Banana, rounded apple, russet pear,
> gooseberry . . . does not all this convey
> life and death into your mouth? It's there! . . .
> Read it on a child's face any day,
>
> when it tastes them. What infinity!
> Can't you feel inside your mouth a growing
> mysteriousness, and, where words were, a flowing
> of suddenly released discovery?
>
> Dare to say what "apple" has implied!
> Sweetness, concentrated, self-repressing,
> slowly yielding to the tongue's caressing,
>
> growing awake, transparent, clarified,
> double-meaning'd, sunshine-full, terrestrial:—
> O experience, feeling, joy,—celestial!

Here, as in the companion poem (I, 15), olfactory sensations are to convey the duality of experience (verses two and three provide a bridge to the orphic idea). Poems like this betray in some way how much a product of the early century, the age of Mach and sensationalist metaphysics, Rilke really was. He goes much further than a refined naturalism, of course; he is not describing the experience, for words are allegedly inadequate (verses five to seven of the second quatrain). Instead, the object creates its own language (not *words* but *discoveries*) in the reaction of the tastebuds to the sweet apple juice. With different technical means Hopkins before him had audaciously identified a sudden illumination with the effect of a sloe bursting in the mouth:

197

> How a lush-kept, plush-capped sloe
> will, mouthed to flesh-burst,
> gush-flush the man, the being with it, sour or sweet,
> brim, in a flash, full!

What a critic has said of Hopkins, in fact, applies to many of Rilke's sonnets and other poems, in that his "words and phrases are actions as well as sounds, ideas and images, and must be read with the body as well as the eye." [33] For a better understanding of the "fruit" sonnet the reader is referred to the correspondence of the following year, where Rilke records the "indescribable penetratingness" of the scent of citrons kept in a glass bowl in his room. Despite their astringent bitterness to the taste, he went on to say, their scent gave him a sensation of "space and openness" which "the fortunate fruit absorbed into its growth by day and night." [34] More importantly, the passage not only explicitly connects the fruit with the life-and-death Orpheus reference but retraces his whole poetic development back to the Paris "lace" poem.

The presentation of this physical impact in an olfactory-visual climax is finely rendered in the closing tercet, where the resulting taste of the fruit is conveyed in three qualifying sequences: first a transference into psychological terms with open *a* vowels (*klar, wach, transparent*), particularly emphasizing the diaphanous in the final loan word. This set of epithets is then subsumed in another order, dealing with aspects of the orphic myth (*doppeldeutig, erdig, hiesig*), where the emotional relatedness of physical sensations to cosmic purposes is well indicated in the ascending vowel scale. The poem's meaning *is* the equating of the taste of a fruit with those elements, usually dropped from consciousness, which are necessary to fuller human stature: sunlit earthiness, now-ness, and the dual partnership of life and death, And, finally, a third series of analogues, ending on the high-pitched rhyme *riesig*, picks up the other two, like the lower basin in Rilke's "Roman Fountain," and gives a substantival summary (*Erfahrung, Fühlung, Freude*).

The *Sonnets* so far discussed have conformed to a more or less recognizable pattern. Others (the mirror, II, 3; breathing, II, 1; dancer, II, 18) are not only more intricate and subtle in meaning but more complex in rhythmic structure. Not infrequently sonnet-form and rhyme are engulfed in irregular verse-lines, and we are more aware of internal than external rhyme:

> Atmen, du unsichtbares Gedicht!
> Immerfort um das eigne
> Sein rein eingetauschter Weltraum. . . .

> Breathing, invisible poem! That great
> world-space, at each inhalation
> exchanged for this human existence. . . .

The efficacy of the "dancer" sonnet, II, 18—group-related to I, 15—derives from a complex of factors: repetitions, broken rhythms, multiple meanings, and image transfers:

> Tänzerin: o du Verlegung
> alles Vergehens in Gang: wie brachtest du's dar.
> Und der Wirbel am Schluss, dieser Baum aus Bewegung,
> nahm er nicht ganz in Besitz das erschwungene Jahr?

> Blühte nicht, dass ihn dein Schwingen von vorhin umschwärme,
> plötzlich sein Wipfel von Stille. Und über ihr,
> war sie nicht Sonne, war sie nicht Sommer, die Wärme,
> diese unzählige Wärme aus dir? . . .

> Dancer: you transmutation
> of all going-by into going: what you have wrought!
> And your finishing whirl, that tree of mere animation,
> how it took over the year you had flyingly caught!

> Did not its crown, that your swaying might settle
> to swarming,
> suddenly blossom with stillness? And above that, too,
> was there not sunnily, was there not summerly warming
> all the warmth that exhaled from you? . . .

The protoform of this "tree of motion" can be traced back to the "Spanish Dancer" of *New Poems*. Here the motion is "transmuted" through various figures into the perfected art at the tree's summit, indicated by the orphic attributes "silence," "sun," "summer," "warmth."

The underlying tension in Rilke's poetry is that found between art and life, permanence and change, the formed and formless, *Lorbeer* and *Schicksal*. His problem is essentially of a linguistic rather than metaphysical nature, to be solved by the transformation of the idea through language into what has been called "absolute art," a kind of "miracle of transubstantiation" effected by the language process itself.[35] To round out the implications of the "dancer" sonnet one might compare it with Schiller's poem "The Dance" (*Der Tanz*), in classical hexameters, or with Keats's "Ode on a Grecian Urn" and Mörike's "To a Lamp." Art as a means of perpetuating what would otherwise be lost in the transient flux is the underlying premise of Keats's lines, "O happy, happy boughs! That cannot shed/your leaves, nor ever bid the spring adieu." There are moral implications in Keats's ode (as there are in Schiller's poem), such as the identification of truth with beauty, while Mörike's poem concludes that beauty is an end in itself. But Rilke, as we have seen, began his career by defining beauty as "something always added, we do not know just what," and toward the end placing it within the purlieus of the terrible. What he conceived as "pure lastingness" (*Das reine Dauern*) is quite different from Keats's attempt to "freeze," so to speak, his pipes and timbrels, the wild ecstasies and ditties of no tone, into a "cold pastoral." His orphic music is the very element calculated to activate rigid space. The dynamism of his sonnet is at the opposite pole to the static quiescence of Keats's poem. Where Keats merely describes the dancing figures on his urn in terms suitable to the "silent form" and "cold pastoral," Rilke fuses both dancer and dance, at once the transient motion and the permanent form. The dance grows actually, step by step, out of the functions of language, as in the two tercets:

> Aber er trug auch, er trug, dein Baum der Ekstase.
> Sind sie nicht seine ruhigen Früchte: der Krug,
> reifend gestreift, und die gereiftere Vase?
>
> Und in den Bildern: ist nicht die Zeichnung geblieben,
> die deiner Braue dunkler Zug
> rasch an die Wandung der eigenen Wendung geschrieben?
>
> Nay, it was able, your tree of rapture, to bear.

Are they not, all its fruits that so peacefully
  shine,
jug streaked with ripeness, vase further ripened, still there?

And does not your mark in their paintings
  still meet the discerning—
that of your eyebrows' darker line
swiftly inscribed on the wall of your own
  swift turning?

Rilke perpetuates the movement of the "finishing whirl" by project-
ing the dancer—a very bold leap—into art-forms (vase, jug). The
image seems borrowed from Valéry ("Asile, asile, o mon asile, o
Tourbillon!"), as indeed the entire sonnet is a glowing tribute to the
author of *L'Âme et la Danse*.[36] The projected dancer, in turn, is ret-
roactively credited with having sprung directly from the dance-tree
without either human or mechanical mediation. Nor is the movement
quiescent even here, not even in the ultimate strophe, for both dancer
and vase are ultimately caught up in the unceasing transformations
of language, the complex Rilkean terminology of sovereign syntactical constructions and metaphoric meanings (*reifend-gereiftere*;
Wandung-Wendung). The result is as close an approximation to
"l'acte pur des metamorphoses," which Valéry's Socrates professed
to see in Athikté's dance, as is admissible within the limitations of
the poetic word: "On ne doit voir son corps qu'en mouvement."[37]
And yet even a cursory review of the poem will show that its basic
materials are the old words, the accustomed images: tree, fruits,
vase, pictures, only now transformed and condensed into a thing of
great complexity.

ORPHIC WISDOM: TRANSFORMATION

German literature has always been rich in rhymed wisdom or
Spruchdichtung, from Walter and Hans Sachs down through Goethe
and Schiller to the present day. The third group of Rilke's sonnets
might be likened to such reflective, often didactic poetry, were there
not danger that such terms might be misunderstood. These sonnets of
Rilkean wisdom count among his best, which could hardly be the
case were his didacticism conspicuous or the ethical content strained.

THE RING OF FORMS

Here, too, the fundamental perception of experience is the same as
in all the mature poetry, the reflective poems merely adding what the
Elegies and *Sonnets* only provide indirectly and by implication:
direct reflection of the poem on the immediate exigencies of our
world. In what strains does the orphic lyre conjure up the problems
of a machine age, the metaphysical problems of time and eternity, of
God and the possibilities of regeneration?

In all of Rilke's poetry the time factor (time and change that are
to be transcended in the timeless permanent) is ever present, and
particularly in this sonnet group. Time enters into the unfolding of
the machine motif at least half a dozen times, into the conception of
historico-cultural evolution (Karnak, II, 22), those "splendid ex-
cesses of our own existence," as well as into our modes of belief: the
genetic evolution of man, who creates his own gods that fate peev-
ishly destroys, is a nonetheless hopeful projection since eternity still
lies before him ("What aeons attend us," II, 24). A long though
familiar bridge is thus thrown from the time-anxiety of *The Book
of Hours* ("You bent me slowly out of time") to the timeless orphic
realm of spatial fullness (Sonnet II, 27):

Gibt es wirklich die Zeit, die zerstörende?
Wann, auf dem ruhenden Berg, zerbricht sie die Burg?
Dieses Herz, das unendlich den Göttern gehörende,
Wann vergewaltigts der Demiurg?

Sind wir wirklich so ängstlich Zerbrechliche,
wie das Schicksal uns wahr machen will?
Ist die Kindheit, die tiefe, versprechliche,
in den Wurzeln—später—still?

Ach, das Gespenst des Vergänglichen,
durch den arglos Empfänglichen
geht es, als wär es ein Rauch.

Als die, die wir sind, als die Treibenden,
gelten wir doch bei bleibenden
Kräften als göttlicher Brauch.

Does it exist, though, Time the destroyer?
When will it scatter the tower on the resting hill?
This heart, the eternal gods' eternal enjoyer,
when shall the demiurge ravish and spill?

Are we really such tremblingly breakable
things as Destiny tries to pretend?
Does childhood's promise, deep, unmistakable,
down in the roots, then, later, end?

Ah, Mutability's spectre!
out through the simple accepter
you, like a vapour, recede.

We, though we wax but for waning,
fill none the less for remaining
powers a celestial need.

The two quartets contain five interrogations which hardly leave the slightest doubt of the answer, even if the reader had not the conclusion of the poem before him. His response will be primarily determined by the rhythm. Since the agents here are *qualities*, not *persons*, the participial substantives used throughout, generally in enjambment, convey to the thought a lingering emphasis. The broken syntax further slows down the pace of the lines to suggest questioning. The retardation at line eight is magnified through the use of dashes, aided by clear intervocalic leaps (u–$\ddot{a}$–i). The twofold repetition in the first verse of each section of the word "really" (*wirklich*)— and what Rilke-Orpheus meant by that—is another ingredient in deciding the tone of the response. And, finally, the abrupt change of rhythm in the tercets comes with a bang as they hurry to the finish, not in interrogations but two apodictic statements.

Some half-dozen sonnets deal directly with the role of the machine in our age, in the context of fretful, aimless motion versus contained repose. The implications of technology were not so foreign to Rilke as one might expect and, in a way, he prepares for Auden with his technical vocabulary of planes, tennis courts, and motorboats. Rilke's attitude toward the machine is moderate and sensible: technology has its function in life as means but not end, as servant but not master (I, 18, 23; II, 10). Sonnet I, 18 contains wry humor and irony—*Zwar ist kein Hören heil* ("To be sure, no hearing is spared/in this confusion")—but *Hören heil*, "spared hearing," is precisely the requirement of the orphic *Innenraum*. It is not surprising, incidentally, that many sonnets deal negatively with the acoustic unpleasant-

nesses of a mechanistic age: the "droning and drumming" of machines, "heavier-growing hammers," even the "splintering wedge of
screaming" of children as opposed to "the bird's clear cry." The
previous figure of mechanistic confusion is ironically played off
against an allusion to the "new" Message of the Wise Men in the
opening lines. The spiritual impasse to which the machine has
brought us is handled in I, 24: we have lost "those primeval friends
of ours, the unfated,/ever unsuing gods"; instead,

Nur noch in Dampfkesseln brennen
die einstigen Feuer und heben die Hämmer, die immer
grössern. Wir aber nehmen an Kraft ab, wie Schwimmer.

In boilers only are burning
the former fires and heaving the heavier-growing
hammers. But we are like swimmers whose strength is going.

In Sonnet I, 23 appears the airplane motif. Speed for its own sake
is set against recognition of a "pure goal" (*reines Wohin*), the successful gadget against the quiet depths of heaven, boyish pride
against accomplished Be-ing (*Dasein*). The uncertainty of the man-
made contraption is revealed in the hovering length of a single conditional sentence of eight lines, and is emphatically dispelled in the last
tercet with its conspicuous end-word *sein* ("be"). In another flight-
sonnet (I, 22), more generally related to the orphic idea, the device
employed to bring out the meaning is again contrast. The antitheses
are openly exposed, each quartet with its pair of opposites, each
tercet balanced against the other, the final one resting solidly on four
noun-symbols of contrasted yet reconciled moments of existence:

Alles ist ausgeruht:
Dunkel und Helligkeit,
Blume und Buch.

Look
how rested all things are:
shadow and fall of light,
blossom and book.

As an appendage to the attack on misapplied technology Rilke
weaves in an old concern (II, 19), a commentary on the money-basis
of our civilization where the gold resting "somewhere at ease in the

pampering bank" is characteristically offset by the figure of the beggar with the "perpetually open hand," a figure reaching back to *The Book of Hours* and other Paris poetry. How sensitively aware he was of the philosophical implications of a scientific age is conveyed through metaphors like "antennae feeling for antennae," "purest tension," "harmony of forces," "configurations." In his last years, when speaking of his own work and the effect of others' work on him, he was fond of using the mathematical-physical term *Schwingungszahl* ("inner vibration-count") as an index of a "true relation" (*wirklichem Bezug*), in the orphic sense.[38]

Escape from Time, the destroyer, is possible through transformation in Orpheus, and some of the finest sonnets are concerned with this theme, none so profoundly as the final ones of Part II, comprising a small cycle of their own. Sonnet 12 urges us to be prepared for transformation, a flame altering all things that slip from our grasp. The theme terminates in a mythological figure, as often in the *Elegies*: Daphne in laurel can only desire that her lover transform himself into the wind that blows through her leaves. Two sonnets (II, 17, 21) describe the inner landscape of transformation—the summer dream-world with continuously watered gardens, as clear as if "poured into glass." The opening note of the first is one of epic rapture: "Sing those gardens, my heart . . . gardens you have not known, transparent, untrampled." These gardens of oriental profusion have symbolical reality for those who, with Orpheus, have advanced into the other dimension of experience (hence "those you do not know," "unattainable," "unexampled").

Sonnet I, 21 is accompanied with one of the rare notes Rilke appended to the collection: "The little spring-song seems to me, as it were, the 'interpretation' of a singularly dancing music I once heard sung by the convent children at a morning service in the little conventual Church at Ronda (in the South of Spain). The children, always in dance measure, sang a text I did not know to triangle and tambourine":

> Frühling ist wiedergekommen. Die Erde
> ist wie ein Kind, das Gedichte weiss;

> viele, o viele . . . Für die Beschwerde
> langen Lernens bekommt sie den Preis . . .

> > Spring has come again. Earth's a-bubble
> > with all those poems she knows by heart,—
> > oh, so many . . . with prize for the trouble
> > of such long learning, her holidays start . . .

The importance Rilke attached to childhood throughout his life and work needs no special emphasis when we recall the *Notebooks*. Malte's tragedy was the failure to utilize this childhood by reconciling it with the orphic double nature of life and death where winter is balanced with spring, age with youth, heaviness with lightness, school-learning with singing. For life, despite Destiny, is "overflowing" (*Überschüsse*) and "glorious abundance" (*die herrlichen Überflüsse*), arranged and ordered through music (II, 22). To carry through the idea of spring in the sonnet, the earth is compared to a child eager to recite poems learned by heart under the strict tutelage of winter. The situation is then transposed to another level by combining the two ideas of arduous grammatical application and charging winter sap in the bold verbal-play of "roots" and "stems." Tone and attitude may recall, for some, Faust's Easter Sunday apostrophe to spring:

> > Vom Eise befreit sind Strom und Bäche
> > durch des Frühlings holden, belebenden Blick . . .

and, for others, echoes of the rose-garden in Eliot's *Burnt Norton*:

> > Quick, said the bird, find them, find them,
> > Round the corner. . . .

and the finale of *Little Gidding*:

> > Quick now, here, now, always—
> > A condition of complete simplicity
> > (Costing not less than everything) . . .

The last four words of the sonnet ("she sings, she sings!") pull the individual poem into the range of symbolical meaning of the entire sequence and of the "singing god" at its beginning, as Rilke's appended note went on to add.

Sonnet II, 13, as well as its predecessor, is concerned with the transformation theme proper. It must be included in any final analysis of the group, since Rilke referred to it specifically as "the most valid" of all. "It contains all the rest and expresses *that* which, although it's at the same time far beyond my reach, might one day be considered my purest and ultimate accomplishment, in the midst of life."[39] It has its further interest for English readers in view of Yeats's famous epitaph "Rocky Face," originally written in a copy of Rilke's late poems and conceived in a moment of rage against his warmer ideas of death: "Draw rein; draw breath./Cast a cold eye/on life, on death./Horseman, pass by."[40]

> Sei allem Abschied voran, als wäre er hinter
> dir, wie der Winter, der eben geht.
> Denn unter Wintern ist einer so endlos Winter,
> dass, überwinternd, dein Herz überhaupt über-
> steht.
>
> Sei immer tot in Eurydike—, singender steige,
> preisender steige zurück in den reinen Bezug.
> Hier, unter Schwindenden, sei, im Reiche der
> Neige,
> sei ein klingendes Glas, das sich im Klang schon
> zerschlug.
>
> Sei—und wisse zugleich des Nicht-Seins Beding-
> ung,
> den unendlichen Grund deiner innigen Schwing-
> ung,
> dass du sie völlig vollziehst dieses einzige Mal.
>
> Zu dem gebrauchten sowohl, wie zum dumpfen
> und stummen
> Vorrat der vollen Natur, den unsäglichen Summ-
> en,
> zähle dich jubelnd hinzu und vernichte die Zahl.

> > Anticipate all farewells, as were they be-
> > hind you
> > now, like the winter going past.
> > For through some winter you feel such
> > wintriness bind you,
> > your then out-wintering heart will al-
> > ways outlast.

      Dead ever more in Eurydice, mount with
        more singing,
      mount to relation more pure with more
        celebrant tongue.
      Here, in this realm of the dwindlers and
        dregs, be a ringing
      glass, which has, even though shivered
        to pieces, been rung.

      Be—and, perceiving in that which is
        being's negation
      merely the infinite ground of your fervent
        vibration,
      beat, through this never-again, to the ful-
        lest amount.

      To the stock of used-up, as well as of
        dumb and decaying
      things within copious Nature, those sums
        beyond saying,
      count yourself joyfully in and destroy the
        account.

The roots of this sonnet extend downward through the years to the poem "Orpheus. Eurydice. Hermes" of 1914. The earlier poem presupposes the orthodox legend and describes how Eurydice, committed to the death-realm with its wider vistas, does not wish to return to life. The role of Orpheus is a complete reversal of his function in the *Sonnets*:

      Voran der schlanke Mann im blauen Mantel,
      der stumm und ungeduldig vor sich aussah.
      Ohne zu kauen frass sein Schritt den Weg
      in grossen Bissen; seine Hände hingen
      schwer und verschlossen aus dem Fall der Falten
      und wussten nicht mehr von der leichten Leier,
      die in die Linke eingewachsen war
      wie Rosenranken in den Ast des Ölbaums.
      Und seine Sinne waren wie entzweit:
      indes der Blick ihm wie ein Hund vorauslief,
      umkehrte, kam und immer wieder weit
      und wartend an der nächsten Wendung stand,—
      blieb sein Gehör wie ein Geruch zurück . . .

The slender husband first, in his blue mantle,
gazing in dumb impatience straight before him.
His steps devoured the way in mighty chunks
they did not pause to chew; his hands were hanging,
heavy and clenched, out of the falling folds,
no longer conscious of the lightsome lyre,
the lyre which had grown into his left
like twines of rose into a branch of olive.
It seemed as though his senses were divided:
for, while his sight ran like a dog before him,
turned round, came back, and stood, time and again,
distant and waiting, at the path's next turn,
his hearing lagged behind him like a smell . . .

His attributes are a complete negation of all the later "singing god" is supposed to symbolize: mute and impatient, bifurcated thought, hearing lagging like an odor; and could any antithesis be more apt than the designation of his hands as "heavy and clenched, out of the falling folds"? It is rather Hermes in the earlier poem, "the god of faring and of distant message," who resembles most the Orpheus of the *Sonnets.*

Let us return to the sonnet, which is didactic and contains at least six categorical commands to the reader (again it is difficult to avoid reading between the lines evidence of the Christian paradox that "he who loses his life shall gain it"). The full scope of the transformation process is contained in the first verse. Its stoic implications in verses two to five could only have been written by one who had transcended immense suffering: to anticipate departure (to say "death" would be an oversimplification) is to be ever ready for transformation into new forms. Whatever ultimate moment of experience this may mean, we are to look forward to it as we look backward at the winter "almost gone." Here is added a memory of one winter, the cruelest of all (perhaps a biographical hint of the "critical years"). The period of drought is expressed in the grammar and word structure of verses four and five (the threefold repetition of *winter* and *über* in various combinations, among which the light word *Herz* is caught as in a vise). In the second quatrain we move from the human to the mythical plane in the second command to be "ever dead in

Eurydice." The poet-god may overcome love that has vanished into the shades by converting it into a different direction, into art. The conquest of loss restores man or the artist to the "pure relationship" which encloses that more adequate and inviolable world we create in ourselves. Verses seven and eight of the second quatrain express the thought that this world is a declining one (a touch of the "cosmic irony" of the twenties) and our realization and full acceptance of this fact is the highest accomplishment, like the fragile beauty of clinking glass even as it breaks. Our submission to this twofold act of "being" and, at the same time, of non-being, of life and of death, raises us above ourselves, completing for once the vibratory spiral of life. By taking count of our inmost "vibrations" we overcome time and destiny, and complete the circle of fullness. To all the countless sums of nature (those already used or those still mute or undiscovered) we are to add ourselves rejoicingly, destroying the arithmetic of Destiny and completing the full Ring of Forms.

For the *Sonnets* as a whole holds true what Rilke considered as his special contribution to "the tradition." [41] An important letter of March 1923 defines what he meant by this term: "not the superficial-conventional" but the "real derivation" from the past ("if not outside us where it more and more disappears every day, at least within us"). The *Sonnets* grew out of "the impetus to contribute to its [tradition's] fulfillment something of my own, something relatively precise." [42] They link up, on one hand, with the transformation theme of the *Elegies*, and on the other, set up monuments to the past, of rather narrow range but extreme magnetic compulsion. These flowers, statues, gardens, and unicorns are salvaged instances of the Western tradition, symbolical rather than representative, no longer seen as isolated things but fitted into a pattern whose inner dynamics are controlled by the singing god.

o͞8 Conclusion

R<small>ILKE</small> continued to write, from the abundant February days of 1922 until his death in 1926, an impressive number of poems, both in French and German, in many ways an afterharvest of the *Elegies* and *Sonnets*. Not only does this poetry reflect back on previous levels of perception and feeling, setting the earlier work in clearer focus, but it more particularly attempts to bring to a reposeful conclusion the tensions and strains that electrified the Duino atmosphere. Whether this attempt was really successful is another question. At any rate, the last poems do not revert to the simple, spontaneous patterns of the early verse nor do they point, as some have held, in a new direction of creative development.[1] The constant circling about among old themes and subjects, even though modulated in a different key, tends to become monotonous; the rhythms seem those of a tired and ill man, dying notes in a great orchestral arrangement extending through a lifetime.

LANGUE PRÊTÉE: CORNUCOPIA

The French poems (*Poèmes Français*)—they include "Vergers," "Les Roses," "Les Fenêtres," "Carnet de Poche," and "Poèmes Épars"—were avowedly a gesture of acknowledgment to the French-Swiss canton of Valais for the friendly hospitality that enabled Rilke to finish the great work of his career. They also represent a kind of feeler or attempt to strengthen his ties with the west which had been

211

severed by the war. Like Nietzsche before him, Rilke came more and more in the end to identify himself with the warm, pagan south, the Latin *Méditerrané*. Over much of the final poetry weaves the spell of Zarathustra's noonday hour and *ce trop de clarté* of Valéry's *Cimetière Marin*, which casts a magic light over the ribbon roads and sloping vineyards basking in the midday heat.

In *The Book of Hours* he had objected to the Renaissance as the mere springtime of God and not His rightful summering. If one were to associate Rilke's own poetry symbolically with the seasons— seasons that radiate so vitally and intricately into the manipulation of language and theme—it would probably be with the fall or winter. But much of the late poetry stands under the full sign of summer in all its ripeness. Here are no unattainable angels or constructed threshold gods, or rather these former symbols seem transmuted into the present moment, harmonized with earth and man. The same roses, angels, fountains, and trees are transplanted from their previous settings of existential strain and anxiety to the warm, peaceful certainties of the Latin south. And, as with most of the French poems, Rilke usually begins directly with invocation:

> Pays, arrêtè à mi-chemin
> entre la terre et les cieux,
> au voix d'eau et d'airain,
> doux et dur, jeune et vieux . . .
> (*Quatrains Valaisans*, II)

The usual paradoxes are conspicuous but mellowed in tone, while Orpheus is fitted into his proper landscape between an existent earth and sky, the earth of the old gods, of the matriarchal reign and the prelapsarian Garden: "C'est la terre contente de son image/et qui consent à son premier jour."

Many old motifs are reworked (fountains, dolls, roses, springs, windows, etc.), with occasional variations on the pure "thing" poem that recall Rilke's and Baudelaire's Paris: "Fragment d'Ivoire," "L'Orphelin," "Hiver," "Ossuaire." Now and then we catch echoes of Mallarmé and Valéry ("Sanglot, sanglot, pur sanglot," which has its German equivalent of these years in "Tränenkrüglein"), or find the poet's epitaph at Raron reworked in "Cimetière" from "Carnet de Poche." Old concerns are repeated, like the animal-consciousness theme of the Seventh Elegy: "broute une présence/qui n'a pas le goût d'ailleurs." The "angel" of the French poems is calm and benevolent, more like the earlier angel figures than the stern Duino symbol. It retains the ambivalence of its predecessors, the paradoxical *présence absente* of the silent pagan deities of the landscape, yet its strict urgency has yielded to a kind of good-neighborliness, with just a suggestion of the orphic mission of the *Sonnets*: "Les Anges, sont-ils devenus discrets!/Le mien à peine m'interroge." The lamented days of Tobias seem actually to have returned in the season of fullness and cheer: "Reste tranquille, si soudain/l'Ange à ta table se décide." Yet the mellow prescience of death is suggested in many passages, like the recall of the Eurydice theme—"Toutes mes adieux sont faits. Tant de départs/m'ont lentement formé dès mon enfance"—and the poignant "Car tu sais, je m'en vais."

Rilke's poetry in the *langue prêtée* has only technical interest in the framework of his poetry at large and does not alter the main orientations of his achievement. At the same time, to call it the product of "off hours" hardly does justice to its delicacy and grace, a sense of profile and repose rarely realized elsewhere. But the French poetry served a much more important purpose by providing an opportunity to make further experimentations with poetic language in a foreign tongue. Rilke's unceasing interest in the capacities of words, their subtle meanings and nuances, found here a welcome field for exploration. Poems written in both French and German on identical subjects, and at roughly the same time, invite careful comparison ("Handinneres" and "Palme"; "Das Füllhorn" and "Corne d'Abondance," as well as the differing versions of "Eros" and "The Magician"). Comparing the German *Elegies* with the French *Vergers*, André Gide wrote the author that the latter possessed "une qualité un peu différente, et plus rare peut-être, plus délicate, plus subtile." [2] Rilke's reply leaves no doubt of his knowledge of the exact angle of this difference: "Cela ressemblait si peu au travail et cela en comportait cependant toutes les découvertes." [3] Writing in French was a further step in Rilke's constant effort to enlarge the potentialities of poetic expression.

These so-called "discoveries" are not to be found among new ideas, new approaches, or new themes but lie in the realm of language. The German "Cornucopia" (*Das Füllhorn*), whose first verse may be taken as symbolic of Rilke's poetic universe ("Schwung und Form des gebendsten Gefässes"), ends in the following quatrain, referring to the Goddess of Abundance:

> Nein, sie steht in Überlebensgrösse
> hoch, mit ihrem Horn voll Übermass.
> Nur das Wasser unten geht, als flösse
> es ihr Geben in Gewächs und Gras.

> Nay, she stands there larger than living,
> high with her horn that overflows.
> Only below the water goes
> and turns to growth and green her giving.

The theme of the French "Corne d'Abondance" picks up this vital excess too great for our hearts but introduces, at the same time, a different set of images and references and, consequently, a new range of emotional experience:

> O corne trop vaste, quel
> miracle par vous se donne!
> O cor de chasse, qui sonne
> des choses, au souffle du ciel!

The German "The Magician," to be discussed later, and the French "Le Magicien" lead, when compared, to similar "discoveries."

Many of the last German poems likewise interweave with the tone of the French verse in reducing inner conflict to a conciliatory attitude toward experience. A note of Goethean clarity and festive mood is sometimes heard (though these qualities are by no means identical) and thus serves to prevent the reflective element in these poems from becoming mere gnomic lyricism. The shorter verses in dactylic meter are particularly buoyant ("Alle die Stimmen der Bäche," "Wann war ein Mensch je so wach," "Quellen, sie münden herauf," etc.), and again emphasize the rejuvenating, restorative forces of earth. Or better, the gods of Hölderlin seem reborn to convert the paradoxical "aridity of trees" into true amethysts and betray a gentle intervention in human affairs, like a breeze turning heavy ears of grain. But

CONCLUSION

their sympathy is still an unpredictable affair, and they still belong, milder replicas of the Duino angel and Orpheus, to another realm "where our own heaven begins." Even in the attempted reconciliation the paradox, the chasm, the Otherness between man and his real cosmos is still present:

> Schweigsam, einfach und heil legt sich an seine
> Errichtung plötzlich ihr anderes Mass.

> Silently, plain and whole, to his rising
> stature suddenly their different meas-
> ure is laid . . .

It is again open to debate whether this later poetry does not rather suffer than gain from the attempted reconciliation of orphic realm with earthly things. Unlike Hopkins, whose very language is identified with sensuous experience, Rilke sees in nature chiefly "directions" and "gestures."⁴ Though the physical body is the primary "plot," as it has been called, of his poetry, one does not feel that his brooks, fountains, trees, and vineyards have really been reborn in the flesh.⁵ Deprived of its dynamic tensions, stresses, and dialectics, this particular late lyric seems rather ineffective and spiritless; something has evaporated which is associated with Rilke at his best. Only in the narrowest sense can this kind of poetry be called one of "accomplishment."⁶

Not all the late poetry is similarly attenuated. A very fine poem, one of the last to be written (August 24, 1926), seems truer to his metaphorical landscaping than the ones just discussed, and convincingly sums up his experience of art-in-life. In the first stanza, the "dove" returning after long absence to its dovecote—an echo of the Prodigal Son as well as the love theme—is the initial concrete figure employed to objectify the poem's essential meaning, which emerges in the second and third stanzas:

> Unter den Tauben, die allergeschonteste,
> niemals gefährdetste, kennt nicht die Zärtlichkeit;
> wiedererholtes Herz ist die bewohnteste:
> freier durch Widerruf freut sich die Fähigkeit.

> Über dem Nirgendsein spannt sich das Überall!
> Ach der geworfene, ach der gewagte Ball,

215

füllt er die Hände nicht   anders mit Wiederkehr:
rein um sein Heimgewicht   ist er mehr.

Of all the doves the   always most protected,
never endangered most,   does not know tenderness;
richest of all hearts is   the resurrected:
turning back liberates,   freedom rejoices.

Over the nowhere   arches the everywhere.
Oh, the ball that is   thrown, that we dare,
does it not fill our hands   differently than before?
By the weight of return   it is more.

Without establishing a correlation between the thought and Heidegger's views on Being and the Nought (fairly evident in tropes like *geworfen, gespannt, Nirgendsein, Überall*), we may follow the thread of conception back to the "ventured" ball of *New Poems*, likewise returned to receiving hands with "added" meaning, while the "homing-weight" carries through the implications of one of Rilke's favorite last symbols, "the scales" (*Die Waage*). Rilke's view of the world ends, as it had begun, with gods and things, but man is still only an existential possibility for whom only the poet-sorcerer can properly balance the scales.

PROSPERO

One of the lesser-known poems of 1913, "The Spirit Ariel," written after a reading of *The Tempest*, is extraordinarily revealing, not only for its radical departure from the customary interpretation of Prospero's role, but especially for the clue provided that suggests what Rilke considers the poet to be. Like Auden in his "The Sea and the Mirror: A Commentary on The Tempest," he was not attempting to interpret either the play or its characters in a new sense but to "use the play's structure as a base from which to deploy his own themes." [7] The crux of the poem is the conception of Prospero as the magician (artist). In order that the Ring of Forms may come into being (*und wir feiern den Kreis*, reads a late poem, "For Nike"), the word can be induced to "sing" only after it has been exalted to the level of magic exorcism (*hebt sich das Wort zur Beschwörung*). The connection of the sorcerer-figure with a theory of poetry leads directly to a group of late poems that relate back to the Prospero

216

theme: "The Goldsmith," "Sorcery," "Le Magicien," "Sorcerer."
In "Sorcerer," for example, Rilke's quarrel with Shakespeare is clear enough. He charges Prospero, in effect, with having renounced his magic (poetry) to become a retired bourgeois puppet when he should have persisted, like Rilke's own sorcerer (*Oh Magier, halt aus, halt aus, halt aus*), and with a liberated Ariel, onward through further stages of transformation. Rilke will have no resignation from the high sorcery of art. The association of Prospero with the discipline of poetry is made emphatically clear in the poem "Magic" (*Magie*), where the transformation theme of the Ninth Elegy is narrowed to the functioning of the poetic word:

> Hier ist Magie. In das Bereich des Zaubers
> scheint das gemeine Wort hinaufgestuft . . .
> und ist doch wirklich wie der Ruf des Taubers,
> der nach der unsichtbaren Taube ruft.

> This is the sorcery: the common word
> appears to rise stepwise to magic state . . .
> and yet is nothing but the male dove's note,
> calling for the invisible mate.

Rilke is not merely stating that the art of poetry *is* Prospero's magic; he goes much further to include within it the realization of those emotions (witness the love reference in the final two lines, which employ imagery similar to the dove-poem already quoted) that have generally been supposed to exist in their own right. No more than the poetry itself are such feelings to be entrusted to "the ordinary word," but are to be heightened and intensified (*hinaufgestuft*) in the realm of art-magic. In this sense it is true that Rilke creates "a new idiom which would neglect the anthropomorphic for the physical basis of language" and that "the commonplace sense of words is neglected for their seeming origin as signs, signifying weight, direction and invisibly orientated gesture." [8] Rilke's word-sorcery brings everything under its sway, the whole complex of human emotions and beliefs that have deteriorated in a godless age and are to be restored in another order. Perhaps Heller was implying something similar by saying that "In the great poetry of the European tradition the emotions do not interpret; they respond to the interpreted world.

217

In Rilke's poetry the emotions do the interpreting and then respond to their own interpretation." [9] So far is his conception of Prospero from Shakespeare's paragon of wisdom or the "close replica of Christ" which G. Wilson Knight professes to find in him, that he is Orpheus and angel, Ariel and Rilke himself, at one and the same time.[10] Our human world seems thus to be in the predicament of Goethe's Sorcerer's Apprentice, until the command of the right word brings the unruly spirits to their knees.

Rilke's statements on the nature of poetic language, often combined with quite original theories of perception, should certainly be collated. The craft-aspect of his work, the creativity of the "word," is the very key to his aesthetic, thought, and "message." To this extent he is like Hopkins in that his poetry appears "not to progress by thought to which word and image are subordinate, rather by word and image distilling thought." [11] No wonder that the wisdom emanating from such premises is somewhat different from what Shakespeare's Prospero had bequeathed the world.

In the beginning was the Rilkean Logos. Eliot's well-known observation in "Tradition and the Individual Talent," that the poet rightfully has no personality to express but only a particular medium, had its characteristic Rilkean formulation a few years later. Thus a young poet is warned against subjectivism: "But if you nevertheless find a pen in your hand, you must forbid it to put down anything 'impressionistic,' compel it to note the facts of your own life and, better still, of a life that is more foreign to you . . ." [12] What immediately follows bears directly on Rilke's own practice of poetry, for the correspondent is also urged to

. . . fashion beside the pen intended to furnish your friends with the signs of your doing and striving, a second pen which you will treat like a tool: and do not let yourself be swayed by what comes from this second pen, be hard towards the least of its products. The workmanlike output which this other pen adumbrates should not work back into your own life, should be a *design*, an *alchemy*, a *transmutation* of which the "I" was only the first and last stimulus . . .[13] (My italics.)

The poet's language, the second pen, produces the art-work of a "thinglike solitude," a mysterious process in which the poet's share is that of "some quiet deputy." "No word in the poem (and I mean every 'and', 'the' and 'that')," he informed another correspondent, "is identical with the same-sounding word in ordinary discourse; the purer ordering (*Gesetzmässigkeit*), the great relatedness and configuration it assumes in poetry and creative prose alters it in the very germ of its nature, rendering it useless and unusable for mere communication, something untouchable and permanent: a transformation . . ."[14] His intimate concern with language, finally, is graphically expressed in a letter of 1920 that substantiates what has been termed the "purely physical process" of his poetry in the effort to achieve "transcendent orientation":

So it frequently happens that one is at odds with the exterior conduct of language when its innermost essence is meant, a very inner language, uninflected, if possible, a language made of *word-kernels*, a language that hasn't been *plucked at the top of the stem* but seized in the very *linguistic seed* itself. Would not the perfected hymn to the sun have to be invented in this language, and isn't the pure silence of love like the *heart-soil* around such linguistic seeds? Alas, how often one wishes to speak a few degrees lower in the scale . . . but one only descends a minimal layer, left to surmise *what speech would be like where silence is* . . .[15] (My italics.)

Such a Prospero is not required to abdicate his magic and return homewards in resignation, however wise in wisdom, for there is only one world, and "once and for all/it's Orpheus when there's singing." Only through transfiguration in the invisible world of the poetic word are Rilke's Ariel and Prospero finally reconciled, and only here, it appears, is created the authentic version of Miranda's Brave New World.

NOTES, BIBLIOGRAPHY
AND INDEX

o͡o *Notes*

Introduction

[1] Bollnow, pp. 347ff.
[2] Hermann Meyer, "Rilkes Cézanne Erlebnis," *Jahrbuch für Aesthetik und Allgemeine Kunstwissenschaft*, vol. 2 (1952-54), p. 70.
[3] Gottfried Benn, "Artists and Old Age," tr. Ernst Kaiser and Eithene Wilkins, *Partisan Review*, vol. XXII, no. 3 (Summer 1955), p. 305.
[4] Karl Shapiro, *Beyond Criticism* (Lincoln, Neb., 1953), pp. 54ff.
[5] *Ibid.*
[6] Richard Hoggart, *Auden: An Introductory Essay* (London, 1951), p. 27. See also D. J. Enright, "Reluctant Admiration: A Note on Auden and Rilke," *Essays in Criticism*, vol. II, no. 2 (April 1952), pp. 180ff.
[7] Hans Egon Holthusen, *Rainer Maria Rilke. A Study of His Later Poetry*, p. 7.
[8] Cf. Erich Simenauer, *Rainer Maria Rilke. Legende und Mythos* (Bern, 1953).
[9] Review of Simenauer's book in the London *Times Literary Supplement*, Jan. 14, 1955.
[10] Cf. Holthusen, *Die Welt ohne Tranzendenz: eine Studie zu Thomas Manns "Doktor Faustus" und seinen Nebenschriften* (Hamburg, 1949).
[11] Meyer, *op. cit.*, p. 69.
[12] Cf. Günther; Guardini; Mason, *Der Zopf des Münchhausen*; and Holthusen, *Der Späte Rilke* (Zürich, 1949).

Chapter I. The Early Workshop

[1] *Wartime Letters*, pp. 225-6.
[2] *Ibid.*
[3] Kohlschmidt, *Rainer Maria Rilke*, pp. 13ff.
[4] Demetz, pp. 23ff. See also Heerikhuizen, pp. 56-8.
[5] Bollnow, pp. 13ff. For a contradictory opinion on Rilke's vocabulary see Belmore, p. 123.
[6] Benn, *Probleme der Lyrik*, p. 16.
[7] Heerikhuizen, p. 38.
[8] *Ibid.*

223

THE RING OF FORMS

[9] *Ibid.*

[10] *Ibid.*, p. 12.

[11] "Preface to the Lyrical Ballads," *Poetical Works of William Words-worth*, ed. Ernest de Sélincourt (Oxford, 1944), p. 386.

[12] Kohlschmidt, *op. cit.*, p. 10.

[13] Angelloz, p. 98.

[14] Critics have pointed to suggestive connections between Rilke's dramatic interests and Hauptmann's *Michael Kramer*, also produced in 1901. Cf. my article, "Rilke and the Theater," *Monatshefte* (Madison, Wisc., 1951), pp. 15–26.

[15] *Ibid.*

[16] *Bücher, Theater, Kunst*, ed. R. von Mises (Vienna, 1934).

[17] *Ibid.*, pp. 174–5.

[18] *Ibid.*, "Der Wert des Monologes" and "Noch ein Wort über 'Wert des Monologes' " (1898).

[19] *Ibid.*, pp. 174–5.

[20] *Ibid.*, p. 193.

[21] Angelloz, p. 104.

[22] Letter to Bodo Wildberg, Jan. 1896, quoted in Heerikhuizen, p. 66.

[23] Rudolf Kassner, *Buch der Erinnerung* (Zürich, 1954), p. 247.

[24] Butler, pp. 43ff.

[25] *Briefe und Tagebücher aus der Frühzeit*, 1899–1902 (Leipzig: Insel, 1942), pp. 174ff.

[26] Heerikhuizen, p. 153.

[27] Frank Wood, "Rilke's Keats-Bild," *Germanic Review* (Oct. 1950), pp. 210ff.

Chapter II. The Dark God

[1] Heerikhuizen, p. 94.

[2] *Tuscan Diary*, quoted in Heerikhuizen, p. 95.

[3] Ellen Key, *Seelen und Werke* (Berlin, 1911), p. 159.

[4] Heerikhuizen, p. 102.

[5] *Briefe und Tagebücher*, p. 16.

[6] Heerikhuizen, p. 97.

[7] *Briefe und Tagebücher*, p. 17.

[8] F. R. Leavis, *New Bearings in English Poetry: A Study of the Contemporary Situation* (London, 1932), p. 19.

[9] Mövius, p. 178.

[10] *Letters*, I, p. 34. To Sofia Schill, March 5, 1900.

[11] *Tuscan Diary*, *op. cit.*

[12] Mason, *Lebenshaltung und Symbolik*, p. 18.

[13] Kohlschmidt, *Rainer Maria Rilke*, p. 53.

[14] "Stundenbuch," *Werke*, II, p. 264.

[15] Heller, *The Disinherited Mind*, pp. 111ff.

[16] Samuel and Thomas, p. 88.

[17] *Rainer Maria Rilke–Lou Andreas-Salomé: Briefwechsel* (Zürich-Wiesbaden, 1952), p. 119.

[18] Klatt, p. 6.

[19] Holthusen, *Rainer Maria Rilke. A Study of His Later Poetry*, p. 7. See also W. H. Auden, *New Year Letter* (London, 1941), p. 24.

[20] *The Notebooks of Malte Laurids Brigge*, p. 187.

[21] Betz, p. 77.
[22] Lou Andreas-Salomé, *Lebensrückblick. Grundriss einiger Lebenserinnerungen* (Zürich-Wiesbaden, 1951), p. 119.
[23] Heerikhuizen, p. 151.
[24] *Briefe*, II, p. 215. To Rudolf Zimmerman, Jan. 25, 1921.
[25] *Selected Poems of Michelangelo*, tr. E. Cheney (Boston, 1885), pp. 68 and 66, respectively.
[26] "Geschichten vom lieben Gott," *Werke*, IV, p. 88.
[27] Kohlschmidt, *op. cit.*, pp. 64ff.
[28] *Ibid.*, p. 62.
[29] Heller, *op. cit.*, pp. 111ff.
[30] Heerikhuizen, p. 146.

Chapter III. Experiment in Objectivity

[1] Betz, p. 77.
[2] Heerikhuizen, pp. 157ff. See his treatment of *New Poems* in Ch. 5, "The Great Conflict."
[3] Cf. C. F. MacIntyre, *Rainer Maria Rilke. Fifty Selected Poems with English Translations* (Berkeley, 1941), p. 13.
[4] *Briefe und Tagebücher*, p. 158.
[5] Hugo von Hofmannsthal, "Versuch über Victor Hugo," *Gesammelte Werke*, Prosa I (Fischer Verlag, 1950), p. 378.
[6] *Briefe und Tagebücher*, p. 206.
[7] *Briefe, 1906–1907*, p. 214.
[8] Duwe, p. 15.
[9] In the matter of influences, see letters to Alfred Schaer, Feb. 26, 1924, and Hermann Pongs, Aug. 17, 1924, *Letters*, II, pp. 333ff. and 345ff.
[10] Stéphane Mallarmé, *Divagations* (Paris, 1932), II, p. 94.
[11] *Briefe*, II, p. 192. To B. K., Nov. 24, 1920. In French.
[12] *Letters*, I, p. 146. To Lou Andreas-Salomé, April 15, 1904.
[13] Cf. Rilke's description of the snail-shell episode in Rodin's garden, *Letters*, I, p. 83. See also Angelloz, Ch. 4, p. 197 *passim*.
[14] Fritz Kaufmann, "Sprache als Schöpfung: Zur Absoluten Kunst in Hinsicht auf Rilke," *Zeitschrift für Aesthetik und Allgemeine Kunstwissenschaft*, vol. xxvii (Stuttgart, 1934), pp. 16, 35ff., 51.
[15] Austin Warren, in *Gerard Manley Hopkins*, by the Kenyon Critics (New York, 1944), pp. 76ff.
[16] John Crowe Ransom, *The World's Body* (New York, 1938), p. 124.
[17] Cf. Wolfgang Kayser, "Eine Unbekannte Prosa-Skizze von R. M. Rilke," *Trivium* (Jahrgang v, 1947), p. 82.
[18] E. M. W. Tillyard, *Poetry Direct and Oblique* (London, 1934), p. 171.
[19] José-Maria de Herédia, *Poésies Complètes* (Paris, 1943), p. 18.
[20] C. M. Bowra, *The Heritage of Symbolism* (London, 1943), p. 67.
[21] Angelloz, p. 219.
[22] *Letters*, II, p. 276. To Ilse Blumenthal-Weiss, Dec. 28, 1921.
[23] Holthusen, *op. cit.*, p. 29.
[24] "T. S. Eliot," in Curtius, p. 300.
[25] *Ibid.*, p. 312. See also my article, "Rilke and Eliot," *Germanic Review* (Dec. 1952), pp. 246–59.
[26] T. S. Eliot, "Baudelaire," *Selected Essays, 1917–1932* (New York, 1932), pp. 343ff.

THE RING OF FORMS

27 *Notebooks*, pp. 52ff.
28 "Rodin," *Werke*, IV, p. 313.
29 *Ibid.*, p. 343.
30 *Briefe, 1902–1906*, p. 98.
31 *Notebooks*, pp. 67ff.
32 *Briefe*, I, p. 207.
33 *Oeuvres de Baudelaire* (Paris: Pléiade, 1935), I, p. 418.
34 Goertz, pp. 39, 50 *passim*.
35 *Briefe*, II, pp. 214ff. To Rudolf Zimmerman, Feb. 3, 1921.
36 Goertz, p. 49.
37 *Letters*, I, p. 287. To Clara Rilke, June 24, 1907.
38 Hermann Meyer, "Rilkes Cézanne Erlebnis," *Jahrbuch für Aesthetik und Allgemeine Kunstwissenschaft*, vol. 2 (1952–54), p. 84.
39 *Letters*, I, pp. 310–11.
40 *Briefe, 1906–1907*, p. 344.
41 *Ibid.*
42 Meyer, *op. cit.*, pp. 74ff.
43 *Letters*, I, p. 311.
44 *Ibid.*, p. 304.
45 *Ibid.*, pp. 306ff.
46 *Ibid.*, p. 308.
47 *Ibid.*, p. 316.
48 Meyer, *op. cit.*, p. 77.
49 *Ibid.*, pp. 84–5.
50 Kaufmann, *op. cit.*, p. 7.
51 Meyer, *op. cit.*, p. 77.
52 Belmore, p. 48.
53 *Briefe, 1907–1914.*
54 Quoted in Belmore, p. 121.
55 See Belmore, pp. 120–55.
56 Holthusen, *op. cit.*
57 *Briefe, 1906–1907*, p. 300.
58 Angelloz, p. 216. The later edition (1952) omits this statement and, in general, evaluates this aspect more moderately.
59 *Ibid.*, p. 219.

Chapter IV. The Autobiography of a Book

1 Betz, pp. 74ff. *et passim*.
2 Simenauer, pp. 457–9.
3 *Selected Letters*, p. 49. To Lou Andreas-Salomé, May 12, 1904; compare with letter to Kippenberg, Jan. 2, 1909, five years later.
4 *Lettres à Rodin* (Paris, 1928).
5 *Selected Letters*, p. 181.
6 *Ibid.*
7 *Ibid.*, p. 184.
8 *Briefe, 1907–1914*, p. 185. To Hedda Sauer, Jan. 28, 1912.
9 *Briefe*, I, pp. 362–3. To Artur Hospelt, Feb. 11, 1912.
10 *Ibid.*, p. 364.
11 *Ibid.*, II, p. 372.

[12] *Notebooks*, pp. 28–9.
[13] Cf. Kohlschmidt, *Rainer Maria Rilke*, pp. 107ff., in reference to Kierkegaard's *Diary of a Seducer*: "Der Malte ist ebenso sehr Konfession wie Verhüllung, radikale Rechenschaft wie reine Phantasie."
[14] Betz, pp. 74ff.
[15] *Ibid.*, pp. 78ff.
[16] Butler, p. 205.
[17] *Ibid.*
[18] *Selected Letters*, p. 157.
[19] Betz, p. 78.
[20] Butler, p. 210.
[21] Bollnow, p. 23.
[22] Rudolf Jancke, "Rilke-Kierkegaard," *Dichtung und Volkstum*, vol. 39 (1938), pp. 315ff.
[23] *Ibid.*, p. 314.
[24] *Letters*, II, p. 256. To Hermann Pongs, Oct. 21, 1924.
[25] *Ibid.*, p. 107. To Helene von Nostitz, Jan. 23, 1914.
[26] *Notebooks*, p. 61.
[27] *Ibid.*, p. 129.
[28] *Ibid.*, p. 52.
[29] *Ibid.*, p. 171.
[30] *Letters*, II, pp. 372ff. To Witold von Hulewicz, Nov. 10, 1925.
[31] *Selected Letters*, p. 391.
[32] *Notebooks*, p. 119.
[33] *Ibid.*, p. 208.
[34] Letter to Ludwig Ganghofer, April 16, 1897; quoted in Heerikhuizen, p. 53.
[35] *Notebooks*, p. 162.
[36] *Letters*, I, pp. 57ff.
[37] *Notebooks*, p. 216.
[38] *Ibid.*, p. 209.
[39] *Ibid.*, p. 26.
[40] *Ibid.*, pp. 75–6.
[41] Francis Fergusson, *The Idea of a Theater* (New York, 1953), p. 173.
[42] Quoted in *Notebooks*, "Notes," p. 223.
[43] *Ibid.*, p. 75.
[44] *Ibid.*, p. 26.
[45] *Ibid.*, pp. 194ff.
[46] *Ibid.*, p. 196.
[47] *Ibid.*, p. 201.
[48] *Ibid.*, p. 202.
[49] *Ibid.*, p. 159.
[50] *Letters*, I, p. 337.
[51] Angelloz, p. 262.
[52] Kohlschmidt, *op cit.*, pp. 108ff.
[53] Butler, p. 211.
[54] F. Martini, *Das Wagnis der Sprache* (Stuttgart, 1954), p. 140.
[55] *Ibid.*, p. 142.
[56] *Ibid.*, pp. 138ff.
[57] *Notebooks*, p. 176.

THE RING OF FORMS

Chapter V. The Critical Years

[1] *Gedichte, 1906–1926*, ed. Ernst Zinn (Wiesbaden: Insel, 1953).

[2] *Briefe*, II, p. 507. June 26, 1914.

[3] Cf. *Letters*, II, pp. 80ff. See also *Briefe an seinen Verleger*, Jan. 7, 1913, pp. 156ff.

[4] *Letters*, II, p. 45.

[5] *Ibid.*, p. 82.

[6] *Briefe*, I, p. 502.

[7] *Rainer Maria Rilke–Lou Andreas-Salomé, Briefwechsel* (Zürich-Wiesbaden, 1952), p. 361.

[8] Cf. *Briefe, 1907–1914*, p. 275. To Karl von der Heydt.

[9] *Rilke-Gide Correspondance, 1909–1926*. Introduction et Commentaires par Renée Lang (Paris: Corrêa, 1952), p. 114n.

[10] Cf. my article, "Rilke's Keats-Bild," *Germanic Review* (Oct. 1950), p. 211.

[11] *Rilke-Gide Correspondance*, p. 159.

[12] *Briefe*, I, p. 413.

[13] *Werke*, II, p. 270.

[14] Cf. Angelloz, pp. 279ff.

[15] *Letters*, II, p. 375.

[16] *Letters*, II, p. 115. To Lou Andreas-Salomé, June 9, 1914.

[17] *Rilke-Gide Correspondance*, p. 66.

[18] Kohlschmidt, *Rainer Maria Rilke*, pp. 133ff.

[19] Rilke's *Taschenbuch*, Jan. 14, 1898. Cf. *Briefe*, I, p. 457.

[20] Quoted in Butler, p. 241.

[21] Friedrich Beissner, "Rilkes Begegnung mit Hölderlin," in *Dichtung und Volkstum*, Bd. 37, H. 1 (1936), p. 47.

[22] *Ibid.*, p. 41.

[23] See also letters to Ludwig von Ficker, Feb. 15, 1915, and Helene von Nostitz, July 12, 1915, *Briefe, 1914–1921*, pp. 36, 57.

[24] *The Life of the Virgin Mary*, with an Introduction and English Translation by Stephen Spender (New York: The Philosophical Library, 1951), p. 8.

[25] Kohlschmidt, *op cit.*, p. 126.

[26] Angelloz, p. 295.

[27] Kohlschmidt, *op. cit.*, p. 126.

[28] Spender, *op. cit.*, p. 7.

[29] *Briefe*, II, pp. 320–1.

[30] Kohlschmidt, *op. cit.*, pp. 127–8.

[31] *Briefe*, I, p. 336.

[32] Spender, *op. cit.*, pp. 7–8.

[33] *Letters*, II, p. 72.

[34] *Ibid.*, p. 70.

[35] *Ibid.*, p. 72.

[36] Hoggart, *Auden: An Introductory Essay*, p. 27.

[37] *Briefe*, II, p. 239.

[38] Gebser, p. 25.

[39] Kohlschmidt, *op. cit.*, pp. 139–43.

[40] *Ibid.*, pp. 119ff.

[41] *Ibid.*, p. 125.

[42] Purtscher-Wydenbruck, p. 274.

[43] *Briefe*, II, p. 119. To Adelheid von der Marwitz, Jan. 14, 1919.

[44] *Ibid.*, p. 120.

[45] Cf. particularly Bassermann, *Der Späte Rilke* (Munich, 1947), pp. 39ff.

[46] *Letters*, II, p. 159.

[47] *Ibid.*

[48] *Briefe, 1914–1921.*

[49] *Letters*, II, p. 204. To Anni Mewes, Sept. 12, 1919.

[50] *Briefe*, II, p. 26.

[51] *Briefe, 1914–1921*, p. 54.

[52] *Notebooks*, p. 109.

[53] Angelloz, p. 289.

[54] Berdyaev, pp. 125–6.

[55] Cf. Simenauer, pp. 529ff.

[56] *Ibid.*, p. 537.

[57] Prawer, p. 218.

[58] Holthusen, *Rainer Maria Rilke*, p. 28.

[59] Laurence Thomas, *André Gide: The Ethic of the Artist* (London, 1950), pp. 49ff.

[60] Theodora Bosanquet, *Paul Valéry* (London, 1933), p. 86.

Chapter VI. Angel

[1] Guardini, pp. 13ff.

[2] *Briefe*, II, p. 485.

[3] *Ibid.*, p. 448. To Countess M., Aug. 9, 1924.

[4] *Ibid.*

[5] *Letters*, II, p. 330. To Nanny von Escher, Dec. 22, 1923.

[6] David Hoeniger, "Symbolism and Pattern in Rilke's 'Duino Elegies,'" *German Life and Letters*, vol. III, no. 4 (Oxford, July 1950), pp. 271ff.

[7] *Ibid.*, p. 272.

[8] *Letters*, II, p. 375.

[9] Purtscher-Wydenbruck, p. 208.

[10] Samuel and Thomas, p. 114.

[11] *Briefe*, II, p. 484.

[12] Schiller, "Die Künstler," *Werke* (Leipzig: Bibliographisches Institut, 1895), pp. 271ff.

[13] Heller, *The Hazard of Modern Poetry*, p. 37.

[14] *Ibid.*

[15] Kreutz, p. 22.

[16] *Ibid.*, p. 23.

[17] "The Marriage of Heaven and Hell," *Poetical Works of William Blake* (London: Chatto & Windus, 1906), p. 242.

[18] Kreutz, p. 31.

[19] Cf. Vaihinger, *The Philosophy of "As If"* (London, 1935), p. 24.

[20] *Letters*, II, p. 342; Leishman's translation of *Sonnets to Orpheus*, Introduction, p. 26.

[21] *Letters*, II, p. 373.

[22] Kreutz, p. 35.

[23] *Paradise Lost*, Bk. IX, *The Poems of John Milton* (New York: Nelson, 1937), p. 36.

[24] Cf. Heller, *The Disinherited Mind*, pp. 109ff. See also *Letters*, II, p. 75.

[25] Cf. *Letters*, II, pp. 374ff.

THE RING OF FORMS

[20] *Biographia Literaria*, ed. W. Shedd (New York: Harper, 1884), pp. 336ff.

[27] Cf. Novalis (Friedrich Leopold, Freiherr von Hardenberg), "Fragmente und Studien," *Schriften* (Leipzig: Bibliographisches Institut, 1929).

[28] *Briefe*, II, p. 341. To Gräfin Margot Sizzo Croney.

[29] Guardini, p. 383.

[30] *Ibid.*

[31] George Santayana, *Dominations and Powers: Reflections on Liberty, Society and Government* (New York, 1951).

[32] *Briefe*, II, p. 485.

[33] Guardini, p. 411.

Chapter VII. Orpheus

[1] *Letters*, II, p. 373.

[2] Leishman, *op. cit.*, p. 16.

[3] *Letters*, II, p. 376.

[4] *Briefe*, II, p. 321.

[5] *Notebooks*, p. 52.

[6] Geering, pp. 16ff.

[7] Rehm, p. 566.

[8] *Ibid.*, p. 562.

[9] *Ibid.*, p. 512.

[10] *Ibid.*

[11] Holthusen, *Rilkes Sonette an Orpheus*, p. 32.

[12] Hermann Pongs, "R. M. Rilke: ein Vortrag," in *Euphorion, Zeitschrift für Literatur*, vol. 32 (Stuttgart, 1931), p. 69.

[13] *Briefe*, II, p. 419. To Gräfin Sizzo, June 1, 1923.

[14] *Ibid.*, p. 326. To Leopold von Schlözer, March 30, 1923.

[15] Belmore, pp. 214ff.

[16] Holthusen, *op. cit.*

[17] *Ibid.*, p. 36.

[18] *Ibid.*, pp. 43ff.

[19] *Ibid.*, pp. 57ff.

[20] *Ibid.*, p. 53.

[21] *Ibid.*, p. 61.

[22] *Ibid.*, p. 65. See also Paul Zech, *Rainer Maria Rilke: der Mensch und das Werk* (Dresden, 1930), p. 134.

[23] Holthusen, *op. cit.*, p. 98.

[24] *Ibid.*, pp. 85ff.

[25] Quoted in Holthusen, *Der Späte Rilke*, pp. 14–15.

[26] *Ibid.*, *Rilkes Sonette an Orpheus*, p. 135.

[27] *Ibid.*, p. 144.

[28] *Ibid.*

[29] *Briefe*, II, p. 402.

[30] Geering, pp. 19ff.

[31] Leishman, *op. cit.*, p. 148.

[32] Tillyard, *Poetry Direct and Oblique*, p. 171.

[33] Leavis, *New Bearings in English Poetry*, p. 172.

[34] *Briefe*, II, pp. 426–7. To Gräfin Sizzo, Dec. 16, 1923.

[35] Fritz Kaufmann, "Sprache als Schöpfung: Zur Absoluten Kunst in Hinsicht auf Rilke," *Zeitschrift für Aesthetik und Allgemeine Kunstwissenschaft*, pp. 16ff.

[36] Paul Valéry, *Eupalinos ou l'Architecte, Précedé de "L'Âme et la Danse"* (Paris: Gallimard, 1923).
[37] *Ibid.*, p. 24.
[38] *Letters*, II, p. 374.
[39] *Briefe aus Muzot*, p. 119.
[40] *The Letters of W. B. Yeats*, ed. Allan Wade (London, 1954), p. 913. To Dorothy Wellesley, Aug. 15, 1938.
[41] *Briefe*, II, p. 401. To Leopold von Schlözer. March 30, 1923.
[42] *Ibid.*

Conclusion

[1] Cf. Bollnow, p. 347. See also Heller, *The Disinherited Mind*, p. 132.
[2] *Rilke-Gide Correspondance*, p. 244.
[3] *Ibid.*, p. 247.
[4] Hartman, pp. 75ff.
[5] *Ibid.*, p. 76.
[6] Heller, *op. cit.*, p. 132.
[7] Hoggart, *Auden: An Introductory Essay*, p. 172.
[8] Hartman, pp. 78, 95.
[9] Heller, *op. cit.*, p. 136.
[10] G. Wilson Knight, *The Crown of Life: Essays in Interpretation of Shakespeare's Final Plays* (London, 1948), pp. 252ff.
[11] Hartman, p. 49.
[12] *Selected Letters*, p. 402.
[13] *Ibid.*
[14] *Die Briefe an die Gräfin Sizzo, 1921–1926* (Leipzig: Insel, 1940), p. 20.
[15] *Briefe*, II.

o͒o Bibliography

The critical bibliography of Rilke to date is so vast that any attempt at inclusiveness would hardly serve a practical purpose. For fuller information the reader is referred to Walter Ritzer, *Rainer Maria Rilke: Bibliographie* (Vienna, 1951). A convenient working bibliography is contained in F. W. van Heerikhuizen, *Rainer Maria Rilke: His Life and Work*, translated from the Dutch by F. Renier and A. Cliff (New York, 1952). The following selected bibliography is restricted to those works which bear more immediately on the text.

For both the prose and the poetry the English translations used in this book, apart from my own, are listed below. Reference is also made to the *Gesammelte Briefe*, I, 1897–1914; II, 1914–1926 (Leipzig: Insel Verlag, 1939); to the original *Briefe* series in chronological volumes (Leipzig: Insel Verlag, 1929–1937); and to the *Gesammelte Werke*, 6 vols. (Leipzig: Insel Verlag, 1927).

Translations

Babette Deutsch. *Poems from "The Book of Hours" by Rainer Maria Rilke.* Norfolk, Conn.: New Directions, 1941.

Jane Bannard Greene and M. D. Herter Norton. *Letters of Rainer Maria Rilke*, I, 1892–1910; II, 1910–1926. New York: W. W. Norton & Co., 1945, 1948.

R. F. C. Hull. *Selected Letters of Rainer Maria Rilke, 1902–1926.* London: Macmillan & Co., 1947.

J. B. Leishman. *Poems.* London: The Hogarth Press, 1934.

———. *Later Poems.* London: The Hogarth Press, 1938.

———. *Selected Poems.* London: The Hogarth Press, 1941.

———. *Requiem and Others Poems.* London: The Hogarth Press, 1949.

———. *Sonnets to Orpheus.* London: The Hogarth Press, 1949.

J. B. Leishman and Stephen Spender. *Duino Elegies.* New York: W. W. Norton & Co., 1939.

Jessie Lemont. *Poems.* New York: Columbia University Press, 1943.

Ludwig Lewisohn. *Thirty-One Poems by Rainer Maria Rilke.* New York: Beechhurst Press, 1946.

M. D. Herter Norton. *Translations from the Poetry of Rainer Maria Rilke.* New York: W. W. Norton & Co., 1938.

232

BIBLIOGRAPHY

————. *Wartime Letters of Rainer Maria Rilke, 1914–1921.* New York: W. W. Norton & Co., 1940.

————. *The Notebooks of Malte Laurids Brigge.* New York: W. W. Norton & Co., 1949.

Leslie Phillips and Stefan Schimanski. *The Lay of the Love and Death of Cornet Christopher Rilke.* London: Lindsay Drummond, Ltd., 1948.

Stephen Spender. *The Life of the Virgin Mary.* New York: The Philosophical Library, Inc., 1951.

Selected Bibliography

Andreas-Salomé, Lou. *Rainer Maria Rilke.* Leipzig, 1929.

Angelloz, J.-F. *Rainer Maria Rilke. L'Évolution Spirituelle du Poète.* Paris, 1936.

Belmore, H. W. *Rilke's Craftsmanship.* Oxford, 1954.

Benn, Gottfried. *Probleme der Lyrik.* Wiesbaden, 1951.

Berdyaev, Nicholas. *Solitude and Society.* New York, 1938.

Betz, Maurice. *Rilke in Paris.* Zürich, 1948.

Bollnow, O. F. *Rilke.* Stuttgart, 1951.

Brutzer, Sophie. *R. M. Rilkes Russische Reisen.* Königsberg, 1934.

Butler, E. M. *Rainer Maria Rilke.* Cambridge, 1941.

Curtius, E. R. *Kritische Essays zur Europäischen Literatur.* Bern, 1950.

Dehn, Fritz. *R. M. Rilke und sein Werk. Eine Deutung.* Leipzig, 1934.

Demetz, Peter. *René Rilkes Prager Jahre.* Düsseldorf, 1953.

Duwe, Willi. *Deutsche Dichtung des 20. Jahrhunderts.* Leipzig-Zürich, 1936.

Gebser, Hans. *Rilke und Spanien.* New York-Zürich, 1953.

Geering, Agnes. *Rilkes Sonette an Orpheus: Versuch einer Einführung.* Frankfurt, 1948.

Goertz, Hartmann. *Frankreich und das Erlebnis der Form im Werke Rainer Maria Rilkes.* Stuttgart, 1932.

Guardini, Romano. *Rainer Maria Rilkes Deutung des Daseins. Eine Interpretation.* Munich, 1953.

Günther, Werner. *Weltinnenraum. Die Dichtung Rainer Maria Rilkes.* Berlin, 1952.

Hartman, Geoffrey. *The Unmediated Vision: An Interpretation of Wordsworth, Hopkins, Rilke, and Valéry.* New Haven, 1954.

Hausmann, Ulrich. *Die Apollo-Sonette Rilkes und ihre Plastischen Urbilder.* Berlin, 1947.

Heerikhuizen, F. W. *Rainer Maria Rilke. His Life and Work.* Tr. F. Renier and A. Cliff. New York, 1952.

Heller, Erich. *The Disinherited Mind. Essays in Modern German Literature and Thought.* Cambridge, 1952.

————. *The Hazard of Modern Poetry.* Cambridge, 1953.

Holthusen, Hans Egon. *Rainer Maria Rilke. A Study of His Later Poetry.* Tr. J. P. Stern. New Haven, 1952.

————. *Rilkes Sonette an Orpheus. Versuch einer Interpretation.* Munich, 1937.

Kippenberg, Katharina. *Rainer Maria Rilke. Ein Beitrag.* Leipzig, 1935.

Klatt, Fritz. *Rainer Maria Rilke. Sein Auftrag in Heutiger Zeit.* Berlin, 1936.

Kohlschmidt, Werner. *Rilke-Interpretationen.* Lahr, 1948.

————. *Rainer Maria Rilke.* Lübeck, 1948.

233

THE RING OF FORMS

Kreutz, Heinrich. *Rilkes Duineser Elegien. Eine Interpretation.* Munich, 1950.

Mason, Eudo. *Der Zopf des Münchhausen. Eine Skizze im Hinblick auf Rilke.* Einsiedeln, 1947.

————. *Rilke's Apotheosis.* Oxford, 1938.

————. *Lebenshaltung und Symbolik bei Rainer Maria Rilke.* Weimar, 1939.

Mövius, Ruth. *Rainer Maria Rilkes Stundenbuch.* Leipzig, 1937.

Pitrou, Robert. *Rainer Maria Rilke. Les Thèmes Principaux de son Oeuvre.* Paris, 1938.

Prawer, S. S. *German Lyric Poetry. A Critical Analysis of Selected Poems from Klopstock to Rilke.* London, 1952.

Purtscher-Wydenbruck, Nora. *Rilke: Man and Poet. A Biographical Study.* London, 1949.

Rehm, Walter. *Orpheus: der dichter und die Toten.* Düsseldorf, 1950.

Salis, Jean Rodolphe de. *Rainer Maria Rilkes Schweizer Jahre.* Frauenfeld, 1952.

Samuel, Richard, and R. Hinton Thomas. *Expressionism in German Life, Literature and the Theater, 1910–1924.* Cambridge, 1939.

Schneditz, Wolfgang. *R. M. Rilke und die Bildende Kunst. Versuch einer Deutung.* Graz, 1947.

Simenauer, Erich. *Rainer Maria Rilke. Legende und Mythos.* Bern, 1953.

○ ○ *Index*

Names

235

Titles and First Lines

237

THE RING OF FORMS